LIGHT UPON A HILL

The University at Chattanooga,
1886-1996

JOHN LONGWITH

The University of Tennessee at Chattanooga / 2000

Copyright 2000 by The University of Tennessee at Chattanooga
All rights reserved.

No part of this book may be reproduced or transmitted in any form or by any means, electronic or mechanical, including photocopying, recording, or by any information storage and retrieval system, without permission in writing of The University of Tennessee at Chattanooga.

FIRST EDITION

ISBN 0-944897-04-5

Manufactured in the United States of America by
Adams Lithographing, Chattanooga, Tennessee

CONTENTS

Foreword iv

Introduction vi

Acknowledgments x

Chapter 1 The Methodist University 1

Chapter 2 A Double-Faced Somewhat 28

Chapter 3 Grit and Grace 49

Chapter 4 Modern Times 78

Chapter 5 Not Just Another Mill Town 91

Chapter 6 Bounds of Place and Time 110

Chapter 7 The Transfer 137

Chapter 8 Growing Up in the System 163

Notes and Sources 180

Selected Bibliography 215

Appendices 221
    A. Chronology 221
    B. Presidents and Chancellors 244
    C. Trustees, 1886-1969 245
    D. Trustees, University of Chattanooga Foundation, 1969-1998 253
    E. Guerry Professorships, 1961-1999 260
    F. UC-UT Merger Agreement, March 4, 1969 262

Index 287

FOREWORD

In the final pages of Homer's *The Odyssey*, Ulysses prepares for yet one more journey of war and peace. Preceding that journey, he said to his son, "Telemachus, now that you are about to fight in an engagement which will show every man's mettle, be sure not to disgrace your ancestors who were eminent for their strength and courage all the world over." Telemachus' reply was to assure Ulysses that he was " in no mind to disgrace your family." This is a conversation applicable to every institutional change. Each generation of faculty, students, board members and friends of this university has rightfully reminded its successors of the eminence of strength and courage of those who loved the university — and worked on its behalf — in previous eras.

The University "at Chattanooga" has had an impressive series of journeys in its history. Those journeys involved different names, missions, directions and, of course, challenges. But in those journeys are lessons of strength and courage, demonstrated by and through eminent persons and programs. We are especially grateful for this history of the university, and, in particular, for the diligent efforts of John Longwith to tell the story of the University. It is a story of strength and courage. It is a history that those of us who come lately to this institution need to know as those who lived our history have come to cherish it. None of our university ancestors would ask that we merely continue to duplicate the past. The voices in this history tell us what has been valued by our predecessors. The voices show us courageous acts to create quality academic opportunities in the liberal arts tradition. We hear the call for access; and we see the extraordinary efforts of presidents and chancellors, faculty and staff, board members and community leaders to sustain the University. Like Ulysses to Telemachus, these pages charge new generations coming to UTC not to disgrace the university. And the response this history reveals is that voiced by succeeding generations down through the ages: We are "in no mind" to disgrace this university.

Those of us privileged to be at UTC now hope it is a tribute to its ancestral memory that there are new generations of faculty, staff, students, administrators, donors and friends of UTC who love the university that has been presented to us. As the University of Tennessee at Chattanooga sets out on its new journeys in the year 2000, we are aware that we face uncertainties similar to those faced often in the first 100 years. The university has fought with courageous intellectual capital to overcome fiscal and other obstacles to academic quality and access and to maintain the institution's integrity. We know with the Pulitzer prize-winning author, Edward Albee, not to cave in to fear. In his play, *Who's Afraid of Virginia Woolf?*, Albee reminds us:

> It's very simple, when people can't abide things as they are, when they can't abide the present, they do one of two things. Either they... turn to contemplation of the past,... or they set about to alter the future.

The new lesson of the 21st century, though, might well be to join our contemplation of the past with our continued zeal to alter the future for Tennesseans. In the lessons of our first century might well lie the principles and policies to alter the ways we prepare our students to improve the quality of life, for others as well as themselves, in the 21st century.

Frederick Obear, Chancellor Emeritus
Bill Stacy, Chancellor

INTRODUCTION

It is, sir, as I have said, a small college,
and yet there are those who love it.
Daniel Webster, arguing before the Supreme Court in the
Dartmouth College Case, 1818

This dear place
UC's late classics professor, Dr. Joseph Callaway,
in conversation with President LeRoy Martin

Without question, the most significant event with which John Longwith has had to deal in this centennial history is the merger in 1969 of the University of Chattanooga and the University of Tennessee. Concomitantly with this merger was that also of Chattanooga City College into the UT system. This centennial history, the account that John Longwith has written, is not a public relations document; he is too honest and too good a research man and writer to fall into that trap. Nevertheless, those of us who have known and loved the University in many ways for many years must face the problem of nostalgia.

Several hundred UC alumni live in the Chattanooga metropolitan area; many of them still long for what they think of as the good old days. They are those who have never acknowledged the wider opportunities that the University of Tennessee system offers UTC as one of its major campuses. It is impossible to read this book without recognizing those opportunities that have opened to us as part of the UT system. There are certainly also those alumni, among whom I count myself, who, given all the circumstances that obtained, accept the merger as both inevitable and beneficial.

Perhaps the more visible advantages the merger made possible were less important than those having to do with educational opportunities in this community, but nevertheless they mattered significantly. If I may be excused for using personal illustrations: when I became chairman of the English department in the summer of 1963, I did not have the convenience of a telephone in my office on the first floor of Race Hall. Dr. Maxwell Smith, who had retired a few years earlier after a long tenure as dean of Arts and Sciences, had an office just down the hall from mine, and he kindly left his office door unlocked so that I could use his telephone.

Nor did I have a dependable typewriter; what I had was an elderly manual typewriter, and when I asked the provost if it would not be possible for me to have an electric typewriter, his laughter was dismissive. Nevertheless within a few days, a portable electric Smith-Corona was delivered to my office. Following the merger, a young IBM sales representative spent so much time on the campus that he was sometimes taken for a new faculty member, hoping for a tenure track position.

A much more important and immediate change was the increase in the enrollment of minority students and the disadvantaged. The merger did not inaugurate the desegregation of UC of course; the graduate programs were desegregated in 1963 and the undergraduate the following year. Sometimes I hear comments that seem to imply that all the faculty and staff were adamantly opposed to desegregation, but that is simply not true. My own experience tells me that we had among us very few determined racists. The opposition to desegregation, such as it was, came from certain of the UC trustees; it was they who vetoed an honorary degree for Ralph McGill, editor of the Atlanta *Constitution*, a native son of Hamilton County, a graduate of McCallie School. McGill's sin, of course, was that he was a racial moderate as demonstrated in his columns in the *Constitution*, and more especially in his book called *The South and the Southerner*, published in 1963, a truly seminal book, especially for those who longed to see the influence of the Judaic and Christian tradition brought to bear on public policy in the United States of America.

I think very often of the passion of the two quotations that serve as epigraphs for this introduction: Daniel Webster's love for Dartmouth College and Joe Callaway's affectionate reference to our own campus as "this dear place." Dr. LeRoy Martin during his tenure as president of UC (1959-1966) on more than one occasion expressed public annoyance at being asked at educational meetings and similar gatherings out of town, how large the University of Chattanooga was. I share vicariously Dr. Martin's annoyance. There are far more important questions to ask — the level of intellectual challenge, the striving for excellence, the willingness to try new measures. Many questions are more important than the size of a school.

In a convocation address in Patten Chapel at the beginning of a fall term, early in his presidency, Dr. Martin's speech was as memorable as any I have ever heard on that sort of occasion. He had a great fondness for students; he and Mrs. Martin had two daughters of their own, and he liked young people. He was interested in the life of the mind, and that convocation address 40 years ago was full of sound and affectionate advice. One point he made, as I recall, is that all the administrative machinery, and all the equipment, have as their role to enhance and facilitate the educational experience. That is the reason for their existence. It is a point to keep in mind in reading this book.

John Longwith's history of the university, both UC and UTC, shows us, I think, that Shakespeare's words in *The Tempest* are validated once again: "What's past is prologue." The present state of the University is an outgrowth of the past, of our history and our traditions. The present is the fulfillment of the past, and in a hundred ways the University continues to deserve our loyal allegiance.

George Connor
Guerry Professor of English, Emeritus

ACKNOWLEDGMENTS

As Bernard De Voto wrote of his epic history, *The Course of Empire*, "This book is a clearinghouse for the books and ideas of others." So, too, in its much more modest way is this book about the university at Chattanooga. Many people have contributed to its final shape, and I am indebted to them for information, ideas, insight, and even the occasional well-timed word of encouragement.

Among those who consented to interviews or otherwise influenced the contents of this book are: Edward Boling, Richard Buhrman, Patricia Bytnar, Edward Cahill, Chuck Cantrell, Susan Cardwell, Roland Carter, Roland C. Carter, George Connor, Annette Conrad, George Cress, James Drinnon, Jr., Louise Griffith, Benjamin Gross, John Guerry, Zan Guerry, Douglas Hale, William Hales, Jr., Thor Hall, Jane Harbaugh, Arlie Herron, Holly Hodges, Ruth Holmberg, Ken Hood, Larry Ingle, Joe Jackson, Joseph E. Johnson, Ziad Keilany, Margaret Kelley, Milton Klein, Lawrence Levine, James Livingood, and David Lockmiller.

And also: John T. Lupton II, Curtis Lyons, June McEwen, Carolyn Mitchell, Fouad Moughrabi, Frederick Obear, David Parker, Vincent Pellegrino, Rickie Pierce, John Prados, William W. Prince, Scott Probasco, Jr., Charles Renneisen, Gene Roberts, Reed Sanderlin, Natalie Schlack, Bill W. Stacy, Robert J. Sudderth, Jr., Timothy Summerlin, Mary Tanner, John Trimpey, Robert Kirk Walker, Dorothy Hackett Ward, James A. Ward, James G. Ware, Thomas C. Ware, Harold Wilkes, and Raymond Witt, Jr.

I also owe a substantial debt to Gilbert Govan and James Livingood, not only for their 1947 history, *The University of*

Chattanooga: Sixty Years, but for the wealth of archival material they unearthed in the process of writing that book. The fruits of their research were my principal source for the years 1884-1941.

Another rich trove of archival material was gathered by George Connor in the early 1980s, when he conducted a series of revealing interviews with faculty and administrators ranging from William Masterson and Edwin Lindsey to Paul Palmer and August Eberle. Those tape-recorded interviews were never far from hand as I worked to understand the interplay of personality and circumstance that shaped the course of events after World War II.

Special thanks also go to Fred Obear, Deborah Arfken, and George Connor for reading and commenting on the manuscript; to Linda Walker, editor of *UTC: A Pictorial Review*, who tracked down and turned over to UTC more than a few of the photographs reproduced herein; and to Peggy Gregory for typing the research notes that formed the substance of this book.

Finally, I am pleased to acknowledge the generous support of the Benwood Foundation, the Hamico Foundation, Mr. and Mrs. Olan Mills II, and the University of Chattanooga Foundation.

April 1999   J.L.

1
The Methodist University

Rebuild thy walls, thy bounds enlarge
And send thy heralds forth
Say to the South 'Give up thy charge'
And 'keep not back, O North!'
– Hymn of the Methodist Episcopal Church (North), 1878 edition

Bishop Isaac Wiley cultivated the more remote, wilder vineyards of the Methodist Episcopal Church North. Recently, he had come back from the mission fields of China to accept dominion over the church's educational work in the American South, where an opening of great promise appeared in 1884. On the afternoon of February 6 in that year, Bishop Wiley stood with a group of his fellow churchmen on a treeless hilltop at the east end of Chattanooga, Tennessee. Here they were gathered to plant a school.

They pictured it as a university of the same academic caliber as their estranged brethren, the Southern Methodists, had brought forth at Vanderbilt in Nashville, or as the Episcopalians had founded nearby at Sewanee. Bishop Wiley was on hand to conduct the groundbreaking ceremony for the school, to be called Chattanooga University. It was to be the Church North's "great central university for the white population... in that [Southern] territory lying east of the Mississippi river."[1]

The school property took in about 13 gently sloping acres and extended two square blocks down McCallie Avenue and two square blocks back to Vine Street. On one edge had been the town hanging grounds. Foundation lines for the proposed building were laid out. On the high ground above McCallie Avenue, a temporary wooden grandstand faced the spot where Bishop Wiley would drive a stake to mark the building's northeast corner. The spot commanded fine views.

From the hilltop, Bishop Wiley looked out over a broad river valley and onto one of the small islands of industrialism in a largely agrarian region. Soot, grit, and coal dust billowed from the railroad yards, blast furnaces, tanneries, and saw mills of Chattanooga. Local boosters spoke of it as the future "Pittsburgh of the South." Already the air had a reddish color about it.[2] In the far distance, Bishop Wiley could see the river basin terminate in steep encircling ranges dominated in the south by Lookout Mountain, in the northwest by Walden's Ridge, and in the east by Missionary Ridge, which Union forces commanded by General Grant had taken on a hazy November morning just 20 years ago.

Joining the group with Bishop Wiley were various local dignitaries who exchanged pleasantries with their northern visitors while they waited for the ceremony to begin. Visions of progress rather than memories of old quarrels animated them; current disagreements were politely left unmentioned. Local initiative and church patronage had brought this diverse group together on this piece of common ground, but not without a long struggle. Three of their number knew just how difficult it had been to advance the cause of Chattanooga University even to this point of inception.

One was Dr. Richard S. Rust, deputy to Bishop Wiley, authority on the church's southern work and staunch advocate of Chattanooga's bid for the "central university." Another was Captain Hiram S. Chamberlain, iron-and-coal magnate who led the drive to underwrite a portion of the school's initial cost through local sources. And there was the Reverend John J. Manker, minister of the town's First Methodist Church, several of whose members, including Captain Chamberlain, formed the essential core of community support for the school. Manker had also played a key role in securing for Chattanooga University the official endorsement of Northern Methodists in the Holston Conference of East Tennessee and surrounding conferences. With Dr. Rust's help, Manker had asserted the primacy of Chattanooga's claim on the Church North until finally outmaneuvering rival claimants from other localities in the area.

By two o'clock on this February afternoon in 1884, the hilltop began to draw a crowd of townspeople, some arriving in carriages but most on foot. Among them were "the intelligence and wealth of Chattanooga," reported the local *Times*. They gathered near the crest of the hill, around the northeast corner point. Many of the onlookers waited expectantly for Bishop Wiley's words, wondering whether he would take hold of a troublesome question. Rumors had circulated for months that Chattanooga University would educate black as well as white students. Local organizers vigorously denied any such intention, but equivocal statements from various agencies of the Church North had kept the issue very much alive.[3]

At 2:30 sharp, Bishop Wiley opened the ceremony with a brief welcome and then started off by telling his listeners that

Chattanooga University was as yet an "incipient movement" whose "bearing on the future" was unknowable. No one could "divine the outspreading consequences" or anticipate the "result of driving this stake and beginning the work of erecting this structure."

While prepared to leave the future to his listeners' imaginations, Wiley reserved for himself the role of defining present intentions and motives. He ventured no closer to the question of the color line than to say that the school was, first of all, "an affair of the city of Chattanooga." Its intentions were strictly honorable. It meant "no harm," had "no hidden purpose." There was, he averred, "no motive other than the common, the highest and best – to rear a university that will stand for ages, disseminating light, intelligence and the higher morality."

Toward the close of his remarks, Bishop Wiley permitted himself a quick glimpse into the future. He visualized for the audience "a cluster of magnificent structures" and an institution dedicated as much to social uplift as to higher education. Chattanooga University would promote sectional reconciliation, become a school of national unity, a noble experiment yielding "the first and best illustration of how we can better understand each other." What more auspicious ground for reconciliation could be found than "in this valley where battles were fought, in sight of the graves of fallen heroes of both sides...where Northern money is placed beside Southern money...where the South and the North meet as brothers"? He concluded by inviting one and all to join in raising a temple consecrated to the Brave New South: "Let us shake hands together, forget the past and feel that we have a common destiny… We will better know each other's minds, our hearts will beat side by side, and there will be no North, no South, no East, no West."

With that, Bishop Wiley lifted up a wooden stake, positioned it on the northeast corner and, while holding it on the spot, raised his eyes upward and invoked divine blessings on the enterprise, then struck the stake three blows, hammering it into the ground.

Wiley next took up a shovel and gouged out the first clump of earth. He passed the shovel along to Chattanooga Mayor Hugh Whiteside, first in the party of officials who each in turn removed a spadeful of earth. Some handled the shovel expertly, while others "manipulated it somewhat awkwardly." When they were through, another prayer was said, and the onlookers slowly began to depart.

And so it was that Northern Methodism embarked on its third attempt to bring forth "a great central university" in East Tennessee. Two earlier attempts had failed for lack of broad popular support. In neither case had the organizers been able to rise above the narrow interests of sect and section. Instead of promoting tolerance and understanding, they often sowed dragons' teeth. As an instrument of reconciliation and enlightenment, the Church North was a blunt tool, its edge dulled by internal dissension and a reputation for combativeness.

The American Methodist movement had split over the issue of slavery in 1844 and, while the nation itself achieved formal reunion in 1877, the sundered halves of the denomination – known in the vernacular as "Methodists North of God and Methodists South of God" – did not reunite until 1939. Any chance of speedier reunion was lost during the final months of the Civil War, when Northern Methodism aggressively expanded southward into territory occupied by Federal forces. Armed with a War Department edict that permitted the seizure of all Southern Methodist "houses of worship… in which a loyal minister… appointed by a loyal bishop… does not officiate," Bishop Matthew Simpson directed a campaign of expropriation with intent to "disintegrate the rival body, and absorb whatever of it shall be worth preserving."[4] Southern Methodist preachers who refused to recant were barred from their church buildings and had to conduct services at makeshift sites such as courthouses, private dwellings, and groves.

Simpson's predatory policy never gained the unanimous approval of his fellow bishops. Moderate counsels eventually prevailed, and by 1876 most of the expropriated churches had been returned to their owners. But there remained bitter memories of the northern church's attempt, in the words of one Tennesseean, "to establish a religion at the point of a bayonet."

Nowhere in the South were those memories more deeply imbedded than in East Tennessee. To the people of that area, the Church North would long be associated with the virulent "Fighting Parson" William G. Brownlow. "I am not a moderate man," he once declared modestly. Whether traveling the backroads as a Methodist circuit rider or later while editing the Knoxville *Whig* or still later when serving as Governor of Tennessee, Brownlow poured a steady stream of scalding words onto the Devil, Southern Methodists, Rebels, Democrats, and other enemies of the "true religion." He excelled at stirring up hate and encouraging vigilante justice, neither of which required much encouragement in upper East Tennessee, where Unionists and Confederates had been bullwhipping, bushwacking, and murdering one another since 1862. In the pages of his Knoxville *Whig*, Brownlow preached a war of vengeance against ex-Confederates who, he wrote, had "forfeited all rights to citizenship, and to life itself."

Actuated by similar motives in 1864, Brownlow rallied Northern Methodist forces throughout East Tennessee, organized them into what would become the Holston Annual Conference, and petitioned the church for recognition. That recognition, granted in 1865, empowered the Holston Conference to manage church affairs within its boundaries, subject to the supreme jurisdiction of the quadrennial General Conference. Under Parson Brownlow's tutelage, the Holston Conference set about cleansing its domain of "rebel preachers." Its "loyal members and ministers" expressed their resolve to "claim and hold... with the Divine Blessing... all property belonging to [Southern Methodism]... and rebuild the waste places of Zion."[5] They seized about 100 Southern Methodist churches in East Tennessee and still occupied 18 of the churches and one parsonage as late as 1873.[6]

Through other means, the Holston Conference also came into possession of a Southern Methodist school, the Athens Female College, in Athens, Tennessee. During the war, the school had run up enormous debts, a large portion of which were owed to its president, Erastus Rowley. In 1865, Rowley renounced the Church South and united with the Holston Conference as a preacher. He thereupon sued the school for monies it owed him and, when the court ordered the school property sold to satisfy debtors' claims, purchased it for considerably less than its estimated value. In 1866, Rowley sold the building, land, and equipment to the Holston Conference.[7] A year later, the state legislature granted to William Brownlow, Thomas H. Pearne, John F. Spence, and other incorporators a charter that conferred upon their school the name East Tennessee Wesleyan College.

Before long, Methodists of the Church North were

congratulating themselves on having established in the South their own "Loyal College... true to science, country, morality and religion." The rejoicing was overhasty, for East Tennessee Wesleyan suffered a chronic lack of both the students and money necessary to elevate its program of instruction above that of "a good village academy." Because of the ties to Brownlowism, the school exerted little charm except in upper East Tennessee and among the Parson's northern friends, who provided the last-minute benefactions that alone sustained the school. Geographically, too, East Tennessee Wesleyan was an isolated outpost. Athens, located midway between Knoxville and Chattanooga, was a drowsy farm town with few resources to lend in the development of a regional college.

Church leaders, recognizing the impediments at Athens, decided to examine the possibility of an alternative venue for the central Methodist university. In 1873, representatives from conferences in the central South elected a committee to determine the most suitable location for the institution. Chattanooga, Knoxville, and Athens emerged as the top three choices. The committee asked for material tokens of interest from each city. Pointing out that "such an institution would bring money into any place," the committee-men intimated to petitioners that the consideration given to their applications would be proportional to their respective donations of cash and acreage. When the committee delivered its report, the prize went to Knoxville, whose merchants and bankers had pledged $50,000 and 40 acres of land.

The projected school, at first called Central Methodist, was chartered as Knoxville University in 1873. Land was acquired and trustees elected before anyone noticed that an embarrassingly large discrepancy existed between the handsome sums pledged and the meager amounts actually being collected. As subscribers defaulted on their commitments, the trustees cast about for "some princely minded friend… possessed of adequate means" and willing to bestow a gift of such magnitude that the proposed university would "cheerfully change its name" in order to memorialize him.[8] That lure, however, failed to catch a Vanderbilt, a Carnegie, or a Peabody. Benevolent agencies of the national church, focused as they were on the stark educational needs of freedmen, declined to rescue the venture in higher education for whites. When, toward the end of 1873, pleas for funds were also ignored by Northern Methodists in places that had been passed over in favor of Knoxville, plans for the school had to be dropped.

East Tennessee Wesleyan remained as it had been since 1867, the denomination's only "high grade" school for whites in all the South; but even that solitary outpost tottered on the edge of bankruptcy in 1875. The miscarriage of Knoxville University and the plight of East Tennessee Wesleyan confounded and disheartened the region's Northern Methodists. They blamed the situation on national church authorities who, by allotting some 80 percent of available funds to the aid and education of freedmen, were "not doing their duty to the white people in the South." A Tennessee cleric indignantly observed: "It is a well-known fact that one-half of the whites are in a condition in reference to education in which it is… as much a Christian duty to aid them as the colored people."

Others were less inclined to appeal strictly on the basis of "Christian duty." Pragmatists argued that the apportionment of funds was inexpedient, detrimental to the church's regional ambitions. The expansion of Northern Methodism was imperiled, said its southern adherents, so long as northern officialdom viewed the southern work as primarily a mission to the black people. The perceptiveness of this reasoning could not be easily faulted after 10 years in which the Church North had struggled in vain to outgrow its status as a marginal, upstart institution in the South. One faction of northern officials had already begun to talk about the necessity of securing "a lodgement... among the ruling classes in the South," but advocates of radical Reconstruction were still in control. [9]

In 1875, the Holston Conference passed a resolution asking that the "next General Conference... so adjust the educational... machinery of the Church as to bestow upon white schools... the material aid which their importance demands." Though besieged by entreaties of that kind from various southern conferences, the General Conference of 1876 could not be persuaded to modify the church's policy.

The plaintive query – "Is nothing to be done for... white people?" – received a more sympathetic hearing at the next General Conference, in 1880, when the assembled delegates sanctioned the development and maintenance of schools for "white members and friends" to the extent possible without compromising "the work among our people of color." Responsibility for carrying out the directive was given to a church agency whose name described its purpose: the Freedmen's Aid Society. Located in Cincinnati, the Freedmen's Aid Society had collected and disbursed $893,918 during the 13 years since its formation in 1866. The Society's financial resources, however, were hardly adequate to sustain the sheer number of its undertakings, which amounted to more than 50 schools of various academic and vocational levels by 1879. In addition to operating the loose network of freedmen's schools, it was now thrust into the business of developing separate schools for whites.

Up until 1874, the Freedmen's Aid Society had enjoyed liberal subsidies from the Freedmen's Bureau, which had exasperated southern whites more than any other Federal agency of Reconstruction, and with which the Society was often confused. Recalling the earlier ties, many native whites regarded the Freedmen's Aid Society and the Church North itself as little more than "the religious auxiliary of the Radical party."[10] That popular conception was a bit timeworn by 1880. The Society's board of managers, taken as a group, displayed a wide and shifting spectrum of attitudes toward their charge. At one extreme, there were those who felt called upon to reshape southern society in the image of New England Methodism, and at the other end there were those who had come to believe that the path of wisdom lay in doing what was possible within the existing social order.

Of those in the latter group, Dr. Richard Rust had the fewest illusions. In 1866, as founder of the Freedmen's Aid Society, Rust had vowed that the South would be evangelized "even should it be necessary… to drench again the land in blood." But 13 years as secretary, or chief operating officer, of the Society had taught him better. Noted for his sagacity, forbearance, and persuasive powers, this one-time apostle of the sword was, in the words of a contemporary, "the veritable Nestor" of the church's educational work in the South.

The decision to include both races within the Society's purview revived hopes for a "great central university." Southern conferences clamored to win Dr. Rust's endorsement of a first-class college in the central South. That territory included seven conferences and extended along the Appalachian corridor from lower Kentucky and Virginia to upper Alabama and Georgia. Politically, this area was dominated by the Holston Conference, which effectively laid claim to the central university. Rust showed interest, provided that Conference members united behind an eligible location where the citizenry would join with the Society to build up the school. His request taxed the Conference's limited capacity to act in harmony. Though Parson Brownlow had died in 1877, his adversarial style was still much in evidence. Dissension within the membership had become so acute by 1878 that Conference leaders, citing "the crowded state of our work," asked that no more clergymen be transferred to the body. Internal strife grew worse, reaching an explosive climax during the early 1890s when, according to a church historian, the Conference was "greatly disturbed... by charges and counter charges [of misconduct], followed by several trials," acquittals, civil suits, and the withdrawal from communion in 1895 of ten disgruntled clergymen.[11]

The underlying personal conflicts surfaced during the early planning stage of the university. Differences of opinion as to its proper location caused divisions that hardened and resulted in a standoff between the defenders of Athens and the advocates of Chattanooga. The Athenian faithful were led by the Reverend John Fletcher Spence, president of East Tennessee Wesleyan. John Spence had been a circuit-riding preacher in Ohio and then a chaplain in the U.S. Army during the war before moving south to cast his lot with the followers of William G. Brownlow. In later years, Spence credited himself with having largely "drafted... the papers that... organized" the Holston Conference, and he reportedly was "very active" in pursuing the Conference's original objective of dispossessing Southern Methodism.[12] Small and compact of frame, Spence stood rigidly erect, with his bearded chin thrust forward. He was a clear speaker and a prodigious worker who "slept, wrote...

planned, and taught classes in the same room" at East Tennessee Wesleyan. The years of single-minded dedication to the beleaguered school had greatly magnified its merits in his eyes. Spence's devotion to East Tennessee Wesleyan was exceeded only by his implacable hostility toward any arrangement that would locate the central university away from Athens and beyond his direct control.

Spence's stand at Athens aroused considerable opposition in the Chattanooga district, notably from one of his own former pupils and allies, the Reverend John Jenkins Manker. A native Ohioan and son of a Quaker convert to Methodism, John Manker had decided upon a religious vocation at the age of 19 and was a seminarian at Ohio Wesleyan three years later when the war halted his studies. Following service as a captain of Federal cavalry, he had moved to East Tennessee, affiliated with the Holston Conference in 1866, and over the next four years served as minister of the Methodist Church in Athens, while also teaching Greek at East Tennessee Wesleyan and completing requirements there for the B.A. degree. He earned an M.A. from Ohio Wesleyan shortly afterward. In 1873, at the age of 33, Manker was elected president of East Tennessee Wesleyan; but, perhaps foreseeing his inability to work with business manager John Spence and other trustees, he turned down the post, which subsequently devolved upon Spence. Manker's aspirations as a college builder lay elsewhere.

After seven further years in pastorates in upper East Tennessee, Manker was transferred in 1880 to the First Methodist Church in Chattanooga. There his ministry flourished as never before. The First Methodist was, he recalled, located on Pine Street in a "decidedly unattractive" frame building with windows "glazed over as though intended for a saloon," and the membership, composed almost entirely of immigrants from the North, numbered no more than one hundred.[13] Though small in size and of humble appearance, the church had a membership list that read like a who's who of Chattanooga's most affluent families: the Chamberlains, Wilders, Pattens, Whelands, Gahagans, Woodworths, and other well-to-do citizens could be found there every Sunday. Within a year, Reverend Manker inspired them to undertake a grand and costly building project. Despite the misgivings of fiscal conservatives, ground was broken at the corner of McCallie and Georgia Avenues and work began on a magnificent edifice, known as the "Stone Church" because it was the first and, for many years, only church building of stone in the area. When completed in 1885, it was said to be "by far the most impressive building in the community."

Manker soon hit upon another project worthy of the potent energies he had awakened among the laity of First Methodist. Well before the Stone Church was under roof, he was urging them to imagine the turrets and spires of a church university rising majestically above their city. The image scratched its way into their fancy, and various members offered to start raising the earnest money needed in order to attract funding from the Freedmen's Aid Society. Chattanooga's initiative provoked a response from the Holston Conference in October 1881. Adopting a resolution offered by John Spence, the Conference declared its preference for Athens as the site of a central university and designated Knoxville as the only other acceptable location. The action excluded Chattanooga and restricted consideration to cities whose superiority was questionable: Knoxville because the University of Tennessee was entrenched there, Athens because the Freedmen's Aid Society was known to be unenthusiastic about it. Spence and those voting with him seemed prepared to do without a central university rather than see it go to Chattanooga.

During the spring of 1882, Manker discreetly put Chattanooga's case before Bishop Henry W. Warren of Atlanta and Dr. Rust of the Freedmen's Aid Society. While they were powerless to overrule the Holston Conference, they could bring considerable pressure to bear on its members. Bishop Warren and Dr. Rust were ready to exercise vigorous guidance when the "Education Convention" of the Holston Conference met in May 1882 to sort out differences prior to the Conference's formal session in October.

With Bishop Warren presiding as chairman, the Education Convention transacted its business smoothly until the Reverend Manker introduced a resolution that would give the Freedmen's Aid Society authority to select the university's location from a list of three cities to be submitted by a screening committee of Central South churchmen chaired by Bishop Warren. This move to circumvent the Holston Conference set off a "stormy debate." Reverend Spence charged that the proposed method of selection was a sham because the Freedmen's Aid Society, which would have the final say, was "prejudiced in favor of Chattanooga." Rust and Manker argued for the resolution. Finally, Bishop Warren made "a few guarded remarks" favorable to the resolution, whereupon, after some parliamentary skirmishes over tabling the measure, it was put to a vote and passed.

Delegates to the Holston Conference, assembling in Chattanooga on October 19, 1882, unanimously approved the method of selection and pledged "to abide by and support" the decision ultimately handed down by the Society's board in

Cincinnati. In a further act of deference, the delegates retracted and nullified "all former expressions of preference made by the conference." Definite traces of preference, however, soon appeared on the freshly wiped slate. Outward harmony gave way to frank and pointed expressions of preference during an address delivered by Dr. Rust. According to a participant, Dr. Rust suggested to the delegates that if they "would unite on Knoxville or Chattanooga at once," the Society was prepared to be most generous. His remark occasioned a lively exchange which, as the participant records it, began when a crusty itinerant in the audience, the Reverend W.H. Rogers, posed this impolitic question: Would not Athens do as well?

Dr. Rust – That is hardly a fair question.

(Voices in the audience – Don't answer it.)

Dr. Rust – Yes, I will; I never did like dodging the question.

My opinion is that Chattanooga is the place.

(Applause by the Chattanooga people.)

Bishop Warren called the site screening committee to meet in Chattanooga on February 28, 1883; only eight of its 16 members showed up, but one held a proxy that enabled them to proceed. Following brief tours of inspection in Chattanooga, Athens, and Knoxville, the committee took its ballot. To no one's surprise, the vote went decisively to Chattanooga as first choice, with Knoxville coming in second and Athens third. It was then left to the Freedmen's Aid Society to name the place which, wrote a jaundiced clergyman, "shall be the fortunate Educational Eldorado of our southern work."

The board in Cincinnati took the matter under advisement while two of its officers, Dr. Rust and Bishop John M. Walden, paid frequent visits to Chattanooga, explaining to Northern Methodists there that a strong display of local generosity would secure the university for Chattanooga. Bishop John Walden was soon to be a prominent figure in district church affairs. He became the district's first residing bishop in 1884 and succeeded Bishop Isaac Wiley as president of the Freedmen's Aid Society upon Wiley's death in Foochow, China later that same year. The sum that Walden and Rust sought to obtain locally was not inconsiderable, except in relation to the Society's own projected expenditure of an initial $70,000. As Walden recalled: "It was thought that if $15,000 could be raised in Chattanooga the Society would be warranted in planting a school [there]."

Within a short time, pledges totaling $13,000 had been received, mostly from the laity of First Methodist, including John Wesley Adams, architect and builder of the Stone Church, the County Jail, and several of the town's finer residences; Andrew Jackson "Jack" Gahagan, lumberman and furniture manufacturer; General John T. Wilder, a promoter who had teamed up with northern capitalists to develop the area's iron and steel industry; Henry Clay Beck, owner of Title Guaranty & Trust Company; David Woodworth, tannery superintendent for absentee owners in the North; and Captain Hiram Chamberlain, an official of the Roane Iron Company and an astute businessman whom the New York *Herald Tribune* identified as one of "the seven millionaires of Chattanooga" in 1892.

Those donors predicted that the full $15,000 would be forthcoming. They were mistaken; only "about $11,000" materialized, but that was inducement enough for the Society.[14] Its board of managers declared their intention to establish a regional college of the church in Chattanooga and in July 1883 paid $31,000 for the 13-acre site where, seven months later, on February 6, 1884, the hosts of Northern Methodism gathered to break ground for Chattanooga University.

Following the ritual of groundbreaking, more than a year passed without sign of construction activity on University Hill. The Freedmen's Aid Society, with its numerous obligations elsewhere and a debt outstanding on the Chattanooga property, was evidently in no hurry to finance a major building project. Not until November 1885, 20 months after Bishop Wiley had driven the corner stake into place, did actual construction begin. Once underway, the work went quickly, and by the spring of 1886 an imposing, four-story structure of brick and cut stone loomed on the hilltop. Its main tower, standing 130 feet high and topped by a gilded spire, commanded the attention of travelers approaching the city from any direction. The ponderous, elaborated facade was variously described as an "admixture of Queen Anne and Gothic," as "French," and still yet as "modified Gothic." Unquestionably, the massive pile of brick and stone was a classic example of architectural taste in the Gilded Age.

Designed and built by John Wesley Adams at the contract price of $40,000, the building was soon dubbed "Old Main." With roughly 7,000 square feet of space on *each* of its four floors, plus a full-size, labyrinthine basement that "resembled the catacombs of Rome," Old Main could and did house the whole works: science laboratories, a chapel seating 400, 39 dormitory rooms accommodating up to 150 boarders, administrative offices, classrooms, a library, dining hall and kitchen, boiler rooms, and apartments for faculty and staff.

Images of Old Main that have survived in writing are no less picturesque and variegated than the building itself. To a memorist who grew up within its walls and later returned as a professor, "the old red brick building" seemed to have been designed by an architect who "belonged literally to the 'dark ages.' While all the rooms on the outside had light and air, inside the monolithic structure there were great areas of darkness… A few gas jets flickered feebly but they gave little light… I'd say they'd rate about 10 candle power each, and when you sat in a chair under one of them and tried to read, you could hardly see the printing in the book."[15]

Others saw radiance through the gloom. For those students who came to Chattanooga University straight off hard-scrabble farms in the coves and pine barrens of Appalachia, Old Main must have been an amazing sight, as wondrous to them as the spires of Oxford would have been to a medieval countryman. It was the most impressive building they had ever seen, their first glimpse of opportunity and an undiscovered world. Some idea of this affective power was captured by a Chattanooga *Times* reporter who, after viewing the building by night, wrote: "This Institution is a light upon a hill, in a literal as well as a figurative sense. It is lighted throughout with gas, and when it is illuminated in the evening, it is truly a light upon a hill, a thing of real beauty."

Furnishing and equipping Old Main increased the total start-up costs to about $85,000, almost 90 percent of which had been contributed by the Freedmen's Aid Society. With so much capital already invested and the likelihood that still more would be needed, the Society and its Chattanooga partners, together with representatives from the six cooperating conferences, met in June 1886 to define their respective rights and duties in the enterprise. Twenty-eight of them agreed to serve as both incorporators of

Chattanooga University and its first board of trustees. John Manker, Hiram Chamberlain, and 14 other Chattanoogans took seats on the board, as did 10 conference delegates. Joining them were Dr. Rust and Bishop Walden, who was elected board president.[16]

The term "board of trustees" was somewhat misleading in this case, since it implied that the trustees governed and directed the university, whereas their function was more nearly that of branch managers. Their decisions were subject to a higher authority, whose home office was in Cincinnati. As the charter stated, Chattanooga University was "owned... [and] under the... control [of] the Freedmen's Aid Society of the Methodist Episcopal Church." The board's subordinate role was spelled out in a contract, undated except for the year, 1886, and headed "An Agreement between the Freedmen's Aid Society... and the Chattanooga University." By its terms, the local board could use and occupy the university property so long as the two parties agreed on matters of school policy and management. In the event of disagreement, either party could terminate the arrangement by giving one year's notice, at which time the property reverted to the Society.

Apart from assuming responsibility for any operating deficits, the Society had few obligations. Its prerogatives were more numerous, including authority to appoint all officers and faculty, fill vacancies on the board (the majority of whose members were to be Northern Methodists), regulate expenditures, approve salaries, and control such funds as might one day go into endowment. Chattanooga University was, in effect, a wholly-owned subsidiary of the Freedmen's Aid Society. The Agreement did, however, contain a buy-out clause in which the Society obligated itself to transfer ownership of the property to the local board, provided that the board built up an endowment sufficient to sustain the school and that it "refunded" all monies invested by the Society.[17]

In accordance with the contract, Dr. Rust, as secretary of the Society, had charge of hiring a faculty and its president. "At least five times as many well recommended persons as [could] possibly be employed" vied for places on the faculty. Rust quickly filled three of the places, announcing those appointments while the search for a president was still underway. He named the Reverend John Manker dean of theology, a post which ranked second to that of president in the hierarchy. Rust chose as professor of natural sciences the Reverend Wesley W. Hooper, then president of Rust University, a school established for blacks in Holly Springs, Mississippi. And he picked Wilford Caulkins, for some years on the faculty of East Tennessee Wesleyan, to be professor of ancient languages. The first-year faculty was later rounded out with four additional appointments: the Reverend Robert Steudel, instructor in modern languages; E.A. Robertson, mathematics instructor; Frank Adams, music instructor; and Mary A. Presnell, professor of English and preceptress.

Besides teaching their courses, the faculty members would live on the premises and act *in loco parentis*. It was their responsibility to oversee student activity in all its particulars, stimulating scholarship and piety alike. They were expected to train the intellects, regulate the behavior, and attend to the moral and spiritual welfare of a large population of boarding students, girls as well as boys. All this would take place in a communal setting where the faculty and their young charges worked, dined, worshiped, and went about their daily lives in close proximity under one roof. "By having the professors and their families live in the institution with the students," the founders aimed, as they put it, "to combine the best advantages of collegiate culture and training with the comfort and watch care of the Christian Home."

In late July 1886, just three weeks before the school was to open, Dr. Rust named as its acting president the Reverend Edward S. Lewis, a native of Massachusetts and a graduate of Boston University (B.A. 1877, M.A. 1881). The Reverend Lewis, 31 years old at the time, had a little less than five years' experience as a college administrator for the Freedmen's Aid Society. He came to Chattanooga from another school operated by the Society, Little Rock University, where he had been president since 1882.

Lewis and his faculty colleagues worked out matters of curriculum, student governance, and academic standards during the first week of September. Their academic blueprint incorporated most of the traditional features of the American college as it had existed, before the trends toward "practical" learning, elective courses, and extracurricular growth began to reshape higher education. Those were trends that Lewis and the faculty wanted to avoid at Chattanooga University. They adopted fixed programs of study in which the fundamental subjects were Latin and Greek. No course of a purely technical or professional nature was offered, but students were given all the ingredients of a liberal education grounded in the languages and literary canon of Western civilization. Instruction in the sciences was less thorough, consisting of three years' work for the Bachelor of Science degree. The "classical course," which led to the B.A. degree, was the only four-year program of study. In it, the successful student had to demonstrate proficiency in, among other things, the languages and literary texts of three cultures, two ancient and one modern, in addition to his own.[18]

Besides the college of liberal arts, there were two other scholastic divisions: a school of theology and a college preparatory department. The School of Theology, headed by John Manker, would function as a denominational seminary, open to any candidate for the ministry who presented letters of endorsement from the appropriate church authorities. Of broader appeal was the "academic," or college preparatory, department. Such departments could be found at most colleges in the South; even Vanderbilt maintained one. Subcollegiate instruction was a necessity rather than an option in a region where public schooling stopped at the elementary level. In the absence of a secondary school system, Chattanooga University had to offer preparatory work; otherwise, few students in the area could have qualified for admission to its collegiate division. The academic department served as a feeder to the college and also generated more tuition income than the two other divisions combined. Preparatory students would vastly outnumber collegians during the early years; and, consequently, the general level of teaching would be closer to that of a high school than to that of a university. It was a "university" only in the fond hopes of its founders. As Dr. Rust acknowledged: "This is called a university. We have named the child ahead."

With prelates of the Church North occupying high positions on the faculty and board, it was inevitable that students would be barred from any activity which might have offended high-toned Methodist sensibilities. The rules governing student behavior contained all the denomination's favored moral prescriptions. There were the usual Methodist prohibitions against such forms of worldliness as dancing, the theatre, cosmetics, many games, "boisterous conduct," tobacco, and intoxicating drink. To members of a denomination that worked harder than any other for temperance laws, youthful experimentation with alcoholic beverages constituted an unpardonable offense. The faculty would deal summarily with offenders, including one Mr. B, who, it was determined, "had returned to the university intoxicated and... passed the night on the reception room floor." Finding Mr. B "guilty of visiting saloons," the faculty sent him packing. More innocent varieties of entertainment would also meet with official displeasure. When P.T. Barnum's circus rolled into town, the faculty placed it off limits to students.

In the early days, extracurricular activities abounded only in the devotional area. Failure to attend daily chapel services carried a penalty of one demerit, and habitual absences could result in suspension. Wednesday evening prayer meetings and periodic revivals, though not compulsory events, were urged on the students. And each Sunday, boarding students were expected to attend church in the company of faculty members, unless their parents had secured permission for them to attend some other than a Northern Methodist church.

The overall program of Chattanooga University faithfully reflected the American collegiate tradition except in one respect. The one great exception was its policy of coeducation. Received opinion had long held that girls neither required nor were fit for serious academic pursuits. The stress of college work could irreparably harm female nervous and reproductive systems, said many educators. Others darkly warned that too much learning would "masculinize" a young woman and, thereby, prevent her from fulfilling her destiny as wife and mother. Her fate, instead, would be an unhappy marriage or spinsterhood. Expanding on that belief, a student at Vanderbilt derisively remarked: "No man wants to come home at night and find his wife testing some new process for manufacturing oleomargarine, or in the observatory sweeping the heavens for a comet."

Given those cultural attitudes, few colleges admitted women on equal terms with men. In Tennessee, for example, not one of the three leading colleges in 1886 – Vanderbilt, Sewanee, or the University of Tennessee – enrolled women as students. At the handful of institutions which did adopt coeducation before the mid-1890's, administrators proceeded cautiously with the commingling of the sexes. Daniel Read, president of Missouri University when it opened to women in 1868, recalled that the change from an exclusively male student body was regarded as a "very bold and hazardous measure," and one which he and his associates implemented "by degrees… carefully feeling our way, as though explosive material was all about us."

Like the officials in Missouri, the faculty of Chattanooga University approached coeducation warily, ever on the alert to stamp out the sparks of student romance. Particular vigilance was demanded of the preceptress, Mary Presnell, who supervised the "morals and manners" of women students. Although the men and women attended class and chapel together and took meals in common, they otherwise were kept apart, restricted to separate study halls and literary societies, partitioned off in separate prayer meetings, and forbidden contact except when supervised by the faculty. A woman who so far forgot herself as to speak from her window to a passing man received five demerits for her effrontery, and the same penalty was meted out to male students guilty of similar infractions. Under no circumstances would the faculty permit boarding students of the opposite sex to visit one another in the dormitories. Men calling on residents of the women's dormitory were turned away by Mary Presnell, even brothers calling on sisters. And as a precaution against attempts to slip through Presnell's defenses, the faculty gave instructions that the dormitory door most vulnerable to illicit entry "be kept permanently locked, and that the corresponding doors on the second and third floors be locked by Mrs. Presnell at 4 P.M. each day, and kept locked until breakfast time the next morning."

Coeducation – albeit within the bounds of Victorian propriety – gave evidence of the founders' resolve to lay the basis for a broadly representative institution, one that catered neither to a single gender nor to a moneyed elite. Their plan called for an institution that would provide "first class... facilities at the lowest possible cost, and thus prove itself the school of the people – good enough for the richest and best, and cheap enough for those of the most limited means." Tuition and other charges were well within the popular price range. As Professor Wilford Caulkins wrote in August to a student prospect: "The Trustees... have fixed the schedule of expenses at... such low figures that it is really cheaper to attend school rather than stay at home.... The tuition is $10 per term, or $30 per year. Board including room furnished, heated and lighted, is only $1.50 per week. 40 weeks board at $1.50 = $60. Add $30 for tuition, and your *entire expense for the whole school year is only $90.*"

The call for students brought a response that exceeded the founders' "most sanguine expectations." On September 15, 1886, Chattanooga University opened with an enrollment of 118 students, and others continued to arrive until, five weeks later, their number stood at 175. Most of them came from parts of East Tennessee outside Chattanooga. Dormitory facilities, designed to accommodate

150 students, soon filled up, and cottages nearby were used to house the influx of out-of-town students.

With boarding capacity stretched to the limit, school and church officials began to talk of expansion. "We stand in absolute need of new buildings," said Bishop Mallalieu, and Acting President Lewis suggested to the Chattanooga *Times* that "additional structures would have to be erected before the close of the first year." Before the close of the first year, however, the school became entangled in a denominational quarrel that blighted its future. At issue was the way that Chattanooga University interpreted and carried out the church's policy on race relations.

2
A Double-Faced Somewhat

Let us be consistent Christian men if the heavens fall . . . .
A lofty consistency is better than Chattanooga University, after all.
While the Methodist Episcopal Church claims the world for its parish,
it cannot pursue a sectional policy anywhere.
– Edward S. Lewis, President of Chattanooga University, 1887

Among the applicants on opening day were two black men, William Wilson and Louis Gibbs, both in their mid-20s and both members of the Methodist Episcopal Church. Wilson and Gibbs presented themselves and their tuition money to John Manker. He asked them whether they were acting on their own or at the instigation of others. They insisted that no one had put them up to apply for admission. "We were not tools in anybody's hands," Wilson wrote, adding that he had sought admission to Chattanooga University "because I preferred to be in school with white boys to test my ability to compete with them in books and by measuring arms with them there."

Manker patiently explained that their applications put Chattanooga University "in an awkward position." Wilson and Gibbs listened as Manker pointed out that the school was intended for the education of whites and would lose its entire enrollment within "less than twenty-four hours" of admitting them or any other blacks as students. He tried to interest them in applying to Dr. Rust for scholarships at a school in Atlanta. They told him that Chattanooga "suited [them] better." He urged them to withdraw their applications, but they refused. "We told him that the faculty must act on them," Wilson recalled. Then, according to Wilson, Manker ended the conversation by saying: "Well, if you can thrust them upon us, we can act upon them."[1]

Manker and the other trustees decided to "quietly pigeon-hole" the applications, hoping to avoid a confrontation, for they knew that two members of the executive committee were eager to make a fight over the admission of blacks. They were Halbert B. Case, a lawyer associated with William Wilson in local politics, and the Reverend Thomas C. Carter, who edited the *Methodist Advocate* and who somehow managed to place himself in the thick of every controversy in the Holston Conference from the time he affiliated with it in 1884 until he angrily severed his connection with it in 1895. Carter and Case were opposed by a solid majority on the board, but the majority hesitated to act for fear that a formal commitment to segregation would raise howls of protest in the North.

Wilson and Gibbs' applications of September 15, together with those made a week later by three black women from Athens, Tennessee, came to public notice on October 9, when a Southern Methodist journal broke the story and drew from it the conclusion that Chattanooga University was "no doubt an expression of Northern sympathy for the Southern negro." In responding to that charge, university officials spoke only in the guise of informed sources, choosing not to be quoted by name. Thus, a university spokesman, identified only as "a gentleman connected with the management," told the Chattanooga *Times*: "Colored people will not be admitted to Chattanooga University; that may be depended upon."

It was a clear signal meant for local ears only, an attempt to reassure southern whites without causing a stir that might antagonize northern patrons of the Freedmen's Aid Society. Pleasing both audiences was a complicated business, as detractors liked to emphasize. A friend of Grant Memorial University (the new name for East Tennessee Wesleyan) used his inside knowledge of Chattanooga University to expose its dilemma, while cloaking his own identity in the pseudonym "REX." In a letter to the *Athenian*, REX gleefully asked John Manker, "If you want your institution to succeed among the whites, why don't you promise them openly and fearlessly, loud enough for the Freedmen's Aid Society to hear you, that they will not have to sit by the side of our brother in black at the table or in the recitation hall?"[2]

Efforts on the part of Manker, Lewis, and Rust to avoid just such an offensive course of action were defeated by a curious incident, which involved a professor of the university, one of its trustees, and a black minister of the Methodist Episcopal Church. On the evening of October 5, Professor Wilford Caulkins stopped by the office of the *Methodist Advocate* to proof an article he had written about Chattanooga University. Caulkins was "in a hurry" that evening, his patience sorely tried by the *Advocate's* editor, Reverend Thomas Carter, who had brought out three issues containing "only a few lines" about the university's opening.

When Caulkins stepped into the office, Carter greeted him and, as they were shaking hands, said: "Professor Caulkins, this is the

Reverend Mr. Johnson." Caulkins looked around and, he related, "saw a colored man whom I had never seen before." When Reverend Johnson responded, "I am pleased to meet you, Professor Caulkins," and extended his hand, Caulkins did not offer his own hand but said, "Good evening, Mr. Johnson," and walked off.[3]

The Reverend Johnson left the office at once, "feeling keenly the rebuff." Caulkins, upon being asked by Carter why he had refused to shake Johnson's hand, explained that he found "any social relation with colored people… distaste[ful]." His behavior toward Johnson, as well as his confession to Carter, did not remain a private affair for long.

Accusations against Caulkins soon reached the ear of Bishop Walden, president of both the Freedmen's Aid Society and the university board. On October 26, Walden instructed Dr. Rust to look into the accusations, discover the facts, and make a full report to the Society's executive committee. Shortly after Rust submitted his findings, Caulkins and the others were summoned to Cincinnati for a hearing before the executive committee. Then, three days after Christmas, the committee reached a verdict. By a vote of seven to four, they decided that Caulkins "did intentionally refuse to shake hands with Rev. B. H. Johnson." More to the point, they judged Caulkins guilty of wrong-thinking, of "entertain[ing] sentiments that unfit him for a position in a school [of] the Freedmen's Aid Society;" and they directed the university trustees to dismiss him "at once."[4]

The university board refused to comply, insisting that the Society reconsider its decision in the case. When the managers in Cincinnati reviewed and upheld their original decision and again called for prompt action, the Chattanoogans once again referred the matter back to Cincinnati, this time with a recommendation from Bishop Mallalieu, of New Orleans, that Caulkins be retained.

As the case of Wilford Caulkins was being aired in the national press, the university board passed a resolution that drew the color line in admissions. The resolution, adopted on January 4, 1887, reads in part: "WHEREAS, It has been again and again definitely and clearly stated by the proper authorities of the Church, and from the beginning has been well understood by all concerned, that the Chattanooga University was designed for the education of white pupils, and was not intended to be a mixed school, and...

"WHEREAS, We are confident that, in the present state of society in the South, the admission of colored students to the Chattanooga University would, on the one hand, be fatal to the prosperity of the institution, and defeat the very object proposed by the Church in the establishment of the school; and, on the other hand, would not only be unproductive of good results to the colored students so admitted, but would excite prejudice and passion, alienate the races, and prove especially detrimental to the interests of the colored people; and...

"WHEREAS, This very question of mixed schools has, by the General Conference itself, been declared to be 'one of expediency, which is to be left to the choice and administration of those on the ground and more immediately concerned;' therefore,

"*Be it Resolved*, That we deem it inexpedient to admit colored students to the University, and that the Faculty be instructed to administer accordingly."

Church law supported the resolution; its claim to legitimacy rested on nothing less than an 1884 General Conference resolution which provided "that the question of separate or mixed schools [is]

one of expediency, which is to be left to those on the ground and more immediately concerned." The language was unequivocal, but so was that of another enactment by the same conference on the same question; it stated that "no trustees of churches, schools, colleges, or universities... should exclude any person... on account of color, race, or previous condition of servitude." The 1884 General Conference had taken a firm stand on both sides of the question. Since neither of those enactments had legal precedence over the other, the Church North was positioned astraddle the color line, condemning segregation and condoning it. As a matter of fact, racial separation was the unwritten rule at Northern Methodist institutions throughout the South, in churches, schools, and universities, and even in the 31 ministerial conferences, 28 of which were segregated.[5]

According to architects of the southern policy, the church was blameless for that state of affairs, because segregation had come about spontaneously, naturally, by the mutual consent of "responsible" whites and "respectable" blacks. Schools "nominally for whites" were not "absolutely closed" to blacks; and, though black applicants were invariably rejected, no one was ever excluded on account of race, insisted one apologist.[6] He spoke for a large number of northern churchmen who reacted with indignation when they learned that Chattanooga University proposed to exclude blacks matter-of-factly. That policy, combined with the board's refusal to give up Professor Caulkins, drew blistering rebukes from the Northern Methodist press. Denominational scribes from as far away as London called for swift action to "vindicate the character" of Northern Methodism and defend the church's honor against the "humiliat[ion]... the shame which Chattanooga University [had] brought" on it.[7]

The faculty and board showed no signs of contrition. Mary Presnell, preceptress and professor of English, spoke out publicly in defense of the university, all but saying that its critics in the North were meddlesome, ill-informed moral parvenus. In a open letter to those critics, which appeared in a church journal, Presnell wrote: "I would like to know, with all due deference, if you seek to hamper the work of missionaries you send abroad, as you do the work of the ministers in the South?... Mixed schools may be right, but it is fully understood by those in the work here that they are not expedient now. Because it is found that two men cannot be educated together, would you leave them in ignorance?"

In late January of 1887, not long after the board declined for the third time to remove Professor Caulkins, the Freedmen's Aid Society faced mounting pressure to crush the rebellion. Only a prompt and vigorous housecleaning in Chattanooga, said some northern clerics, would save the Society from a searching inquiry at the next General Conference. The school had become an embarrassment to the Society, and its board in Cincinnati was ready to overturn the university's position on biracial education, force the ouster of Professor Caulkins, and lop off one or two other faculty heads for good measure. Of this the trustees were certain. They had it on the authority of Dr. Rust, who advised them to break away from the Society before the axe fell. During the first week of February, members of the executive committee proposed to buy out the Society, reportedly offering $75,000 for clear title to the school. As part of their proposition to the Society, they pledged to continue operating the school under church auspices.

The bid for limited independence died abruptly on February 24, when the board of managers in Cincinnati, after deliberating for two days, passed judgment on Chattanooga University. As elected representatives of the General Conference, they were speaking not just for the Society but also for the church as a whole. Their ruling had the force of law and specified the penalty for non-compliance. While they affirmed that the General Conference had sanctioned segregated schooling, they found the university's overt policy of excluding blacks to be a violation of "prevailing sentiment" in the General Conference. As before, they did not call for the admission of blacks but ordered an end to the avowed policy of racial exclusion. Further, they ruled that the "best interests of the Society and the Church" demanded the resignation of Professor Caulkins. They expressed themselves in a series of resolutions that concluded with this ultimatum: "RESOLVED, That if the Chattanooga University fail to secure the resignation of Prof. Wilford Caulkins, to take effect at a date not later than the close of the present school year, and to so modify its action as not to exclude… students on account of race or color… we [do then] instruct our Executive Committee to secure, by agreement, if possible, with the Trustees of said University, the immediate termination of the contract… and, in case of termination… be not secured by mutual agreement… [then] to notify the Trustees… within sixty days from this 24th day of February, 1887, of the termination of the contract…."

On March 24, the trustees acquiesced to those terms with obvious misgivings. They flatly declared themselves "unwilling to concede" that Professor Caulkins merited dismissal; but, "for the welfare of the church," they agreed to request his resignation, which was forthcoming. They also promised an "earnest and faithful effort" to act in harmony with the Society on the race question; but, since students currently in attendance had enrolled "with the understanding that the school would be... for white[s] only," they postponed any changes until the start of the next academic year in September. In the meantime, however, they pointedly reserved the right to terminate the contract and "surrender to... the Society... control of the school, the building and grounds."

Although the board had conceded no more than was absolutely necessary in order the retain church patronage, its action "fell on the people of Chattanooga like a thunderclap," wrote one observer. Whites jumped to the conclusion that the board had lost or given up a battle to uphold the color line. That misperception gained currency when two trustees, attorney Creed F. Bates and the Reverend T.C. Warner of the First Methodist Church, handed in their resignations on the same day Caulkins was given notice. Their departure increased the feelings of "uneasiness" and "apprehension" among students, which had already led six of the 15 seniors to withdraw from the university. One of them confided to the *Times* reporter that they had been advised to leave by the Reverend John Spence, president of Grant Memorial University in Athens. Three of the students entered Grant Memorial, and others soon followed.

The *Times* repeatedly accused Spence of working to undermine Chattanooga University, even reporting that Spence had once stated his intention to "skin Dr. Rust and break up the school." If there was a "sharp contest" between the two schools, said Bishop Walden, then "such an unfortunate fact should not be received as evidence that the educational work of our church is divided against itself." Officials of Chattanooga University regarded John Spence as an enemy and made no secret of their belief. As President Lewis remarked in 1888, "Chattanooga University has been hounded by friends of the Athens school, who never failed to do what could be done by suggesting and urging the color question."

At the Athens school, Spence had perfected the art of restricting enrollment to whites in such a way as never to embarrass church authorities, who insisted that their institutions in the South were open to all. Color-blind principles were thus reconciled with segregationist practice. This casuistry, however, was more than some loyal clergymen could swallow. They had a term for their church's policy on race. "A double-faced somewhat," they called it.[8] The trustees of Chattanooga University had attracted national attention to that "double-faced somewhat," by invoking the church's own expediency doctrine to exclude blacks instead of relying on the more discreet methods being used to accomplish the same end at Grant Memorial and other Northern Methodist schools in the South.

None of the inner circle at Chattanooga University, including Bishop Walden and Dr. Rust, seems to have fully anticipated the importance that their co-religionists in the North would attach to preserving appearances. Looking back on events, President Lewis wrote: "It did not seem wrong to us when two colored men were refused admission last year, but that act shocked the moral sense of all Christendom."

When he wrote those words in September 1887, Lewis had reached the conclusion that Chattanooga University was seriously, if not fatally, compromised – its usefulness forfeit to the overriding interests of the church. With stoic fortitude and no trace of intentional irony, Lewis wrote: "It is a hard thing to have a cause for which we have toiled and sacrificed beyond the knowledge of those who would instruct us, placed at the mercy of an exceptional few applicants in whose sincerity we have no confidence. It takes a large measure of grace to sacrifice Chattanooga University to a 'sensitive and refined brother' who lives in Chattanooga and knows full well the gravity of the present difficulties of his Church, and yet insists upon his rights to enter the University, resisting to the end the kindest advice of a well-known friend of his race, for the sole reason, 'I prefer to be in school with white boys to test my ability to compete with them in books and by measuring arms with them there.' But a lofty consistency is better than Chattanooga University, after all.... Let us be consistent Christian men if the heavens fall.... If disaster results the Church is innocent."[9]

For all the good it did black people, the admissions controversy might as well have been an argument over the doctrine of infant damnation. The color line at Chattanooga University would remain inviolate, but public skepticism about its holding power had a chilling effect on enrollment. In September 1887, school opened with 104 students, a number well below the previous year's total of 175. "Until the question of a mixed school is settled once and for all, the university cannot hope to command the patronage it would otherwise receive," the *Times* commented.

Punitive actions taken against two members of the faculty also hurt the school's standing. During the summer of 1887, the managers in Cincinnati discharged Professor Mary Presnell, apparently for having expressed her views on the feasibility of biracial education. And they dropped John Manker as dean of theology, naming him assistant to Edward Lewis, who was elevated to president and made dean of theology. Manker's demotion mollified a group of influential northern churchmen who were clamoring for his dismissal.[10] In 1889, Manker would lose his staff position as well as his seat on the board.

The purge of schoolmen did not end with John Manker. Its most notable victim was to be Dr. Richard Rust.[11] Never one, in his own words, "to dodge the question," Rust had put himself on the line for Chattanooga University, standing up for the trustees even at hazard to his position with the Society. In May 1888, the General Conference elected to replace Rust as secretary of the Society (which was renamed the Freedmen's Aid and Southern Education Society). To succeed Rust, the delegates appointed the Reverend Joseph Crane Hartzell. A pioneer in the mission fields of Africa, where the Republic of Liberia had made him "Knight Commander of the Order for the Redemption of Africa," the Reverend Hartzell – later Bishop Hartzell – superintended changes at Chattanooga University that weakened the school and seemed calculated to eliminate its potential to cause further embarrassment to the church.

One of Hartzell's first steps was to push for a merger of Chattanooga University with Grant Memorial. Chattanooga was more or less bound to follow the lead of Cincinnati in such a transaction. That, however, was not the case with Grant Memorial, which was owned by the Holston Conference. Relations between conference and school were harmonious and cooperative. In order to bring about a merger of the schools, Hartzell needed John Spence to say the words that would cause the Holston Conference to deed Grant Memorial to the Society. This gave Spence a strong bargaining position.

The Holston Conference endorsed the proposed consolidation in mid-October 1888; and four months later, representatives from each school, meeting under the direction of Hartzell, worked out a plan of consolidation. It specified that Chattanooga and Athens would be "co-ordinate in educational importance" but distinct in educational focus, with no overlapping collegiate-level programs to incite competition for students. Chattanooga would maintain the college of liberal arts as well as develop professional schools of law and medicine, while Athens would operate the school of theology and organize a "school of technology."

Agreement was reached to incorporate the consolidated schools as Grant Memorial University, and 17 men, who would serve as the first board of trustees, affixed their signatures to the charter application on March 26. Of these consolidator-trustees, five were associated with the Chattanooga faction, six with the Athens faction, and the other six were managers of the Freedmen's Aid and Southern Education Society. Their relations were strained from the outset. At their first board meeting, on May 2, 1889, they split along the old lines of conflict. Tempers flared, and one of the Chattanoogans, A.J. "Jack" Gahagan, tendered his resignation before the trustees had even gotten around to the really treacherous business of electing the school's chancellor. The outcome of that contest left Chattanoogans feeling hoodwinked and betrayed.

Under the headline "SPENCE GOBBLED IT," the *Times* carried the story of John Spence's election as chancellor of the new school, adding this editorial comment: "Athens and Chancellor Spence now have possession of Chattanooga and the Chattanooga University property. The game has been remarkably well-played. The men who built the university have been shoved aside."

Those sentiments, couched in more diplomatic language, were transmitted to the Grant Memorial board by a delegation of prominent Chattanoogans. They asked for two concessions in view of the advantage Athens had gained through Spence's election. First, they proposed that the board expand its membership to include three additional Chattanoogans: Hiram Chamberlain, Henry Clay Beck, and John Manker. The board refused to elect either Beck or Manker but did give Chattanooga the three additional seats, which were filled by J.F. Loomis, Dr. Richard Rust, and Hiram Chamberlain, who was elected board president. Second, the delegates from Chattanooga asked that the school's name be changed from Grant Memorial, the trademark of Athens, to some other name less likely to give the impression that Chattanooga University had been swallowed by Grant Memorial rather than consolidated with it. After some discussion, the board approved a semantic compromise: the new name, legally adopted on October 28, 1889, was U.S. Grant University.[12]

Despite the last minute concessions wrung from the board, many Chattanoogans still saw the consolidation as a bad bargain, since Chattanooga University has ceased to exist as an official entity, and the administrative headquarters of the newly-created institution would be located in Athens. "At last the great transaction's done," wrote the editor of the *University Lookout*, published by Chattanooga students. "We are theirs and they are theirs also…. The coming commencement will close the history of Chattanooga University."

The charter of U.S. Grant University placed the college of liberal arts in Chattanooga, while establishing Athens as the seminary and technical school. Only at Chattanooga would a "full college course" be offered. That, at least, was what the Chattanoogans assumed.

In the fall of 1890, however, the Athens campus enrolled 62 liberal arts students including 22 entering freshmen. Secretary Hartzell of the Society let this charter violation pass. His failure to call John Spence's hand convinced many Chattanoogans that the Society has thrown its support to Athens. Local suspicions on that score had first arisen in March, when it became generally known that Hartzell was making arrangements to sell the lower, undeveloped portion of the Chattanooga campus. The property in question, which amounted to about one-half of the school's total acreage, consisted of the two city blocks bounded by Douglas, Oak, Baldwin, and Vine Streets.

Hartzell initially offered that piece of land to John Wesley Adams, architect of Old Main and one of Chattanooga University's incorporators. When Adams rejected not only the offer but also the idea of selling off part of the campus, Hartzell turned to John Spence. In short order, Spence assembled an investment syndicate which offered to pay $90,000 for the property; and in late April, Hartzell wrote to Spence congratulating him – "that is, you and your syndicate" – on the purchase of the property.[13]

Before the deal could be consummated and the deeds forwarded to Spence, a group of Chattanoogans, headed by John Wesley Adams, sued the Freedmen's Aid and Southern Education Society, petitioning for an injunction against the sale. They charged "some ministers" of the church with having "tried to break down and destroy their own school," and with having "secretly agreed to sell the largest portion of [the campus]… leaving for the purposes of a great central university a strip of land 300 x 520 feet."[14]

Chancery Court granted the injunction on April 30. But then the case was transferred to Federal District Court where, on August 14, Judge David M. Key ruled that the Society had the right to sell the property and the syndicate the right to buy it. Unmoved by that decision, Adams and the others appealed to the Supreme Court. Their appeal tangled the property in legal complexities, effectively blocking the sale. The effect was more than temporary. When Hartzell belatedly saw that the complainants meant to put their own church authorities in the dock, he gave up on the sale. Toward the end of 1890, he took the school property off the market, and a few months later the complainants withdrew their appeal.

Several of the trustees were sharply critical of John Spence for his part in the attempted sale. They judged it improper for Grant University's chief administrator to participate in speculative transactions involving the Chattanooga campus. Hartzell came to his friend's defense. At a university board meeting in May 1890, Hartzell secured passage of a resolution endorsing Spence's conduct. "We declare our conviction," the trustees resolved, "that Dr. Spence has… [not] sought to secure personal profit from the transactions conducted by him in behalf of the Society; that, on the contrary, he voluntarily pledged beforehand… that he would turn over any margin realized over and above the price fixed… into the building fund of the institution."

Spence's role in the transactions cost him the few scraps of credibility he had with the Chattanooga trustees. Their earlier sufferance of him gave way to demands for his removal. Hartzell tried to smooth over the difficulties; but at the next annual meeting, the trustees voted Spence out of office. Though they gave him the title of president, his duties were those of financial officer and field agent. The board elected as his successor a compromise candidate, Bishop Isaac Joyce, who accepted the chancellorship as a necessary addition to his other responsibilities as resident bishop of the area.

The change in chancellors was, at best, a symbolic victory for the Chattanooga trustees. Nothing had changed in Cincinnati. The Society, through Secretary Hartzell, had settled upon a policy of turning the Chattanooga campus into a branch of the Athens school. Administrative control of the liberal arts college had already slipped from local hands. When Edward Lewis, dean of faculty and liberal arts, resigned in 1890, the deanship had gone to Dr. George Ackerman, who carried out his duties in Chattanooga while maintaining his residence in Athens and staying on as professor of systematic theology there. Even more bewildering was the fact that Ackerman was actually dean of two competing liberal arts colleges, the chartered one in Chattanooga and the unchartered one in Athens, which accepted 21 entering freshmen in the fall of 1891. Among the majors available in Athens was one styled "Political Science and Temperance."

A solution to the liberal arts muddle was near at hand, Hartzell suggested in a letter of March 1892 to Hiram Chamberlain, board president of Grant University. Hartzell began the letter by informing Chamberlain that the demotion of John Spence had caused distress among the Society's managers, who regarded the action as "unfair" to Spence. Cincinnati was also disappointed by the small attendance at Chattanooga. In view of that, Hartzell warned Chamberlain to expect some major developments touching on the college of liberal arts.

Two months later, when the General Conference got underway, complaints were lodged against the administration of Grant University. Conference delegates from Minnesota and Michigan, whose acquaintance with the situation in Chattanooga was probably limited to information fed to them by the Reverend Hartzell, gained approval for an investigation into charges that the Chattanooga school "had squandered a great deal of money... [and] employ[ed] a faculty larger than necessary."

The charges of waste and overstaffing provoked an editorial blast from the Chattanooga *Times*. Resources and opportunities were indeed going to waste and would continue to trickle away, argued the *Times*, so long as growth was blocked at every turn by the misbegotten merger of 1889. As the *Times* put it: "The so-called consolidation of the alleged Chattanooga and Athens Universities... was never a consolidation; it never can be.... The plan was an absurdity from the beginning. Neither school (they are nothing but fairly good academies) will do its best work or grow toward anything larger, under the existing regime. Why? One reason may be made plain by a simple instance: the dean of the Chattanooga faculty [Dr. Ackerman] is Professor of Theology at Athens, and necessarily spends a large part of his time at Athens, where, we believe, his chief interests are. The real manager of the two schools has all his personal interests in Athens. In short, the arrangement is without possibility of harmony in its parts, an absurdity in business, and hence a foredoomed failure...."

A committee of the General Conference probed the affairs of Grant University and issued its report on May 20, 1892. The report, which was adopted in full by the Conference, stated that expenditures at Chattanooga were too high in relation to the number of students enrolled there. Consequently, the Freedmen's Aid and Southern Education Society was instructed to "adjust the various departments" so as to attain the "greatest possible economy and efficiency."

The critical adjustment was made promptly on June 7, when the university board, at the Society's behest, decided on a charter amendment that transferred the liberal arts college to Athens. Another adjustment occurred the following year (1893) when the academic department at Chattanooga was discontinued and all preparatory work consolidated at Athens.

With those changes, Chattanooga surrendered the last remnants of its 1886 franchise: no longer was it the church's regional seat of higher learning. That distinction now belonged to Athens, in fact if not by decree. The reversal of fortune must have delighted John Spence, but he would not have long to savor it. His contentious ways had exhausted the patience of one group of trustees. They insisted that he go, and in 1893 the board terminated his connection with Grant University. Embittered and quick to show his resentment, he immediately set to work organizing a rival school, the American Temperance University, in Harriman, Tennessee.

Although Spence was gone, his followers in Athens and associates in Cincinnati retained control of the Chattanooga campus. Their actions excited scant enthusiasm in Chattanooga. As token compensation for the loss of the liberal arts college, Chattanooga was given the school of theology, which had been moved to Athens in the consolidation of 1889. Possession of the theology library did not follow automatically because, as officials at Athens assured students, the theology school would fail in Chattanooga and be returned to Athens just as the college of liberal arts had failed and been returned.[15] When it opened at its new location in September 1892, the school of theology enrolled a total of four students.

With nothing much to offer in place of the discontinued collegiate and preparatory work, the institution was all but dead so far as most Chattanoogans were concerned. In an effort at resuscitation, some of the trustees tried to build a new program around professional courses of study. The result, however, was a ragtag assortment of specialty schools, hastily improvised and short-lived for the most part. A law college, organized and run by local attorneys in their spare time, opened in 1891 and lasted until 1894. Colleges of pharmacy and dentistry appeared in 1891 but vanished a year later. Only the medical college, formed in 1889 by local physicians, managed to take hold, though its facilities and standards were of the most rudimentary sort. Applicants who lacked college credentials were routinely admitted into a two-year program leading to the M.D. degree. Their opportunities to gain clinical experience were limited not only by the relatively abbreviated course of study but also by the absence of a municipal hospital. The medical college, located in makeshift quarters away from campus, was a proprietary school owned by its faculty and operated under the trademark of U.S. Grant University.

By 1895, the Chattanooga institution had been reduced to a small denominational seminary loosely affiliated with a homegrown medical college. Administrators left and were not replaced; when Bishop Joyce's episcopate was transferred from the Chattanooga area in 1896, he stepped down as chancellor, and the post was left vacant. Faculty members were seldom paid on time or in full. One professor of theology was in the habit of taking a leave of absence each school year because he "could not afford to teach."

Little remained to suggest that Chattanooga had once been designated as the site for a "great central university." The "light upon a hill" burned only for a handful of seminarians who moved through the cavernous spaces of Old Main like visitors at some ancestral mansion now empty save for a few old family retainers. The shape of things to come was plainly visible to the faculty. In their book of minutes, they noted that the school displayed "unmistakable signs of approaching dissolution."

At that low point, an important change took place at the executive level of the Freedmen's Aid and Southern Education Society. In May 1896, Joseph Hartzell was elevated to bishop, and, shortly thereafter, he retired as secretary of the Society. His successor was Dr. John W. Hamilton. It was Dr. Hamilton who, 10 years earlier as editor of the New York *Independent*, had led the attack on Chattanooga University's policy of admitting whites only. Since then, however, Hamilton and his fellow churchmen in the North had made peace with the color line.

Ironically, the former chief nemesis of the school now became its champion. Hamilton believed its problems could be best worked out by able leadership within the school itself, not by more tinkering from afar with relations between Athens and Chattanooga. Unlike his predecessor, Hamilton refused to play the role of broker to the factions contending over Grant University. Instead, he appointed as chancellor-president an outsider whose youth and lack of executive experience at first caused local observers to take him for just another church functionary passing through the university on his way to a better assignment elsewhere. They were greatly mistaken. By wisdom or luck or a combination of the two, Dr. Hamilton found the very man to break the school loose from the grip of the past.

3
Grit and Grace

Very deep is the well of the past. Should we not call it bottomless?
— Thomas Mann, *Joseph and His Brothers*

One September morning in 1897 a young minister in Binghamton, New York opened a telegram from Dr. Hamilton and read, "WOULD YOU CONSIDER FAVORABLY CHANCELLORSHIP GRANT UNIVERSITY? ANSWER CINCINNATI IMMEDIATELY."

The offer came as a surprise to its recipient, the Reverend John H. Race. *Grant University?* Race "had scarcely heard of" the school and he wired back: "TOO SUDDEN. MUST HAVE TIME FOR THOROUGH INVESTIGATION."

Hamilton encouraged Race and his wife Alice to visit the university at the Society's expense, adding that the position there carried with it "all the honors, duties, and responsibilities of Chancellor, President, Dean, Financial Agent, Faculty, Trustees, and almost the whole business." The Chancellor's main duties, wrote Hamilton, were "to teach… meet the necessities of the school and the Faculty… be present in the pulpit every Sunday [and visit] the patronizing territory, drumming up students, preaching, raising money, etc." The salary was one-third what Race was earning at the time.

John Race was the son of English immigrants who had crossed the Atlantic and settled in Pennsylvania four years before his birth in 1862. A career in business initially appealed to him more than anything else he could think of doing. He had majored in business at Wyoming Seminary in Pennsylvania and then gone to work for a lumber company, where, in a sawmill accident, he lost his left hand. The accident, according to a biographical sketch, "marked a turning point in his life." After convalescing, he re-enrolled at Wyoming Seminary and prepared himself to enter Princeton University, where he received the B.A. degree in 1890. That same year he was ordained a minister of the Northern Methodist Church and returned to Wyoming Seminary as a teacher of Greek and rhetoric. Besides his classroom duties there, he organized the school's first newspaper and its first baseball team, while also earning an M.A. degree from Princeton in 1894. He was in his fourth successful year of a possible five-year assignment at the pastorate in Binghamton when Dr. Hamilton's telegram arrived.

Race visited Grant University with his wife in November 1897, looked over the two campuses, met with the faculty, and saw for himself the "signs of approaching dissolution": run-down buildings at both Athens and Chattanooga, poorly-paid teachers who "thought of giving up," an unsympathetic populace in Chattanooga, the incessant struggle to beg and borrow enough to cover basic operating costs, dwindling enrollments in the collegiate program, a board of trustees caught up in the partisan rivalry between Athens and Chattanooga. Race did not have to be told that he was being asked to accept a rescue mission. It would be easier, he told a friend, to build a new school from the ground up rather than attempt to salvage Grant University.

By some artful dodge, Race might have sidestepped the assignment, but that was not his way. Nor could he find good and sufficient reason to decline the post, which he came to view as an "opportunity to do a really constructive educational task." Back in New York, he sent off a letter accepting the job of "president" – the title he preferred to that of "chancellor." Though by no means confident of success at Grant University, he closed his letter to Dr. Hamilton with this assurance: "Into the work I go… with all there is of me."

President and Mrs. Race completed their move to Grant University in August 1898. They took up residence in Athens. For three months they lived in Athens, and then they packed their things and moved to Chattanooga. By changing his address, Race succeeded in transferring the school's headquarters back to Chattanooga, where he thought it belonged. He spoke of the need for other changes as well, starting with the re-establishment of the college in Chattanooga and conversion of the Athens campus into a "high-grade preparatory school." The Athenians implored him, for the sake of harmony and the effectiveness of his own administration, not to revive a troublesome issue that had been debated vigorously and settled authoritatively many years ago.

Though Race was a newcomer and an outlander, he quickly traced the problems at Grant University to their source. A "monumental mistake" had occurred. "I understand it thoroughly," he remarked. "I know what would happen if the Southern Methodist Church should try to establish such a school in New England, and especially would it be fatal to such an institution if it [were] give[n] the name of a Confederate general."[1] And so he urged friends of the university to work toward the day when it would be owned and controlled by local trustees who were attuned to prevailing sentiment in the resoundingly non-Northern Methodist region. He also insisted that the name Grant University had to go.

Those plans hit an unexpected obstacle in the fall of 1898, when Race learned that the Freedmen's Aid and Southern Education Society had lost title to the lower, undeveloped half of the Chattanooga campus. The property, bounded by Oak and Vine Streets, had been acquired by the State of Tennessee in forfeit for $5,559.67 in back taxes.

"That was school property for school purposes... and it was neither kind nor just to tax us for it... when nobody else in the state pay[s]... taxes on educational property," complained Dr. Hamilton in a letter to Race. (The State argued that the parcel of land was taxable because it had been devoid of educational facilities for over 10 years while rapidly appreciating in value.) "There seems to be a bent purpose to drive us out of [Chattanooga]," wrote Hamilton, who concluded that the only recourse was "to go into the United States Courts and get a decision." [2]

Local and state officials were less obdurate than Hamilton had supposed, and in early 1899 the parties reached an agreement whereby taxes were remitted and title restored to the Society in return for its pledge to develop and use the property for educational purposes "in the immediate future." An intact, tax-exempt campus was assured, so long as the Society constructed and equipped a school building on the contested land without undue delay. How that would be accomplished was more than anyone could say just then. The Society would underwrite a new building only if matching funds came from patrons in Chattanooga, but trustees in Chattanooga advised Race that the time was "inopportune" for raising money locally. Race had a year, perhaps 18 months at most, in which to put the lower campus to use or else risk losing it.

The tax agreement displeased some board members who had wanted to resolve the matter by transferring the school's Chattanooga departments to Athens. Race had held out for the negotiated settlement and, shortly afterwards, he confronted his opponents on the board. At the annual meeting in May 1899, he called upon the trustees either to support his program of change or replace him as president of the university. Though "various opinions seem to prevail concerning the future of the University," declared Race, "there is no doubt in my own mind as to the future policy." Consequently, he told them, "If we are not in harmony then relations between the Board and the President of the University during the past year may be adjusted or dissolved."

He challenged them to face up to reality. "Let the ancient history of this institution be what it may. This condition confronts us: After thirty-two years of effort we have a collegiate department this present year of thirty-nine students."

The institution was a university in name only, and perhaps not even that for much longer because, as Race informed the trustees, the accrediting agency of the Church North had given fair warning that Grant University would be downgraded to the status of an academy, or secondary school, unless deficiencies in college-level English, modern languages, and science courses were corrected. "The collegiate department that should be the strength, the vertebral column, is lamentably weak," said Race. "Our professional departments are stronger than our College of Liberal Arts. We are in a top-heavy condition. The remedy is to divorce the College of

Liberal Arts from the preparatory department, remove the college to Chattanooga, [and] concentrate our attention at Athens on preparatory work."[3]

After hearing Race out, a majority of the board endorsed his plan of reorganization and drafted a petition to the "participating" conferences asking that they approve the plan. Their response was to avoid being sucked into the controversy. One after another, the conferences simply referred the matter back to the university board, either without comment or with the observation that Grant University was free to proceed with the reorganization whenever the means to do so were available at Chattanooga.

Removing the liberal arts college to Chattanooga and upgrading its program would cost, Race estimated, an additional $10,000 a year for five years. The price might as well have been 10 times that, for the Chattanooga trustees were in no mood to raise the money, and the Freedmen's Aid and Southern Education Society had financial problems of its own. As Dr. Hamilton explained to Race: "You must remember, my brother, I am standing by you, but [the Society is] more than $200,000 in debt... and we are tying to get relief.... Some of us will have to get by on less or swamp in the midst of the stream." Furthermore, Northern Methodist schools in Tennessee already received $20,000 to $25,000 yearly, or one-quarter of the Society's annual expenditure in the South, a situation which, wrote Hamilton, was drawing "criticism... from every quarter on our locating too much money with a state filled with innumerable small schools."[4]

Turned down by both Cincinnati and Chattanooga, Race decided to try his luck as one among the throng of petitioners seeking a word with the nation's foremost philanthropist, steel baron Andrew Carnegie. Carnegie, a freethinker and critic of organized religion, was a long-shot prospect for the clergyman-president of an obscure denominational college. Somehow, though, Race managed to secure an appointment to see Carnegie in New York; and on December 7, 1900, accompanied by three other Chattanoogans, he had "a very pleasant interview" with the industrialist. Carnegie declined to aid Grant University on that occasion, but he did make a gift of $50,000 toward construction of a public library building in Chattanooga, and he invited Race to call on him again in a year.

Race discerned at once how the gift could work to the advantage of both town and gown. Back in Chattanooga, he went to the city fathers and suggested that they build the projected Carnegie Library on one corner of the lower campus, which would take Grant University off the hook with the taxman; but "certain members of the city council" objected to that location, and a site downtown was chosen.

A few weeks later, those same councilmen began to talk of initiating condemnation proceedings against the lower campus, where they had plans to develop a municipal park. Race considered the property as good as lost unless the conditions imposed by the tax agreement, still unmet after 18 months, were promptly satisfied. The Society's board of managers concurred and, in June 1901, authorized construction of a building on the lower campus for use by the medical school, the one unit of Grant University with growing enrollments and some support from local patrons. The cost, which was to be borne equally by the Society and the local trustees, was set at $20,000, and a contract was signed in July for an unadorned square brick building.

One small but important modification in its original design was made at the urging of Dr. E.A. Cobleigh, dean of the medical school.

Owing to the intense aversion among laymen to the practice of dissecting cadavers, Dr. Cobleigh deemed it "indispensable" that the new building have "a drive way right into the basement, whereby wagons can drive *out of sight* at night with their burdens, for anatomy. It must be so that unloading can be done leisurely, out of range of curious eyes, and so as never to attract anyone to stop, or a crowd to gather to interfere. We have had dangerous trouble about this every season, and particularly this winter. Personal courage alone saved us from a mob once this winter." [5]

The case for reorganizing the liberal arts college grew more compelling in 1902, as enrollment and tuition income at Athens dropped to an all-time low. From 114 undergraduates out of 303 students and income of $4,200 in 1880, the numbers were down to 20 undergraduates and $3,000 of income for the 1901-1902 academic year. Officials in Athens saw no connection between this pattern of decline and their commitment to uphold the sectarian and sectional policies of a bygone era. In 1902, as in 1867, the school's promotional literature emphasized that its students came largely from families which had been "loyal to the Union" during the Civil War, and alongside each year's list of graduates was a list of students "converted" – presumably to the Church North.[6]

At the board meeting of May 1902, President Race freely expressed his conviction that the liberal arts college could not survive in a denominational enclave. Noting the rise of other colleges in East Tennessee, many with resources surpassing those of Grant University, he told the trustees: "Church loyalty cannot be relied upon to furnish us students unless we can offer advantages equal to other institutions in the same… territory." Those other institutions included not only the University of Tennessee at Knoxville, which was experiencing phenomenal growth under President Charles Dabney, Carson and Newman College in Jefferson City, Tusculum College near Greeneville, and Washington College near Jonesborough, but also a remarkably large assortment of schools sponsored by the Church North. Where once Grant University had enjoyed "the right-of-way throughout all East Tennessee among the people identified with the Methodist Episcopal Church," said Race, "there are now six other schools drawing students from our constituency. In a word, seven institutions under the patronage of the Methodist Episcopal Church are soliciting... within the boundaries of the Holston Conference. This is a matter for serious consideration!"

To the Athenians, Race's position smacked of secularism. They contended that their distinctive denominational emphasis answered a crying need not being served by other schools, not even by the branch in Chattanooga. And they offered to assume financial responsibility for their school if permitted to manage its affairs as they thought fit. Their bid for independence was coolly received by the majority of board members.[7] Race, making no attempt to hide his frustration, retorted: "I am well aware that there are some few people who cling tenaciously to the old ideas. But this board is practically a unit for the development of the university along broad lines. Everybody knows that as soon as we can secure the support, the collegiate department is to be established in Chattanooga."

Privately, though, he was less sure of the outcome. After almost four years in office, he wondered how much longer it would take his backers in Chattanooga and Cincinnati to provide the money needed to carry out his program, and he knew that his detractors in

Athens were watching for any opportunity to discredit him. Though he had been "clear and open" about his intentions from the beginning, his efforts thus far had, he recalled, "evoked the bitterest kind of opposition" from Athens. So conscious was he of the ill-will that he and his wife Alice had never felt comfortable enough to unpack all their household goods, most of which remained where they had been since 1898, stored in the basement of Old Main.[8]

Late in the spring of 1902, as Race felt himself sinking into the muddle of Grant University, he was tossed a lifeline by his old church in Binghamton, New York. Its congregation invited him to return as pastor, and, after conferring with the residing bishop in East Tennessee and the one in Southeast New York, Race accepted the offer. He obviously was delighted by the prospect of going back to a place where he and Alice had many friends and a useful vocation. Perhaps, too, he had hopes that his Chattanooga friends would treat his resignation as a friendly ultimatum.

If that was his strategy, it succeeded admirably. The board of Grant University voted not to accept his resignation and, together with managers of the Freedmen's Aid and Southern Education Society, petitioned the board of bishops to retain Race in Chattanooga, because "he has undertaken important projects which are incomplete, and which his removal would put in jeopardy." Shortly thereafter, a committee of the bishops informed Race of their decision that he stay at Grant University.

Their action was in effect an endorsement, from the top-most ecclesiastical echelon, of John Race's administration at Grant University. And the man most responsible for bringing about that endorsement was now ready to take the lead in financing Race's program. He was John Alanson Patten.

John A. Patten was a widely known figure in Chattanooga and in the high councils of Northern Methodism. His father-in-law, the Reverend John Manker, had been among the founders of Chattanooga University in 1886, and a future son-in-law, Alexander Guerry, would be the university's seventh president. Active in a variety of commercial enterprises such as the Volunteer State Life Insurance Company, the Chattanooga Savings Bank, and the Stone Fort Land Company, Patten was probably best known as the head of the Chattanooga Medicine Company, a manufacturer of herbal tonics and elixirs with names like Black Draught and Wine of Cardui. Patten and his many relatives were, noted Jonathan Daniels, "the big folk of Chattanooga. And no wonder. Women all over the South, high up the creek and close to Courthouse Square, scribble their dates with stub pencils in the Cardui Almanac and at the proper time of the moon buy that bottle of Cardui. It is, as the benevolent Indian maiden on the bottle seems to be promising for the Pattens to the pained and pleading pale face female, excellent for Functional Dysmenorrhea from puberty to menopause. In half of Dixie that whole period belongs to the Pattens."[9]

A trustee of Grant University since 1894, Patten gave Race little more than encouragement until 1902. That October, when the board's campaign to underwrite half the cost of the medical school building ran out of steam $6,000 short of its goal, the Society made clear that authorization to establish the undergraduate college at Chattanooga would not be forthcoming if the local trustees failed to cover their share of the medical building's cost. The $6,000 goal seemed out of reach until Patten and another trustee, J.E. Annis, pledged the full amount themselves, on condition that plans to bring the college to Chattanooga move forward to a speedy consummation. Their gift was a striking demonstration of faith in Race's program, and it had a bandwagon effect on other patrons. Within a year, the Society appropriated $5,000 for support of the college, and Race secured local pledges of $7,000 annually for the same purpose. In May 1904, school officials announced that college work would again be offered at Chattanooga beginning in September. The start of classes, however, was delayed by a legal contest over who would control Grant University.

Athenian loyalists, convinced that the majority will of the board amounted to a "colossal folly," took their arguments out of the boardroom and into the courtroom.[10] On August 15, 1904, President Race and other trustees were named as defendants in a suit brought before chancery court at Athens by trustee John W. Bayless and another Athenian, former trustee Robert J. Fisher. The two plaintiffs sought, first, a complete separation between the Athens and Chattanooga branches of the institution; second, an injunction barring Race and others from interfering with the management by Athenians of the school there; and third, an injunction against the opening of a college of liberal arts at Chattanooga.

As counsel for the defense pointed out, nothing in the charter of Grant University gave officials at either branch the right to withdraw from the corporation and form with its property a school of their own. Besides that, the plaintiffs' request for a complete separation from Chattanooga was incompatible with their request to stop the opening of a college at Chattanooga. In that one particular, the chancellor sided with the defendants. Otherwise, though, he ruled in favor of the plaintiffs, granting them the right of separation and issuing a temporary injunction preventing Race and other trustees living outside his jurisdiction from exercising any control over the Athens school.

The ruling was promptly struck down on appeal, but the plaintiffs thereupon laid their case before the state supreme court. Neither side showed the least inclination to compromise. In Athens, Dean William Wright, Professor David Bolton, Trustee George Lockmiller, and others of influence were determined to break free of "coercion" from Chattanooga and Cincinnati.[11] Race was equally determined to crush what he regarded as a rebellion against the duly constituted authority of the board. The Society cut off all funding to the Athens school, and Race severed official relations with its administrators, refusing to visit their campus or even sign the diplomas they issued.

Both sides held their ground for more than a year, waiting for the Tennessee Supreme Court to render its decision in the matter. Finally, in November 1905, the court dismissed the appeal entered on behalf of Athens, thus confirming Race and the board's authority over each and every part of Grant University. The game was up for the dissidents, who realized, as one of them put it, that "further opposition… would be useless."[12] Their hold on the school was broken; never again would Race find his position threatened by a disgruntled minority.

At the board's direction, the Athens branch conferred its last bachelor's degree on commencement day 1906, and then began to operate strictly as a preparatory school and junior college, subject to oversight from Chattanooga. That arrangement would last into the 1920's. By then, the old rivalry for pride of place had cooled enough for officials at both places to acknowledge that the union of Athens and Chattanooga served the interests of neither. In June 1925, the university board approved an agreement of separation through which friends of the Athens school took charge of its affairs and reorganized it as an independent school they named Tennessee Wesleyan College.

On October 5, 1904, the new undergraduate college of Grant University opened at Chattanooga with ceremonies attended by local and church dignitaries. Many of them, who had gathered on this very spot 12 years earlier at the groundbreaking ceremonies for "a great central university," could readily appreciate the sad irony as well as the bright promise of this occasion. It was the most encouraging development to come out of the school in longer than most of them cared to remember, and their optimistic predictions of what the day foretold were borne out by events. As historians looking back on the occasion would conclude in 1947, it marked "the real beginning" of the university.[13]

For President Race, the future of Grant University depended on its college of liberal arts, its "vertebral column," the one part by which the strength or weakness of the whole would be judged. All else – the preparatory department, the medical and law schools, even the school of theology – was tangential, if not a drain on precious resources needed to make a success of the college.

Race's plan for creating a strong program in the arts and sciences was given form and substance by the professor he appointed dean of the college: Wesley W. Hooper. Students who took courses in ethics, economics, or sociology from W.W. Hooper could recall decades later his "idealism" and "deep social insight in[to] human problems" – qualities forged out of experience and observation of human nature from a variety of acute angles, as a foot soldier in Grant's army during the bloody battle of Shiloh and later as an ordained Northern Methodist minister and president of a church school for freedmen in Mississippi. Since that time, Hooper had been a faculty member of Chattanooga University during its brief existence; and, when college and preparatory work was discontinued at Chattanooga, he had taught at the college in Athens, earning praise at each location, while staying out of the public quarrel between the two. His first loyalty had always been to classroom teaching; he once wrote that the best teachers were not only "thorough scholars, but… possess[ed] high ideals as to the worth and possibilities of the human soul, and [were] able to inspire each pupil to his highest and best endeavor."

Although Hooper and the college's other nine faculty members saw a first year enrollment of only 49 students, the lopsided ratio of faculty to undergraduates began to assume more pleasing proportions as the number of students rose to 88 the following year. They each paid tuition of $30 a year to enter an academic program modeled after those at colleges where $30 just might have made the down payment on a year's tuition. Degrees offered were the A.B, B.S., and Litt.B., all entailing four-year courses of study and all except the Litt. B. demanding a more than casual familiarity with languages both ancient and modern. Candidates for the A.B. and B.S. were required to demonstrate proficiency in English as well as "a good working knowledge" of Latin, German, and one other language chosen by them from the curriculum. The quality of work aimed for in the classroom was evident as early as 1906. That year, as Dean Hooper noted in his annual report to the board, the course in mathematics had been patterned on the one at Cornell University, the sophomore class in physics had covered the material and taken virtually the same examination required of their counterparts at

Johns Hopkins University, and Professor Walter Hullihen's first and second year Latin classes had passed the same examinations used at the University of Virginia.[14]

The Cornells and Virginias of higher education served the faculty as touchstones inside the classroom but not outside it. In the realm of student activities, an undergraduate's options were a good deal closer to those available at the American college of 1805 than 1905. Extracurricular pursuits centered around the debating clubs, or "literary societies," with their weekly programs of public speaking, reading, and debate. To encourage student participation, several of the trustees offered cash prizes each year to the winners of forensic and declamatory contests. These annual competitions drew large crowds and excited the sort of rivalries, loyalties, and pageantry increasingly associated only with intercollegiate athletics. In 1906, for example, an orchestra played during interludes in the competition, flowers were presented to each contestant, and groups of students rose from the audience to deliver their class yells. The law students boomed out

>   Circuit, Criminal, Chancery courts,
>   Contracts, evidence, bailments, torts,
>   Pleading, practice, equi-tee,
>   Clear 'em, Hang 'em, Get your fee.
>   LAW! LAW! LAW!

And the medical students, not to be outdone, countered with

>   Well man, sick man, dead man, stiff;
>   Dig 'em up, cut 'em up, what's the diff?
>   Fractured femurs, fix with sticks,
>   Chattanooga's medicos, nineteen-six!

On most college campuses, literary societies had long since given way to Greek-letter societies, and the contests that tickled the fancy of most students and patrons occurred between the goal posts of a football field. Those pasttimes received little, if any, encouragement at Chattanooga. The faculty placed a five-year ban on the formation of "secret societies," not only because those societies seemed to them like Freemasonry in a toga but also for practical reasons as well. They did not want to see fraternities and sororities competing for the meagre personal resources available on a campus where some 90 percent of the students were delivering newspapers, cleaning houses, clerking in stores or offices, or working whatever jobs they could find to put themselves through college. Although the ban on secret societies expired in 1909, the campus' first nationally-chartered Greek-letter society, Phi Beta Gamma, was not organized until 1921. (Most undergraduates would continue to hold jobs in the years ahead, with over 80 percent employed as late as 1990. The university has never attracted children of the leisure class in significant numbers.[15])

The faculty also used its considerable authority to regulate development of the football program. A full schedule of seven games was played for the first time in 1905, by a team wearing the blue and gold colors of Grant University and coached by Dr. Walter Hullihen, professor of Latin and Greek. The team created a sensation locally, losing only one game and even scoring an upset victory (5-0) over the University of Tennessee Volunteers.

That string of victories might have prompted university officials to see how strong a football program could be built if, copying practices common at other colleges, they hired a professional as coach at double or triple the salary paid to the finest teachers and enrolled exceptional athletes irrespective of their academic abilities or ambitions. Instead, the faculty imposed tight controls on intercollegiate athletics: financial inducements to players were forbidden, teams were allowed to travel away from campus for no more than seven school days a season, and eligibility was restricted to full-time students with passing grades in all courses.

The new rules, which took effect in December 1910, were meant to root out the growing "evils of low scholarship" among football players before their example corrupted the innocent. In the words of a faculty resolution: "The man who is a star on the gridiron and is therefore naturally popular among students is not a good influence in college halls among classmates when he is either incapable or willfully negligent of his classroom duties."

Recognizing that a team purged of classroom scofflaws probably had no business going up against the superior might of uncleansed opponents, the faculty suspended intercollegiate football competition for 1911; that season an inexperienced squad of 13 men played a reduced schedule of five games against local athletic clubs and the Sewanee scrub team.[16] The faculty's crusading zeal diminished after 1911, and eligibility standards were relaxed, but a precedent had been set. As President Race put it: "The athletic sports have been established upon a strict school basis. All our teams have consisted of *bona fide* students.... There will be no matriculating at the University just for the purpose of playing on some of the athletic teams."

The school's athletic standing concerned Race far less than did its financial condition. Financially, Grant University was in much the same plight as most of its peers in the region. In 1900, not one of the 18 American universities with endowments of $1.5 million or more was located in the South. Only two southern universities – Vanderbilt and Tulane – had endowments of as much as $1 million, and the combined endowment income of the 24 colleges in Tennessee was $138,653, or $5,777.20 a year on average.[17] Grant University, with a productive endowment of just $15,000, had investment income well below the state average, probably not more than $1,000 yearly. The combination of negligible endowment income and low tuition charges kept the school in a state of perpetual want. To cover basic operating costs, the school depended on a $3,000 yearly subsidy from the trustees and a $12,000 annual appropriation from the Freedmen's Aid and Southern Education Society.

But funding from Cincinnati could not be relied upon much longer, for the Society had undergone a thorough reorganization in 1904 and was now preparing to clear the books of a good many schools it maintained in the South. Among them was Grant University. Cincinnati made its intentions clear to Race. "Just as soon as possible," he told the trustees, "we must place Grant University on a self-supporting basis." To him that meant raising an endowment of $200,000 right away and another $300,000 soon afterwards. It had to be done quickly. "The aid now given through the [Society]," Race confided in a fundraising letter of January 1905, "cannot in the very nature of the case be continued much longer."

The letter went out to a retired Chicago industrialist, Daniel Kimball Pearsons, whose hobby was giving away chunks of his $6 million fortune to small colleges in the Midwest and South. Philanthropy, said Pearsons, was "greater sport than baseball and more fun than any other entertainment." Race presented the case for Grant University in his letter to Pearsons and sent out similar appeals to several dozen other multi-millionaires, any one of whom could offer a contribution large enough to set in motion a major campaign for endowment. Race met in person with some of them, including Daniel Pearsons. But they all put him off with suggestions that he come back in three months or in a year or, as one wrote superciliously, whenever his school's "endowments give proof of its permanent success."

Then, "suddenly," Race received a "very agreeable surprise" – a letter of April 1, 1905 from Daniel Pearsons in which the 85-year-old philanthropist wrote: "I am ready to make you this proposition: I will give you for the endowment of Grant University $50,000, if your people will raise $150,000 for the same purpose, perpetual endowment. I will give you one year to raise the money and no longer. All the $200,000 must be kept forever, only the income can be used."

Pearsons had baited the hook with $50,000 and given Race one year to fish for another $150,000. After doing some quick mental arithmetic, Race felt confident that he could bring in $50,000 from Chattanooga. He was less confident of his ability to raise the remaining $100,000 from sources outside the local area. His doubts as well as his determination showed in his reply to the proposal. On May 1, he wired Pearsons: "GIFT DEEPLY APPRECIATED. CONDITIONS WILL BE MET IF GRIT AND GRACE HOLD OUT."

Local generosity got the campaign off to a strong start. John A. Patten gave $10,000, and other members of the First Methodist Church contributed $30,000 more. The university's own students collected $5,000, which, as an observer noted, was "as much for them as it would be for the students of Harvard to raise a quarter of a million." All told, Chattanoogans gave $60,000 toward the $150,000 goal. And when local generosity ran out, Race went to work on his friends in the North and on complete strangers there: $11,000 came in from Miss Addie Danforth of New York, $5,000 from Mrs. G.W. Swift of Chicago; $16,000 from Joseph Worthington of Ohio; $5,000 from J.B. Russell of New York.

By late February 1906, a month before Pearson's offer expired, $120,000 had been raised, but the campaign was stalled $30,000 short of its goal. It was then that Race's earlier contacts with Andrew Carnegie paid off; in March 1908 Carnegie gave Grant University the final $30,000 it needed to land the $200,000 endowment fund.

The outcome seemed astonishing to the editor of one church journal. "Who really *believed*," he asked, "that [Grant University] could secure an increase of $200,000 permanent endowment? A few *thought* it could be done… and a certain number of those responsive souls who felt both that it should and would be done diffused an atmosphere of expectancy wherever they moved, but who believed?"

John Race and his colleagues on the board had not only concluded a remarkable endowment drive – they had also started a campaign to win home rule for the university. That campaign picked up momentum when Cincinnati approved Race's oft-repeated request for a change in the school's identity. By charter amendment of June 18, 1907, the local board retired the name U.S. Grant University, replacing it with the name by which the institution would be known for the next 62 years: the University of Chattanooga.

Looking beyond the immediate horizon, President Race foresaw the day when the University of Chattanooga would outgrow its 12-acre campus on McCallie Avenue. Realizing that the site was "too small" and "too valuable" for long-term use, he made plans to move the university north of the river to a 100-acre tract of ground in a section of town later known as Riverview. His idea was to acquire an option on the tract, with expectations of occupying it in a few years, at which point he hoped to develop the 12 acres on McCallie into income-producing rental property. "You can readily understand what this will mean fifty years from now for the university," he told the board.[18]

While Race dealt with strategic issues, Dean Hooper and his faculty colleagues gradually brought academic standards up to the level ordinarily achieved only by much larger and wealthier colleges. In a study of 46 Northern Methodist colleges conducted in 1910, the University of Chattanooga ranked first academically, 46th in tuition income, and 31st in general equipment. Tuition charges were among the lowest in the area and admission requirements among the highest. In fact, the superintendent of county schools reported in 1910 that none of the 65 members of the graduating class at Central High School could qualify for admission to the University of Chattanooga.

Students who succeeded in completing one of the degree programs did not come along very often during these early years. For the years 1905 through 1910, the university had a total of 32 graduates. The numbers were "too small," said Race, who believed that the school would not be taken seriously by most philanthropists and educators until it began to produce "at least twenty-five" graduates a year. Degree requirements, however, were to remain the same, regardless of how many or how few students could satisfy them. Rather than lower their standards, Race and the board were willing to wait until students rose high enough to meet them. As a committee of trustees advised in a report to the board: "... Be patient. There are states in the Union where the same amount of work that has been done here would produce a student body of at least five hundred.... Our growth must be more gradual than in localities where education has become a universal passion among young people.... We are confident that we are working on the right lines."[19]

Confirmation of the soundness of their approach came when the university was invited to join the prestigious Southern Association of Colleges and Secondary Schools (SACS). Organized in 1894 largely through the efforts of Chancellor James Kirkland of Vanderbilt, SACS had evolved into a regional accrediting agency whose collegiate members agreed to establish uniformly high academic standards and to abolish all subcollegiate classes. In 1906, fewer than 20 of the South's 115 institutions of higher learning had satisfied those basic requirements. The second requirement delayed the university's own admission until 1910, when all preparatory work was dropped and the institution joined distinguished company as the 21st collegiate member of SACS.[20]

With some $250,000 of endowment to its credit, the university was able to capitalize on a change of policy within the Church North's Board of Education. That agency had taken over the operations of the Freedmen's Aid and Southern Education Society in 1904 and, four years later, ruled that ownership of any school under its aegis could be transferred to local trustees at such time as those trustees held enough endowment to make their school self-supporting. The Chattanooga trustees immediately petitioned to have title to the University of Chattanooga transferred to their authority, and the Board of Education, after studying their request for almost a year, granted it. On May 21, 1909, the holdings at

Chattanooga and Athens were deeded over to the local board. With that, the university became genuinely Chattanooga's own.

"This day is the best day that the university has known," Race declared at a dinner given to celebrate receipt of the deed. John A. Patten called on all present to join him in expressing, in a tangible and lasting way, their gratitude to the man chiefly responsible for bringing this day to pass. Then and there a "whirlwind campaign" got going to raise $20,000 and build a residence on campus for President and Mrs. Race. Pledges for the entire amount were collected within three days, and a building site was chosen at the corner of Oak and Douglas Streets. When completed in 1911, the president's house would serve not only as an official residence but also as a social center for students and faculty alike.

By the time the president's house was ready for occupancy, the president himself was away on the fundraising trail more than he was at home on campus. In years past, Race had repeatedly tried to win financial backing from the nation's largest philanthropic organization, the General Education Board, of New York. Created in 1902, with a $46 million gift from John D. Rockefeller, the General Education Board bestowed $3 million on southern colleges during the first 12 years of its existence. Between 1902 and 1924, it would contribute $60 million to a select group of colleges that managed to raise an additional $140 million in matching gifts.

Like the Carnegie Foundation and other giants in the field of educational philanthropy, the General Education Board was designed not so much to aid individual colleges as to standardize American higher education, putting it on a "nonpartisan, impersonal," business-like basis, similar to what John D. Rockefeller had achieved in the petroleum industry with his Standard Oil Company.[21] The small denominational college, hardly a model of efficiency and pragmatism, generally had no place in that masterplan. Indeed, as one scholar has observed, both the Carnegie Foundation and the General Education Board "tried to... kill off the weaker denominational colleges... which for decades had simply defied all reason and... refuse[d] to die."[22]

In October 1907, Race had met for the first time with Wallace Buttrick, the "plump and benign" secretary of the General Education Board. Before Race got around to asking for a specific dollar amount, Buttrick advised him that is was "practically useless" to apply for Rockefeller funds so long as the University of Chattanooga maintained a school of theology. He also suggested to Race that the proprietary schools of medicine and law at Chattanooga did not reflect the high caliber of instruction the Board had come to expect of the institutions it assisted. Nevertheless, Race went ahead and asked Buttrick for $200,000. That, Buttrick assured him, was "out of the question."

A year later, Race had gone back to Buttrick, only to be given the same advice as before: come back when you have eliminated your schools of theology, medicine, and law. Though Race had been advocating that very course of action since 1904, some of the trustees were reluctant to part with the professional schools, which boosted enrollment, looked impressive on paper, and gave the institution some claim to the status of university.

The issue took on critical importance in 1910. In May of that year, John A. Patten and another trustee, Bishop William Anderson, conferred with Wallace Buttrick in New York and left his office with the distinct impression that he had just promised to assist the university if it eliminated the professional schools. They wired the good news to their fellow trustees in Chattanooga, who thereupon voted to drop the professional schools as soon as the General Education Board committed itself to the university. But they had dodged the issue, not settled it. Their decision to delay action on the professional schools pending a favorable response from the Board in New York was unacceptable to Buttrick. He told Bishop Anderson that the university trustees must act on the matter forthwith if they expected any consideration at all from the Board.

His demand sent the trustees into a special called meeting on May 30, 1910. During the course of their deliberations, President Race expressed his own views on the question before them. "We are face-to-face with a very vital problem," he began. "The appeals for financial aid made to men of modern ideas – and they are the men who have money – are met by the statement that we are top-heavy, that we have no right conception of the logical steps to be taken in developing the University.... It is well nigh the universal conviction of educators today that the college stands at the center of every educational activity, and that the organization controlling it should undertake no professional work until the college is thoroughly developed....

"Appeals for money to support our college would receive much more ready and hearty response if we confine ourselves to this one undertaking. To put it frankly, it is my deep conviction that we should at this time cease attempting to operate professional schools. The only rational way open to us as it seems to me is to confine our efforts to the development of the college, suffering such temporary losses as may result, meeting in a statesmanlike way such criticism as may result, and appealing confidently to the friends of advanced educational efforts... to cooperate with us... in developing a real college from the fine plant we have in this strategic center."

After hearing Race out, the trustees voted to close the schools of medicine and law and to transfer the school of theology to Athens within 30 days. That action satisfied all of Buttrick's requirements except one. The university's location on McCallie Avenue, so close to downtown and so accessible to students, seemed ideal to Buttrick. Convinced as he was that a great university could not be developed in "secluded spots," he extracted from Race a promise to keep the campus where it was, "right in the heart of the city," rather than move north of the river to the 100-acre site in the country.

Little did Buttrick imagine how quickly the city would spread into the country, turning "secluded spots" into subdivisions. Had Race been free to carry out his original plan, the University of Chattanooga would have relocated to a site on or near the one presently occupied by the Chattanooga Golf and Country Club.

In October 1910, after three years of bargaining, Buttrick delivered the goods, handing Race the means to start up the largest capital-funds campaign ever seen in Chattanooga. The goal was $500,000, 30 percent of which was payable if the university produced the other 70 percent in two years' time. To receive a gift of $150,000 from the Rockefeller Foundation, the trustees obligated themselves to raise $350,000 by November 1, 1912.

Unlike the endowment campaign of 1905-1906, which had run almost entirely on the energy supplied by Race and his inner circle, this campaign drew energy from the community. Joining the endeavor was a special committee of the Chamber of Commerce composed of prominent townspeople such as Mayor T.C. Thompson; bank presidents Harry Probasco, T.R. Preston, and Walter Sadd; newspaper publisher George Fort Milton; and manufacturers J.J. Mahoney and W.E. Brock. The joint effort of town and gown generated contributions of $200,000 from Chattanooga, or quadruple the amount collected there during the earlier campaign.

Race gave up the comforts of the president's home for weeks on end as he went after prospects in the North, appealing to them in his "earnest, high-toned, business-like" manner. During the two years allotted to the drive, thousands of prospects were canvassed; and on the appointed date of November 1, 1912, the university board reported that pledges for the entire $350,000 had been secured. That brought the university's total capital resources to $750,000. The future had never looked better to the trustees.

Their confidence was jarred a few months later when one of their number submitted his resignation. At the board meeting of April 1913, John Race officially announced that he was leaving to accept assignment as co-director of the Church North's extensive publishing enterprise.

Race had guided the university through 16 years of groundbreaking, often tumultuous, change, and that perhaps was long enough for anyone to serve in such trying circumstances. He had met challenges that would have overwhelmed most other college heads, and the new assignment was a well-deserved respite after the years of grinding labor at Chattanooga.

Tributes to Race and expressions of regret over his departure streamed in from trustees, faculty, students, townspeople, and even from a gentleman who had once been among his most outspoken critics. "I shall miss you," wrote Trustee J.W. Fisher of Newport, Tennessee. "The University will miss you. Many will miss you who would have stoned you a few years ago. You will pardon me if I say you are the University to me."

To John Race more than to anyone else must go the credit for transforming a fractious, debt-ridden pseudo-university into a genuine liberal arts college backed by close to $750,000 in capital funds. The school he left in 1913 was essentially his handiwork, and it would stand the test of time. As historians of the university wrote in 1947: "Whatever else the modern University of Chattanooga may be, it is a monument to the genius of John H. Race."

4
Modern Times

No denomination can in the future expect to control a college and at the same time call on the public to support it.
– Henry Smith Pritchett, The Carnegie Foundation (1908)

The search for a new president went on for almost a year as John A. Patten and John Race sized up numerous candidates whose names were passed along to them by various hierarchs of the Northern Methodist Church. Early in 1914, they settled on a 39 year-old Indiana minister who had been recommended to them by an editor of the *Western Christian Advocate*, and in April the board duly elected as university president Fred Whitlo Hixson.[1]

Small and compact of frame, the Reverend Hixson carried himself like a military man, though the only soldiering he had ever done was in the cadet corps at Depauw University, where he had earned his Phi Beta Kappa key. In manner he was austere, in appearance exceedingly dignified. While most of the other trustees dressed in standard business suits, President Hixson favored the frock coats, stand-up collars, and striped trousers seen more often at the Court of St. James than at functions of the University of Chattanooga. He was meticulous and cautious, anxious to make good in this his first posting as a college executive.[2]

Hixson took office during the initial phase of a construction program that would physically transform the campus. In June 1914, ground was broken at the corner of Oak and Baldwin for a "commodious and substantial" gymnasium, the first of five projected buildings to be financed in part with $200,000 from the $750,000 raised during the administration of John Race.

Plans called for the main group of buildings to rise on the hillside overlooking McCallie Avenue. The building committee, headed by Harry Probasco, at first proceeded on the assumption that the new structures could be tied in with Old Main, but they began to have second thoughts when Probasco found out that it would cost as much to overhaul Old Main ($60,000) as to construct a new building. Moreover, fashions in collegiate architecture had veered away from the Gilded Age mannerism of Old Main. It bristled with so many turrets, towers, gilded spires, arches, and porticos that it looked as if it had not been built of brick and stone but squeezed out of a pastry tube. Even if remodeled extensively, the massive pile would still "possess no architectural excellence," the trustees concluded. In the interests of economy and aesthetics, they decided to have Old Main demolished as soon as new facilities were ready for use.

A tight cluster of buildings began to take shape on the hillside around Old Main in the fall of 1915. Designed by Atlanta architect W.T. Downing in the style known as collegiate Gothic, the structures would form three sides of a quadrangle opening out onto the urban landscape in the foreground and Lookout Mountain in the distance. On the west flank of Old Main was the Administration Building or, as it was later called, Founders Hall. Connected to it and running behind Old Main was a classroom building, named John H.

Race Hall in 1950. And extending out along its axis was Science Hall, later renamed Wesley W. Hooper Hall. A cloister led from it to the quadrangle's terminus, the John A. Patten Chapel. Built at a cost of $75,000 and dedicated in 1919, it was a gift from Edith Manker Patten and her children in 1917.

The year before, John A. Patten had died suddenly at the age of 48, after enduring two public controversies that may have hastened his end. For many years, he had been a leading parishioner at Chattanooga's First Methodist Church, the largest contributor to its budget and teacher of a Sunday school class which met in the sanctuary. To all appearances, he was a pillar of the church, but the pastor of First Methodist in 1913, Charles Haven Myers, thought otherwise. Declaring that the Pattens' immensely profitable Wine of Cardui was a tonic of "questionable value and high alcoholic content," the Reverend Myers accused John A. Patten of "hypocrisy" and took his Sunday school class away from him.[3] Patten retaliated by having Myers removed from the pastorate of First Methodist; but when the young minister left, he took with him enough parishioners to organize the Pilgrim Congregational Church.

No sooner did the uproar subside than Wine of Cardui was lambasted in the *Journal of the American Medical Association*. Patten, summoning his lawyers to the Chattanooga Medicine Company, filed suit in Chicago against the American Medical Association, seeking $3 million in damages. Although the court would decide in favor of Chattanooga Medicine, it awarded the company token damages of only one cent, and this partial victory came too late for Patten. In April 1916, while the case was being heard, John A. Patten fell ill in Chicago and died shortly after undergoing surgery for a perforated ulcer.[4]

In April 1917, two months before the groundbreaking ceremonies for Patten Chapel, the United States declared war on Germany. Patriotic passions ran high as the nation mobilized men and resources for a war that President Woodrow Wilson said would be fought "to make the world safe for democracy." A resolution passed at a mass meeting in Chattanooga concluded: "From now on there can be but two classes of people in America: Americans and traitors." Placards on the city's main streets demanded to know "Where is your Liberty Loan Button?"

Chattanoogans embraced the Allied cause with a fervor that seemed to Jerome Hixson, son of President Fred Hixson, "almost fanatical" in retrospect. The wife of a university professor was widely rumored to be a fifth columnist, simply because she happened to be of German origin. Mozart, Beethoven, and Bach were also suspect. "Music by German composers was banned," Hixson recalled, and "some street names were changed, Bismark Avenue becoming Pershing." In those days, Hixson remembered, it even "seemed right to find" inside downtown stores large canisters bearing the printed message: "Deposit your peach pits here, to make cyanide gas to poison Huns."[5]

If there were opponents of the war at the University of Chattanooga, they kept their mouths shut. No one wanted to be thought of as a *slacker*: "Every man has been careful to stand in a position which could justify no criticism of his patriotism," President Hixson assured the trustees in June 1918. By then, every able-bodied male student above the age of 21 had gone into the armed forces, and many of the younger men had left to work in some branch of the civilian war effort. Women joined the Red Cross, enrolled in home nursing courses, and fell to rolling bandages and knitting sweaters, socks, and mufflers for the American troops in France. Collegiate enrollment dropped to some 30 percent of its pre-war level. The varsity athletic teams, the fraternities, and the literary societies all suspended their activities.

The university itself probably would have suspended or curtailed operations had the trustees not meshed the school into the nation's machinery of war. In 1918, the War Department decided to form Student Army Training Corps (SATC) units on many campuses, thereby converting colleges into military posts. On October 1, the university received a SATC unit consisting of about 50 student soldiers. Billeted in Science Hall, they followed a full military regimen and took academic courses which the faculty had revamped in accordance with Army specifications for officer trainees. In no time, however, the Armistice of November 12 eliminated the need for SATC, and the unit was demobilized on December 7, after little more than two months at the university. For that brief stay on campus, the War Department paid the university $12,609.

In many respects, the University of Chattanooga coped with the dislocations of war better than it did with the revolution in manners and morals that took place immediately after the war. Forms of conduct once relegated to the margins of society began to enter the mainstream. There were supposedly "nice" girls who all of a sudden bobbed their hair, raised their hemlines, smoked cigarettes in public, and engaged in the unspeakable practice of necking. There were speakeasies and flappers; the Lost Generation; screen stars like Theda "The Vamp" Bara whose most famous line was "Kiss me, you fool"; backseat romancing and marathon dancing; and the pulsating rhythms of jazz – all vying for the attention of a nation fed up with war, bored with President Wilson's League of Nations, and ready to have a good time.

At the University of Chattanooga, students grew restive under conditions designed to swaddle them in "the watch care of the Christian home." More than 80 percent of them voiced dissatisfaction with the limited range of social activities on campus. They asked for the chance to organize hikes, picnics, athletic events, and periodic festivals; and they asked for a student commons furnished with "comfortable chairs, pianos, victrolas, telephones, popular books and magazines, and a billiard table." More than anything else, though, they bridled at the prohibition against dancing.[6]

In 1915, the students went so far as to hold an impromptu dance in the new gymnasium. School officials intervened to break up the illicit affair, but not in time to prevent it from embroiling the Hixson administration in a major crisis. News of the incident traveled through the Holston Conference, and soon President Hixson's desk was piled high with letters from men of the cloth who were scandalized by the horrible affront to Methodist mores.

The *Methodist Advocate* pilloried school officials, suggesting that they lacked the resolve to prevent similar transgressions in the future. District conferences lodged "vigorous protests" on the basis of rumors that "public dancing" was being "tolerated and encouraged" at the university. And the rural gentry solemnly lectured President Hixson on the reactions to be expected when two healthy young bodies started moving in time to the music. "In a dance, and especially in the unbelievable intimacies and liberties of some of the modern dances," one correspondent warned Hixson, "passions are set aflame which prove uncontrollable save in the anemic and the stalwart.... It is the story of the moth and the flame."[7]

Hixson never entirely quelled the protests coming from the East Tennessee countryside. Even in 1919, three years after he had stated publicly on the floor of the Holston Conference that neither he nor the faculty permitted or encouraged dancing among students, there were still those who regarded the university as a hotbed of liberalism, fated to "go the way of Vanderbilt, forsaking the Church that produced it."[8]

All the while, Hixson faced mounting pressure from students who insisted that the ban on dancing be lifted. Reconciling their demands with those of rural patrons was impossible; both groups wound up feeling shortchanged. In January 1920, Hixson and the faculty granted a student petition to hold three chaperoned dances a year but refused to permit the dances to occur on campus. The university thus achieved an uneasy truce with the 20th century.

Fred Hixson departed the university in July 1920 to accept the presidency of another church school, Allegheny College in Pennsylvania. In selecting his successor, the trustees once again went through a year-long process of evaluating candidates offered to them by the Church North, and from that group they chose the Reverend Arlo Ayres Brown, a native of Illinois who was superintendent of teacher training for Northern Methodist Sunday schools.

The new president possessed a "warm, natural dignity," recalled a faculty member,[9] and was "most tactful, not a strident Wesleyanite," said another, who also commented that President Brown conducted faculty meetings in the manner of "a nice little Methodist Sunday school class."[10] All in all, Arlo Brown made a graceful transition from heading up the training of Methodist Sunday school teachers to heading up the University of Chattanooga.

Perhaps the toughest assignment handed to him by the board was that of enlarging the school's local constituency. Relations with the community had thawed during the presidency of John Race, but large segments of the populace remained cool toward the university. Many townspeople with long memories still referred to it as the "Yankee Methodist University." "They felt that it was a sort of missionary school for mountain whites," recalled Jerome Hixson, "and assumed a somewhat condescending attitude, sending their young people to Southern colleges like Vanderbilt and Agnes Scott, and letting those who could not go elsewhere use the Yankee university."[11]

Progress in bringing about a more perfect union with Chattanooga would be slow during the 1920s, in part because the Church North continued to dominate the school's management. It reached out for wider support yet held fast to narrow denominational prerogatives. President Brown, like all his predecessors, had been assigned to the university by church officialdom, and he reported to school trustees who were compelled by a provision in the charter to elect at least two-thirds of their number from members of the Northern Methodist Church. With its own members casting the decisive vote on any question, the church occupied the position of a majority stockholder in a closely-held enterprise. Non-Northern Methodists could not very well be barred from most top posts at the University of Chattanooga and still be expected to close ranks behind it.

Community outreach during the 1920s was carried on through an array of new academic programs designed to meet local needs and, not coincidentally, to satisfy the university's own pressing need for larger enrollments. The summer school, an innovation of the Race administration, reopened in 1925. (It had been discontinued during World War I.) Intended primarily for the continuing education of local high school teachers, it attracted 128 students in 1926. Another popular addition was the program leading to the Bachelor of Business Administration degree, initiated in 1923, and in such demand two years later that the department needed four professors to handle the teaching load. The curriculum was further enlarged to make room for the fine arts; in 1928, a major in music was offered, a major in art was developed by Professor Frank Baisden, and a program in dramatics featuring performances by the University Players began under the direction of Mrs. David Cornelius. This venture into the fine arts reflected the university's intention, as Arlo Brown put it, to serve Chattanooga as "a beacon of culture."

The integrity of scholarship mattered to President Brown. He proved himself an able defender of academic freedom during the campaign to force the teaching of a biology which conformed to the account of man's origins set down in the first chapter of Genesis. In July 1925, four months after the Tennessee legislature had outlawed the teaching of Darwinian evolution in state schools, John Scopes was brought to trial in nearby Dayton, Tennessee, for the crime of teaching his high school biology class the theory that man had "descended from a lower order of animals." The eight-day trial would become one of the biggest news stories of the decade, as more than a hundred reporters converged on the quiet town to file blow-by-blow accounts of the courtroom battle between Clarence Darrow and William Jennings Bryan.

The University of Chattanooga, a private institution, was not subject to the state's anti-evolution law, but the trial in Dayton inflamed hard-line Methodists in the area. From the small towns of East Tennessee arose a hue and cry against the teaching of evolution at the University of Chattanooga. President Brown, however, refused to place Darwin off-limits to students; he held to the view that it was Chattanooga's "duty" to "explain and discuss with its students every theory of vital concern to them." The board backed him up, even when the small town Methodists took their protests public, labeling the university a "hot-bed of infidelity." Brown made no effort to appease them. In a chapel sermon delivered at the height of the controversy, Brown left no doubt where he stood on the issue. "Anyone," he told his audience, "who says that a man cannot be a Christian and at the same time believe in Theistic Evolution is either ignorant or dishonest."[12]

His forthright stand against the tyranny of popular opinion won Brown high marks from the faculty. Professor Edwin S. Lindsey, whose career at the university stretched from 1924 to 1968, would remember: "When I came here, the university was an island of modernism in a sea of – I shouldn't say this – ignorance."[13]

Unmoved by the clamor of rural Methodists, President Brown encouraged freedom of inquiry and a spirit of liberalization on campus. In 1924, he permitted the students to hold their first sanctioned dance in the school gymnasium. He also presided during negotiations which freed the university from its troublesome connection to the Athens school. And he gathered support for a revolutionary curricular change in 1928, when, "after long… heated" exchanges between traditionalists and modernists on the faculty, the requirement of Latin or Greek for the B.A. was eliminated.

The decision was a belated acknowledgment of reality: the university could not get enough students with high school preparation in those languages; Vanderbilt had scrapped its own Greek-Latin requirement for the same reason in 1919. Only Chicago among the nation's major universities still had a Greek requirement. Chattanooga could back away from its classical emphasis without endangering its academic reputation. It belonged to the Association of American Universities, which meant that its credits were accepted at face value by universities worldwide, and its former students were compiling excellent records in graduate schools at Vanderbilt, Chicago, Wisconsin, Harvard, Yale, and Columbia.[14]

The elimination of required Latin or Greek, together with the new programs in business administration and the fine arts, stimulated record growth. Enrollment more than doubled, going from 261 students in 1920 to 676 in 1928. The faculty grew from 17 to 27 members, and the typical graduating class increased from fewer than 10 seniors to more than 50.

Arlo Brown's accomplishments at Chattanooga did not go unnoticed by Northern Methodist officials. They decided that he was ready for a position of even greater responsibility, and in January 1929 Brown left the university to accept appointment as president of Drew Theological Seminary. Chattanooga's long line of Methodist clergyman-presidents ended with Arlo Brown – at least temporarily. Not until 1959 would another Methodist minister serve as university president.

There were signs that the commercial-civic elite of Chattanooga wanted to play a larger role at the university, both in its financing and in its management. In 1927, for example, the Kiwanis Club had collected just over $60,000 for the construction of a brick stadium along the Oak Street side of Chamberlain Field; the new stadium, with seating for 5,000 spectators, was a gift to the university made "without any restrictions" by the donors. Local civic clubs also had taken part in a capital funds drive for $850,000 in 1922. Under the leadership of Trustee William E. Brock, a Southern Methodist, members of those clubs raised a sizeable portion of the sum sought. Although a large percentage of the pledges turned out to be uncollectible, and though the fees paid to a professional fundraising organization were high in proportion to the amounts actually collected, the university still managed to add $250,000 to its productive endowment, bringing the total to more than a million dollars by 1927.

The finance committee, composed of W.E. Brock, Z.C. Patten, Paul Kruesi, Scott Probasco, John Fletcher, Z.W. Wheland, and other trustees, watched over the $1 million endowment. It generated annual income of more than $50,000, which paid one-half of the school's operating expenses, while tuition and fees covered roughly the other half. In their investment strategy, the trustees aimed for maximum return, passing over blue chip stocks and bonds in favor of high-yield investments. In fact, almost 95 percent of the endowment had been placed in real estate or in real estate participation certificates (REPCs).[15]

The REPC, sold by several local financial institutions, represented shares in various pools of first mortgages on improved real estate. Although the instrument had been around for years, its recent surge in popularity was breathtaking; the volume of REPCs offered nationwide in 1919 was probably only $50 million, while by 1923 it had risen to $500 million and by 1925 to $1 billion. REPCs were tempting because they earned interest of six percent or more at a time when savings accounts paid about four percent. The demand for new issues was immense and growing. To satisfy it, several banks and savings associations in town amassed vast real estate holdings against which to issue REPCs.[16]

One of them was the First National Bank, of which at least two of the university's trustees were substantial shareholders. First National had merged with the Chattanooga Savings Bank in 1928 to form the state's third largest bank, with resources of $32 million. Among those resources was the entire endowment of the University of Chattanooga.

Thus did the university have close to $1 million tied up in a single bank and riding on the real estate market. Dependence on one financial institution and on one investment market can be risky in the best of times. It proved downright foolhardy in 1930, when the economy plunged into the longest and deepest depression in the nation's history.

5
Not Just Another Mill Town

The University of Chattanooga is an area college.... Its campus is to a large degree the whole area....Its privilege and responsibility are to create in this section of the nation an example of what civilization ought to be.
– Alexander Guerry, president, University of Chattanooga (1937)

In June 1929, six months after Arlo Brown's resignation, the trustees gathered to elect his successor. They had looked for someone who could take the university beyond its sectarian origins, and they counted themselves fortunate in having secured the services of an outstanding local educator who, they noted with satisfaction, "instantly meets the unanimous approval not only of the Board of Trustees but also the unanimous approval of the community at large." He was Alexander Guerry, the first layman, non-Methodist, and Southerner to be named president of the university.

Alex Guerry came to the university from the headmastership of Chattanooga's Baylor School. There his ambition and vision, combined with the generosity of Coca-Cola bottling magnate John Thomas Lupton, had transformed Baylor's hole-in-the-corner operation on Palmetto Street into a thriving preparatory school located on a 100-acre campus overlooking the Tennessee River.[1]

Guerry drove himself hard and was intolerant of anything short of success. He espoused lofty educational principles in a way that inspired businessmen and academicians alike, and he would risk failure rather than compromise those principles, believing that "there is always victory even in defeat for those who uphold a worthy cause."[2]

Born in 1890 at Lincolnton, North Carolina, Alexander Guerry grew up at Sewanee, where his father, the Reverend William Alexander Guerry, was chaplain and professor of theology at the University of the South. The family had little in the way of material advantages, but their home was culturally and intellectually rich, and in it great value was placed on service to others. All three of Alex's brothers became Episcopal priests, and Alex would be a steadfast defender of the liberal arts, believing that the true purpose of higher education was not to equip students for a profession but to give "training and preparation for a finer and more useful service to the nation."

In 1910, upon graduating from Sewanee, where he was a member of Phi Beta Kappa, Guerry had come to Chattanooga as a teacher at McCallie School, living in the dormitory. "He was the youngest teacher we had," said Associate Headmaster Park McCallie, "and a brilliant teacher, well beloved by boys and faculty." He demonstrated versatility at McCallie, teaching Greek and Latin and coaching tennis and football, though his employers did overtax his resourcefulness on one occasion. As he later reminded them: "Never shall I forget the German class which I undertook reluctantly upon your insistence that every boy in the group would be infinitely more ignorant of the language than I and so I could keep ahead. You will recall, of course, my consternation when I discovered that one of the students in the class had lived eight years in Germany."[3]

Guerry attended the Chattanooga College of Law at night, taking an LL.B. degree in 1914 in the same class as two of his close friends, Ed Finlay and Phil Whitaker. Finlay and Whitaker would establish flourishing legal practices, and Guerry also contemplated a business career. After his first year at McCallie, he resigned and together with another teacher tried his hand at selling insurance in Memphis. He returned to McCallie in 1912; but, for someone with his ambition and talent, the family-owned and family-operated McCallie School was a dead end. In 1913, he joined the Baylor School, where there was opportunity aplenty for anyone who could breathe new life into the dying school.

That same year he found a partner who would share and encourage his ambitions: Charlotte Holmes Patten. Her father, John A. Patten, held controlling interest in the Chattanooga Medicine Company, whose booming business in herbal elixirs and tonics had made the Pattens, as Jonathan Daniels described them, some of "the big folk in Chattanooga." Socially, Charlotte Patten and Alexander Guerry were from different worlds, and neither of their families encouraged the romance that developed between them. But both of them were strong-willed and independent. In December 1913, they were married in what the Chattanooga *Times* called "a brilliant wedding" ceremony. Following the honeymoon, they settled into a modest house near Baylor School, resisting the temptation, said one observer, "to reside in splendor on Lookout Mountain with Charlotte's friends."

Instead, Charlotte Guerry would entertain students and guests of the school with a flawless and seemingly effortless grace calculated to render their stay unforgettable. More than just a brilliant hostess, she also would be an ever-present, behind-the-scenes participant in her husband's decision-making. Apart, they each stood out in a crowd; together, they were a formidable team – he with his burning idealism and she with her money and quiet pragmatism.[4]

By the time of their marriage, Guerry had assumed the duties of associate headmaster at Baylor, becoming the school's chief disciplinarian, business manager, and recruiter, besides continuing to teach, coach, and direct athletics. On top of all that, he put together a comprehensive plan for moving Baylor out of the deep rut it was in. In its cramped location downtown and with its uncertain trickle of tuition money, the school could do little more than hang on from one year to the next. Guerry's plan called for refinancing and reorganizing the school on a grand scale.

Such a possibility had long been a dream of others at Baylor, but it remained only a dream until Alex Guerry won the confidence of a benefactor who operated on a grand scale. In 1913, while courting Charlotte Patten, Guerry had met her kinsman by marriage, John Thomas Lupton, who owned immensely profitable Coca-Cola bottling plants throughout the South and West. At the time, Lupton was interested in the Baylor School only because his son, Cartter, was a student there. Guerry caught his eye, however, and Lupton soon saw in him a hard-driving, determined young man whose vision of Baylor's future was worth investing in. Between 1914 and 1925, Lupton contributed at least $250,000 toward the cost of rebuilding the Baylor School on a spacious tract of land which surpassed in size and scenic grandeur the campuses of many colleges, including the University of Chattanooga.[5]

At Baylor, Guerry had become skillful at leading his fellow board members by cultivating and guiding their understanding of the issues. And at the university, he quickly took the initiative in the boardroom. On the very day of his election to the presidency, Guerry outlined for the trustees three of his immediate goals. First was an adjustment in athletic policy.

The football program had generated much excitement and a sizeable deficit since 1925, when the pressure to field a winning team led to the hiring of a high-powered head coach, Frank Thomas, who had played at Notre Dame under Knute Rockne and would accept the head coaching position at the University of Alabama in the fall of 1929. During Frank Thomas' last three seasons at Chattanooga, his teams had lost only four games and were S.I.A.A. conference champions in 1927 and 1928. The new emphasis on gridiron glory, with the attendant necessity to recruit and compensate star athletes and coaches, seemed ill-advised to President Guerry. He was one of the few educators in the South who insistently called for a return to strictly amateur athletics in the region's colleges and schools. As he put the case: "Second-rate institutions win prestige and standing not only in the eyes of the American people but in their own eyes by first-rate, bought football teams. Thus, they destroy a sense of values among their students and for themselves. It is the most costly price being paid for glamour in America today."[6] To remove that temptation at Chattanooga, Guerry cut the football budget back to pre-1925 levels, bid farewell to Coach Thomas, and expanded intramural athletics to involve a larger number of students in sports and physical education.

Another of Guerry's immediate goals was to provide the students with the place of their own that they and their predecessors had so often requested: a student commons. It opened in the fall, with a cafeteria and three clubrooms, in the previously unused space beneath Oak Street Stadium. That same year, the restrictions which had driven students to hold dances off campus were finally lifted; proms, cotillions, and similar social events now became a normal part of campus life.

On his first day in office, Guerry also told the trustees of his plan to initiate a series of scholarly conferences under the rubric of an Institute of Justice. Patterned after the Institute of Public Affairs at the University of Virginia, these biennial conferences would bring eminent scholars and public figures to campus for a week-long program of lectures and roundtable discussions on vital topics of the day. During the Institutes held in April 1930, 1932, and 1934, Guerry assembled the most distinguished group of intellects ever gathered in Chattanooga. Among them were Roscoe Pound, dean of the Harvard Law School; Henry R. Luce, publisher of *Time* magazine; John Erskine, novelist and professor at Columbia; Admiral Richard Byrd, leader of five expeditions to Antartica; David Lilienthal, director of the Tennessee Valley Authority; Adolph S. Ochs, publisher of the New York *Times*; and Norman Thomas, political activist and Socialist Party candidate for many offices including the presidency. Their lectures and group discussions were open not only to the faculty but also to students and townspeople. Looking back on the Institutes many years later, an alumnus still marveled at the fact that students were given the chance to "meet and interact with those luminaries." [7]

The Institutes enlivened the intellectual atmosphere on campus, added luster to the university's reputation in academic circles, and demonstrated its commitment to serve as a "beacon of culture" in the Chattanooga area. Further evidence of that commitment came during Guerry's first year in office, as he extended academic programs to reach thousands of the community's working adults. In his view, the university was obligated to make "education a continuing process for all ages through all ages." In years past, there had been sporadic, half-hearted attempts to organize night classes, but nothing of consequence resulted until the Evening College was opened in September 1930. It had an enrollment of 249 students by 1931 anwould eventually develop into the Continuing Education Division, which offered 616 courses with an enrollment of 4,946 students in 1991.

In a still more inventive approach to adult education, the University of Chattanooga took to the air waves, broadcasting programs of classical music and faculty lectures twice-weekly over radio station WDOD. As the university began to project itself into community life, the community itself started to draw closer to the school. In November 1930, the Chattanooga Art Association located its gallery in a building on campus, which also soon became headquarters to the Chattanooga Astronomy Club as well as to the town's Chemistry Club, Radio Club, and Archeology Club.

No sooner had Alex Guerry begun the first year of his administration than signs appeared that the American economy was locked into a collision course with disaster. An industrial boom in the early 1920s had turned into a speculative binge as the conviction spread that everybody ought to be rich. The bandwagon of prosperity, which had taken America to the highest standard of living any people had ever known, originally rolled off the assembly lines of Detroit and other centers of invention and technology. But then it headed into the fantasyland of margin and leverage.

By 1928, the New York Stock Exchange was outperforming all other segments of the economy. Capital and excess profits were pouring into the stock market, driving stock prices higher and higher while industrial output actually leveled off. U.S. Steel shot up from $160 to $268 a share in three months of frenzied trading. Radio Corporation of America leaped from $85 to $420, even though it had never paid a dividend. But an investor who bought 10 shares of RCA early that year, putting up $100 on margin and borrowing the rest from a broker, could have sold the shares at year's end for $4,200.

Such miracles were enough to convince millions of people that, somewhere over what one brokerage firm called the "ever ascending curve of American prosperity," there awaited an inexhaustible pot of gold. "Nothing," declared a business leader, "can arrest the upward movement."

But suppose that an unusually large number of investors decided to take their profits instead of holding out for more. And suppose that they all picked the same moment to cash in.

When that happened on Thursday, October 24, 1929, the New York Stock Exchange broke, then rallied briefly before collapsing under an avalanche of sell orders. RCA plummeted to $28, and many stocks could not be unloaded at any price. The repercussions were immediate and disastrous. Reacting to the crash, business reined in spending, consumers tightened their belts, banks curbed lending, government put the lid on deficit spending, and in no time at all the economy ground to a halt.

From the top of prosperity in early 1929 to the bottom of depression three years later, production fell to less than it had been in 1913. The number of new automobiles coming from Detroit decreased by 80 percent. Investment all but ceased, falling from $162 billion to $800 million. The gains of a decade were wiped out.

The only ascending curves were those charting human misery. Unemployment soared from 3.2 percent to 24.9 percent, and six million men tramped the streets looking for work, for a soup kitchen, for a bread line. Another million men and boys drifted aimlessly across the country, riding the rails and living in hobo jungles. Each day over one thousand families lost their homes in foreclosures.

The desperate times stirred men to desperate actions. Groups of angry farmers arrived at foreclosures and, brandishing pitchforks and hangman's nooses, persuaded sheriffs to call a halt to the proceedings. In May 1930, a thousand New Yorkers standing in the bread line suddenly stormed two bakery trucks that were making deliveries. Two years later, when 15,000 unemployed veterans descended on Washington and demanded payment of their World War I bonuses, the U.S. Army drove them away with tanks, tear gas, and fixed bayonets.

Taken altogether, it was the worst crisis since the Civil War.

Teachers, hourly laborers, and farmers were among the first groups to feel the impact of the Great Depression. Many cities stopped paying their teachers or else paid them in scrip, which merchants and bankers often refused to honor at face value. At the University of Chattanooga, debts were piling up as early as 1930. By the end of academic year 1931-1932, the accumulated deficit totaled $15,900. The finance committee recommended that this shortfall be referred to the executive committee "with instructions to deal with it as best they can."

Waging the struggle to hold down expenditures was Stanley F. "Jack" Bretske, who had left Brock Candy Company in 1924 to become the university's business manager. An expert in thrift and economy, Bretske could, said one professor, "make a nickel go a long,

long way." The board would recognize his contributions by naming a dining facility, dedicated in 1947, Bretske Hall. Jack Bretske guarded every nickel at the university as if it were the school's last. His knack for saving a few dollars here and a few dollars there was never more essential then in 1933, when the steady stream of endowment income dwindled to a slow, intermittent trickle.

The First National Bank, where the university's endowment was invested largely in first mortgages and real estate participation certificates (REPCs), had seen its once profitable portfolio of real estate loans become a drag on earnings. Many hard-pressed borrowers could no longer keep up the payments on those loans, and their defaults jeopardized millions in REPCs, which in turn were secured by increasingly unmarketable property. Caught in the squeeze, First National had been forced to dip into reserves in order to pay interest on its more than $10 million in outstanding REPCs.[8]

As word of First National's condition spread, wary customers began to move their deposits out of the bank. The steady erosion of deposits turned into a landslide during December 1932, when the rate of withdrawals accelerated sharply; from a high of $26 million in 1928, deposits would sink to less than $12 million in early 1933.

Attempting to shore up public confidence, the directors shed their bank's 67-year-old name and spun off the non-accruing real estate loans into a wholly-owned subsidiary. On January 1, 1933, customers of First National learned from determinedly upbeat news reports that they were now doing business with a *"new"* bank: the Chattanooga National. The public was not reassured by that cosmetic change.[9]

The economy hit rock bottom in early March 1933. On the morning of March 2, Chattanooga National failed to open its doors to long lines of customers; thousands of other banks, including some of the nation's oldest and largest, had also closed their doors to customers desperately trying to withdraw their savings. President Franklin Roosevelt, acting within hours of his inauguration, ordered a banking moratorium during which federal examiners would determine which banks were sound enough, or could be made sound enough, to open for business again.

The Chattanooga National Bank failed to reopen after the moratorium, and most of its assets passed into the hands of receivers appointed by the Reconstruction Finance Corporation. The collapse of Chattanooga National left the University of Chattanooga with a nonproductive and rapidly depreciating endowment that would have to be liquidated at a fraction of its face value.

With some 80 percent of its capital resources locked up in REPCs, the university was in one of the worst investment positions imaginable in 1933. Marketable only at a steep discount, the REPCs represented a net loss that would cut deep into endowment principal.[10] Of more immediate concern was the loss of endowment income, which had been funding one-half of annual operating costs. Revenues and expenditures were now dangerously out of kilter.

In June 1933, when the university's bank account showed a balance of $1,987, President Guerry cut faculty salaries by 30 percent and his own salary by 80 percent, a figure the board reduced to 40 percent. Cost-cutting alone was not enough; to cover expenses, the board used $30,000 of endowment principal and borrowed $15,000 from the American Trust and Banking Company. (As collateral the university put up $25,000 in Chattanooga Medicine Company stock, which, according to numerous but unverifiable accounts, belonged to Charlotte Patten Guerry.)

So grave was the situation that the trustees considered the possibility of reducing the university to the status of a junior college; that, they agreed, would be their option of last resort. "While I can say most definitely that we will operate next year and the year after for the full college year… I can say, and most truthfully, that the University financially is in a critical condition," Guerry told the board on June 5.

"The hour of opportunity and crisis" was at hand. It was the university's duty "to meet disaster with a triumph wrought out of its own spirit and determination to live and serve its students and its people." The triumph that Guerry referred to was one of overcoming financial adversity without sacrificing educational quality. Notwithstanding the economic pressures, he was determined to uphold academic standards. As he told other trustees:

> In spite of our financial problems we have not lost sight of the principle of true learning and sound scholarship. The University of Chattanooga desires above all to be an institution of merit and excellence. The curse of the South is mediocrity in education. The curse of education is mediocrity, a low level of work and a lack of real scholarship.
>
> There is something dangerous about mediocrity in education. The low level, the low standard, the lack of scholarship can bring harm instead of good, can be destructive instead of constructive, can level all people, all principles down instead of being the inspiration that draws upward, can wipe away the difference between good and evil, the right and wrong, the beautiful and the ugly, instead of bringing to a people the ability to discriminate,

to appraise correctly the value of life, to know the good, to follow the good, to strive for the good....

The University of Chattanooga... seeks quality of attainment in education.... If this Institution is true to this concept of education, the financial and commercial storms that beat upon us will find the foundation strong and indestructible. I bring to the Trustees these few words about quality in education because loyalty to an ideal of an institution of merit and excellence, during these times, is our first obligation.

That these were not merely brave words was evident even to skeptics by the spring of 1934, when the university's biennial public affairs institute was held on schedule and praised for bringing a variety of expert opinion to bear on a vital issue of that day. Known as the Tennessee Valley Institute, it focused on the economic and social objectives of the newly established Tennessee Valley Authority. All three directors of TVA – Arthur Morgan, H.A. Morgan, and David Lilienthal – were among the featured speakers. Others included Secretary of Labor Frances Perkins, Phillip LaFollette of Wisconsin, Dean Roscoe Pound of Harvard Law School, and Governor Hill McAllister of Tennessee.

TVA's plans for flood control, rural electrification, and agricultural development in a seven-state area roughly the size of England and Scotland were the subject of much public debate, political in-fighting, and legal challenges mounted by the private power industry. Opening up the University of Chattanooga to a symposium on the red-hot issues raised by TVA was a bold move in

1934, particularly since more than a few of the university's own trustees were adamantly opposed to the New Deal agency. But it was also a distinctively un-Yankee Methodist way to engage the university in regional life. Commenting on the Tennessee Valley Institute, the student newspaper at Vanderbilt called it "the outstanding event of the year in Southern education."

In another move to link the school more closely with regional interests, the trustees severed their last formal connection with the Church North. On February 27, 1935, the board dropped the charter requirement that two-thirds of its members be Northern Methodists. As a source of funds, the church had long ago ceased to provide support commensurate with its representation on the board, and university officials were weary of trying to explain to prospective supporters from other denominations why two-thirds of the boardroom seats were reserved for Northern Methodists only.

By ending that practice, the trustees resolved the identity crisis that had kept the university balanced more or less uncertainly between church and community ever since 1886. The trustees had foresworn fence straddling, and now they could ask the community for an equally clear-cut response to the school's financial difficulties.

Though still solvent, the university was desperately short of cash and taking huge investment losses in the process of exchanging REPCs for cash or income-producing assets. To raise $60,000 for ordinary expenses during 1933 and 1934, university officials had dipped into the endowment, liquidating a quantity of REPCs for 32 cents on the dollar. An additional $731,000 in REPCs was exchanged for real estate with a book value of $341,492. By June 1936, when nearly all the REPCs had been swapped for cash or real estate, the $1.1 million endowment of 1929 had shrunk to a book value of $520,000.

On top of that loss, debts began to pile up: $10,000 owed to the American Trust and Banking Company; $27,700 owed to the Commercial National Bank; and $85,000 owed to the Interstate Life and Accident Insurance Company. In 1937, those debts would be consolidated into a ten-year $130,000 loan negotiated with the Hamilton National Bank. Securing the note was a mortgage on the entire campus of the University of Chattanooga.[11]

Those borrowed funds, together with about $30,000 raised locally each year during annual sustaining fund drives first launched by Alex Guerry in 1934, were what allowed the university to continue as a four-year college through the depression years. Both the city and county governments appropriated funds to aid the university, and there was only a temporary drop in enrollment. The number of full time students fell to 423 during 1933-1934 but rose to 605 in 1937-1938, with 446 others enrolled either in the evening college or summer school.

President Guerry carried on the policy of vigorous community outreach, even though it put additional strain on annual budgets. There were no cutbacks in extension services, not in the evening college or in the summer sessions for local teachers or in the radio broadcasts of classical music and faculty lectures.

In fact, the university undertook several new extension projects during its years of greatest financial uncertainty. In the fall of 1934, the university became the sponsor of a new civic institution, the Chattanooga Symphony Orchestra, whose membership drew heavily on university students and faculty. And in 1935, discussions between Alex Guerry and the proprietor of a local school of music,

Ottokar Cadek, led to a joint endeavor operating as the Cadek Conservatory of the University of Chattanooga. Accredited by the National Association of Music Schools in 1935, the conservatory received a Julliard Professorship of Music the following year.

By 1937, it was no exaggeration to call the University of Chattanooga a "beacon of culture" to the surrounding area. Had the university's offerings in collegiate instruction, continuing education, the performing arts, and the fine arts been subtracted from the city's total cultural capital, there would not have been much left to distinguish Chattanooga from many another smokestack town in Southern Appalachia.

That point was brought home vividly to a member of the faculty, Joe Callaway, during an annual sustaining fund drive. Professor Callaway sometimes solicited contributions for the university, and one day he happened to be speaking with a woman, not intending to ask her for money, when she volunteered to make a contribution to the sustaining fund. Callaway knew she could not afford it, that she was giving the proverbial widow's mite. So he asked why she was doing it, to which she replied: "Without the university, Chattanooga would have been just another mill town." [12]

His success at the University of Chattanooga had not diminished Alex Guerry's appetite for new fields of endeavor; the challenge that interested him most would always be the next one. And the next one came for him in December 1937 when he received, for the second time in two years, an invitation to become administrative head of his *alma mater*, the University of the South.

When on December 17, he submitted his resignation to the board, efforts were made to keep him in Chattanooga. A group of local businessmen offered to underwrite whatever salary he asked as head of the University of Chattanooga. A local rabbi wrote him: "You must not leave. As long as you are here, my people have nothing to fear." But the University of the South, all but bankrupt and with enrollment down to 200, presented a challenge that the genius at reviving moribund schools could not pass up.

Long after the depression was over, Alex Guerry would be remembered as one of the university's foremost leaders by the severest critics of leadership at the university, its faculty. "We hated to see Dr. Guerry go," said Professor Frank Prescott in the 1980s. "He and Jack Bretske had held the university together.... I don't know what we'd have done without him." And Professor Edwin Lindsey, who watched presidents of the university come and go from 1924 until 1968, said of Guerry: "He was a great man. He really made the university. More than anybody else he encouraged the idea of excellence."

On June 21, 1938, six months after Guerry's resignation, the trustees elected his successor. Their choice was Archie M. Palmer. A native of Hoboken, New Jersey, Palmer held degrees from Cornell and from Columbia, both of which had employed him in alumni affairs and as a fund-raiser. He had also spent two years in the sales research department of Proctor and Gamble.

President Palmer formulated and at once set to work on an "eleven point program" that consisted mainly of upgrading the university's alumni office along the lines of those at Cornell and Columbia. When not engaged in such plans, Palmer checked on construction work underway on the first new building on campus in two decades. The three-story structure, a co-operative undertaking of the university, the City of Chattanooga, Hamilton County, and the U.S. Public Works Administration, would house both the public and the university libraries. Located on university property at the northeast corner of McCallie and Douglas Streets, the library opened in February 1940 with a collection of just over 100,000 volumes.

By then, World War II had begun in Europe, and the United States, though proclaiming its neutrality, was embarked on a massive program of rearmament and aid to France and Britain. The fall of France in June 1940 convinced most Americans that war with Hitler's Germany was inevitable. "We were all waiting for the other shoe to drop," recalled George Connor, a student at the university in 1940. After passage that year of the Selective Service and Training Act, older members of the faculty began to conduct registration for those of draft age among the students and faculty.

With America's declaration of war on Japan and Germany in December 1941, university officials expected a precipitous drop in enrollment and higher operating costs. Those looming problems would demand a concerted response from all levels at the university, the kind of united effort that the trustees doubted President Palmer could bring forth. The approach to management that Palmer had learned at Proctor and Gamble proved ill-suited to the university. As one professor observed: "Archie Palmer believed in moving the university onto the efficiency basis like a business. You can't do that. Professors are individuals. They're not any good if they're not [permitted to be individuals]."[13]

Palmer's credibility with the faculty suffered irreparable damage when he attempted to dismiss a professor of religion for the offense of having made remarks in class that drew fire from one of the school's local patrons.[14] Students, too, held Palmer in low regard, as they demonstrated when they bestowed the ivy on him, a tradition in which the senior class honored a faculty member with the gift of an ivy plant. In Palmer's case, however, the student, instead of presenting the usual garden variety of ivy, handed Palmer a poison ivy plant.[15]

Soon after Pearl Harbor, several of the trustees came to the conclusion that Archie Palmer was needed in the nation's war effort. One of the trustees, as the story goes, secured a desk job for Palmer in Washington, D.C. With a leave of absence granted by the board, Palmer departed from the university in late March 1942 and in May formally resigned to accept an "important post" in the Food Administration Division of the Office of Price Administration.

6
Bounds of Place and Time

... individuals are so nicely adjusted to a system, and systems to one another and to a whole, that, by stepping aside for a moment, a man exposes himself to a fearful risk of losing his place forever.
– Nathaniel Hawthorne ("Wakefield," 1835)

Our main purpose in life was to survive.
– August W. Eberle, provost,
University of Chattanooga (1957-1965)

In mid-May of 1942, as the trustees began their search for a new president, a Chattanooga insurance executive and influential alumnus of the university, Edwin O. Martin, received a letter from a friend of his in the political science department at North Carolina State College of Agriculture and Engineering in Raleigh. To Ed Martin the professor wrote: "I have a good position and a lifetime contract here, but I would welcome a larger field of service in my native State. I am sure I would like Chattanooga and the University and I know I would do my best to make good.... I will greatly appreciate any good word you may be able to say in my behalf."[1]

Ed Martin said a great many favorable words about Professor David Lockmiller, and in August the trustees unanimously elected Lockmiller president of the university. A native of Athens, Tennessee, the university's new president was the son of George F. Lockmiller, one of the trustees who had tried to stop John Race from transferring the liberal arts college from Athens to Chattanooga in 1904. He was a Methodist raised in the Church North. His ties to the church and to the Athens school almost certainly would have been unacceptable to the board that elected Alex Guerry president in 1929, but this was not 1929 or even 1939.

Though, by his own admission, Lockmiller "didn't know a thing in the world about being a university president," he was a fast learner and his academic credentials, including an earned doctorate, outshone those of his eight predecessors in office.[2] He was the author of three books, including *Sir William Blackstone*. A member of Phi Beta Kappa, he held B.A. and M.A. degrees from Emory University and an LL.B. from Cumberland University in Lebanon, Tennessee. After practicing law for four years in his wife's hometown of Monett, Missouri, he had enrolled in a doctoral program at the University of North Carolina, earning a Ph.D. in 1935 and joining the faculty of North Carolina State College the same year.

In his first address to the university community, President Lockmiller sounded a theme that would resonate down through the many years of his administration. It came near the end of his remarks, when he said: "[The University of Chattanooga] believes that the fundamentals are eternal, but it knows that change is ever present and that it must adapt itself to its day and generation."

The immediate challenge was to survive the loss of virtually every able-bodied male student. Before the last of them departed, the university managed to secure, on February 19, 1943, a contract with the War Department for one of the College Training Detachments (CTDs) of the Army Air Force. The first group of 350 cadets would arrive in March, which gave school administrators about 30 days to find a way to feed and house the troops on a campus where dormitory facilities were limited to a few rooms in Oak Street Stadium. With no time to lose, the board authorized the purchase and remodeling of the former Third Presbyterian Church at Oak and Baldwin Streets; the cadets were quartered there and in prefab barracks erected on the football practice field and elsewhere on campus. The student commons in Oak Street Stadium was converted into a temporary commons room for the civilian students.

Within the span of 30 days, a campus having an enrollment of 95 percent day students was retrofitted to accommodate an enrollment of 60 percent boarding students. Much of the credit for that speedy conversion went to Comptroller Jack Bretske. Recognizing his achievements, the executive committee bestowed the title of vice president on Bretske. This promotion merely confirmed what was already obvious to insiders, that Jack Bretske's authority on campus was second only to that of President Lockmiller.

Under the War Department contract, the university was to receive 350 Air Corps trainees every five months. Besides accumulating several hours of flight training at the municipal airport, they took courses in history, English, geography, mathematics, and physics taught by the faculty. They attended class apart from the regular students. "In other words," one professor observed, "the college operated in two shifts, one for the regular students and the other for the cadets." By July 1944, when the CTD program was discontinued at Chattanooga and other participating schools, 1,234 cadets had received pre-flight training at the university. During those 16 months, the campus was alive with marching units, bugle calls, military drills, and night patrols.

The military contract saved the school from a crippling deficit in 1943, when the number of regular students fell to 339, most of them women. "We turned into a women's college," a staffer remarked.[3] Masculine influences such as fraternities and intercollegiate football were casualties of war; and, in 1943, Judy Smith became the first woman in the school's history to be elected president of the student body.

In that year of the vanishing male undergraduate, new academic programs sprang up in fields of particular interest to women. A two-year program in home economics, organized and headed by Georgia Bell, appeared in September 1943, as did a program in secretarial science, also two years in duration. The following year, through an agreement with the School of Nursing at Baroness Erlanger and T.C. Thompson Children's Hospital, the university began offering basic science courses for pre-clinical students of nursing.

The quiet campus of 1944 changed abruptly after V-J Day in August 1945. A month later, the first wave of returning veterans pushed enrollment to an all-time high of 959 regular students. Passage of the Servicemen's Readjustment Act of 1944, better known at the "G.I. Bill," made higher education affordable to untold thousands of veterans who otherwise could only have dreamed of attending college; and they registered in massive numbers at the nation's colleges. By the fall of 1947, there were 1,500 full-time students attending the University of Chattanooga; and it was rumored, quipped a faculty wit, that President Lockmiller would soon "whistle-stop across the country interviewing prospective faculty members" and give serious thought to "putting traffic control lights in the corridors of the classroom buildings."[4] That proved unnecessary, for enrollment leveled off in 1951 and ran consistently in the 800-1000 range until the baby boomers reached college age in the early 1960s.

The post-war decade brought the applied arts and sciences to a place of prominence in the curriculum. Traditionally, the university had pinned its hopes on the liberal arts college, but the many years of sluggish enrollment growth had caused some to question whether the concentration on liberal arts was suited to local needs and interests. One of the questioners was President Lockmiller. "I believe in the liberal arts," Lockmiller would later say, "but I also believe in the importance of the applied arts. Chattanooga was an industrial town. I was interested in trying to instruct the common people. I wanted to fix it so graduates could get a job in the community."[5]

Under President Lockmiller, the university held to its exacting standards of liberal arts instruction while also developing into a center for vocational, technical, and pre-professional studies, becoming, in the words of a 1955 brochure – "a proven and dependable source of the trained minds that our dynamic economy needs."[6] Purists would sniff at "creeping vocationalism" in academia, but in Lockmiller's view "the academic man is part of the work-a-day world, and to the gain and loss of the campus, he is essential in industry, business, scientific research and affairs of state."[7]

After inaugurating the programs in home economics, secretarial science, and pre-clinical nursing during 1943-1944, the university and several Chattanooga industrialists joined forces to organize the Industrial Research Institute in 1946. Operating out of a 3,000-square-foot building on campus, it provided research services to local manufacturers such as the Chattanooga Medicine Company, Brock Candy Company, Peerless Woolen Mills, and Gilman Paint and Varnish.

Other forays into the applied arts followed in rapid succession: majors in general engineering (1947), industrial management, industrial engineering physics (1951), and social work (1953); a unit of the Reserve Officers Training Corps in 1950; a master's program in education in 1948, and a 3-2 engineering program with the University of Tennessee in 1954.

Those vocational offerings soon drew more students than did the liberal arts program; by 1954, 64 percent of the graduating class majored in some branch of the applied arts.[8] Vocational areas of study would be the fastest growing segment of the curriculum for decades to come. Quantitatively, the liberal arts college of yesteryear was gradually eclipsed as the university's technical and vocational programs multiplied. They were accorded college status in 1950, with formation of the college of applied arts under Dean Paul L. Palmer. Maxwell A. Smith, *Docteur de l'Université de Paris*, continued as dean of the liberal arts college, a post he had held since 1929.

A significant change in academic administration occurred in 1957, when Professor James W. Livingood succeeded Smith as dean of liberal arts, and August W. Eberle, formerly professor of education and director of college placement at Indiana University, became acting dean of applied arts as well as the university's first provost.

As chief academic officer, August Eberle was an able and determined leader who spoke his mind and inspired loyalty among some of the best and brightest faculty members. "If you had an idea about something to do, he never worried about precedent," a professor recalled.[9] "His philosophy was that when people came to him they were to get an answer," said his administrative assistant. "If we didn't know the answer, we were to get it, and not just send them somewhere else."[10] A professor who arrived at the school in 1957 remembered that Eberle "wouldn't have an air conditioner in his office because not every office on campus had an air conditioner. That was not a calculated move. It was him."[11]

Having worked his way through college, earning a Ph.D. at the University of Wisconsin in 1952, and having climbed the academic ladder from the principalship of a Kansas high school to the assistant deanship of a Kansas junior college and on to the position at Indiana University, Provost Eberle identified with the popular demand for colleges to serve as instruments of upward mobility, preparing the vast majority of their graduates for specialized jobs in business, education, and technology. This he considered one of the legitimate functions of higher education; and he tried diligently to make his view felt at the University of Chattanooga, which still billed itself as essentially a liberal arts college despite the fact that almost 70 percent of its students were majoring in the applied arts. Eberle brought an outsider's perspective to the university, seeing as weaknesses what many others had come to accept as strengths.

Some policies and practices gave him pause. In his own words: "The institution had been run pretty much by the president – and he travelled quite a bit... made a lot of world tours[12]– and by the chief business officer... Jack Bretske.... The faculty felt little freedom to do things on their own.... Some academic decisions were being made by the chief business officer... and many faculty members were upset by this....

All my life had been spent in public institutions, and this one touted itself as a small, independent college.... I kept hearing about this small, liberal arts college, but the reality was that we were serving a cross-section of the population of the area. We weren't really a classic, small, private, liberal arts college. And our main purpose in life was to *survive*."[13]

As Eberle suggested, President Lockmiller was not inclined to delegate authority broadly. Department heads ordinarily did not participate in formulating their departments' annual budgets, nor were they often granted the privilege of recommending salary increases.[14] An efficient and effective administrator in his own fashion, Lockmiller excelled at handling matters where his actions required the approval of no more than three or four members of the executive committee, among them Morrow Chamberlain, Paul Kruesi, John Fletcher, and Lupton Patten. They "really ran the university," Lockmiller observed, adding that he never lost a motion or suffered a reversal before the full board, because he "knew the leaders and talked in advance with them until [he] had their support."[15] Though he forged an alliance with those long-time members of the executive committee, some of the younger trustees felt, as one put it, that the board was a "closed shop" and that Lockmiller was too much the "autocrat."[16]

A distinguished member of the faculty remembered that President Lockmiller always seemed "more the lawyer than the Ph.D.," noting, however, that salaries and benefits rose appreciably during his administration.[17] He also earned respect as a defender of academic freedom. In 1955, the demons of McCarthyism were still loose in the land, but Lockmiller refused to play ball with those who defined a "communist sympathizer" as anyone whose political views were objectionable to the John Birch Society.

On one occasion during the era of loyalty oaths and Congressional assaults on un-American activities, a faculty member stated during class discussion that wealth and power in Chattanooga were concentrated in the hands of a few families living on Lookout Mountain or in Riverview. This remark came to the attention of certain community leaders, including local newspaper publisher Roy McDonald, who sat on the university board. McDonald decided to take the matter up with President Lockmiller. So annoyed was McDonald by the professor that, as he gave Lockmiller to understand, he would submit his resignation from the board unless Lockmiller obtained the professor's resignation from the faculty. Given such a clear-cut choice, Lockmiller told the irate publisher: "Roy, I'm not going to put a gag rule on the faculty. I'd be sorry to lose you, but it's a free country and if you want to resign, you ought to do so." McDonald left the board shortly thereafter.[18]

In September 1957, when August Eberle arrived as provost, the university was in the midst of a campaign for $5 million – the first such effort since 1927. Incredibly, almost 30 years had slipped by since the last major drive for endowment. During the 1940s, two campaigns had netted a total of roughly $500,000 in capital funds; but most of that amount had gone into bricks and mortar: Pfeiffer Hall, a women's dormitory completed in 1949; Bretske Dining Hall, opened in 1947; the Stadium-Dormitory with 61 dorm rooms for men, football bleachers seating 6,500, and an R.O.T.C. armory (1948); and Brock Science Hall on Vine Street, completed in 1949.

Between 1906 and 1928, the university accumulated more endowment – $1.01 million – than it had accumulated during the entire period from 1929 through 1955. In 1955, the endowment stood at $1.7 million. That amount fell short of the sums held by many other small southern colleges: Furman had $4.2 million, Berry $4 million, Southwestern (now Rhodes) $2.7 million, Centre $2.5 million, and even Maryville College had $2.2 million.

Of the $5 million that Chattanooga set out to raise in 1956, no more than $3 million had been gathered when the campaign was suspended in mid-1959. At that point, the endowment aggregated $2.7 million, placing Chattanooga last among 12 other universities of comparable size and scope in the South. Operations were undercapitalized, and, barring a sudden outpouring of large gifts from foundations and individuals, the outlook was none too good. "Growth is limited… [and] the academic program will be in jeopardy in the future," the university frankly told patrons in a 1959 brochure.[19]

Evidence of financial malnourishment could be found throughout the campus. The library, with a full-time staff of four and a budget of $42,703 in 1957-1958, had never opened its stacks to students. The salary of a full professor, despite substantial pay hikes earlier in the decade, was 26 percent below the national average in 1959. Telephone service finally reached the office of the English department chairman in the early 1960s, and most members of the department would live to see the day, a few years later, when the chairman's office was equipped with an electric typewriter.

As American higher education entered the computer age, the University of Chattanooga made the leap from manual to electric typewriters. Whether a department's budget would allow for the purchase of an I.B.M. Selectric was a mystery to most department heads, and they would seek enlightenment from Comptroller Bretske, much as the early Greeks consulted the Delphic Oracle. George Cress, chairman of the art department from 1951 to 1984, recalled the time he broached the subject with Bretske. "Oh," Bretske responded, "I didn't know that artists needed a typewriter." Then he peeked underneath his desk blotter and announced, "You have $33 left in your budget." [20]

George Cress could have written his own ticket elsewhere; but, like many of his colleagues on the faculty, he took the scant resources available to him at Chattanooga and produced results that often were the envy of professors at much more affluent universities. In 1955, *Life* magazine identified Cress as one of the South's leading artists; his paintings, abstract landscapes for the most part, would be included in collections at the High Museum, the Birmingham Museum, the Georgia Arts Commission, and the Vincent Price Collection.

Moreover, the art department under Cress attracted an exceptionally large number of students who went on to become artists of note far beyond Chattanooga. Among them were Barry Moser, book designer, printmaker, and recipient of the American Book Award; Robin Hood, winner of the Pulitzer Prize for feature photography in 1977; and Herbert Shuptrine, American genre painter, Pulitzer Prize nominee, and collaborator with poet James Dickey on *Jericho*. Shuptrine, speaking in 1988 about his student days at Chattanooga, said: "The University of Chattanooga had one of the finest art departments in the Southeast – no question about it. I transferred from [the University of Tennessee in] Knoxville in the fall of 1955 and studied here for four years. George Cress's influence has stayed with me all these years. He taught us to get out of the studio and actually experience [painting on site]. That, of course, has been the whole basis of my work. He was truly a great teacher."[21]

Another teacher who accomplished much despite paltry resources was Dorothy Hackett Ward, head of theatre and speech. From 1940 until her retirement in 1975, Ward directed and sometimes acted in a dazzling succession of plays. Her directorial range extended from Shakespeare to Tennessee Williams; the campus facilities at her disposal, however, seldom rose above third-rate. Her theatre for many years was a converted assembly room in Hooper Hall. The stage rested on sawhorses, the lighting was miserable, and the proscenium opening, just 19 feet in height, made it tricky to stage a balcony scene without using dwarfs or large puppets. And yet, "what she could do on that tiny stage was not to be believed without being seen," said George Connor, who played Mercutio in Ward's 1941 production of *Romeo and Juliet*. "She demanded of us the very best we were capable of delivering…. To this good day, when I think of the line from *Romeo and Juliet* – 'O she doth teach the torches to burn bright!' – I see that stage."[22]

Although theatre and speech probably suffered from underfunding more than most departments, budgets were tight all over, even in football. Financial pressures had been responsible for the university's decision to transfer its athletic department to an outside organization in 1947. That year a group of local businessmen and football enthusiasts, collectively known as the UC Athletic Association, had assumed a bonded indebtedness of $600,000 incurred during construction of the Stadium-Dormitory on Vine Street. At the same time, the Association also assumed responsibility for managing and funding intercollegiate athletics. This shifted the financial burden, as well as control, of the program away from campus. Vice President Bretske sat on the Association's board; and its president, Everett Allen, served on the university's board. For all practical purposes, however, the school had spun off its varsity sports program. While conceding in 1959 that this was "not in accord with the best collegiate practice," university officials pointed out that it had "worked remarkably well."[23]

Its success was attributable, in large part, to the head football coach, Andrew Cecil "Scrappy" Moore, who had come to the university as an assistant to Coach Frank Thomas in 1926, after playing football at the University of Georgia and semi-professional baseball with the Birmingham Barons. A wiry, excitable man with a high-pitched voice and cackling laugh, Scrappy Moore compiled a record at Chattanooga that earned him a place in the National College Football Hall of Fame. A standard history of football in the South would rank him as one of the four most successful coaches at universities not affiliated with the major conferences.[24] "Scrappy was the Bear Bryant of his league," said Harold Wilkes, who played for Moore in the 1950s and succeeded him as head coach in 1967.

"We had to scrounge for beds and food," recalled Wilkes. "Sometimes the food was so bad it was laughable.... [Scrappy's friends] Bear Bryant and Wally Butts sort of helped him get players.... We used to go into a season with 25 or 30 players total, and they doubled as the basketball team."[25]

To make ends meet, Moore would schedule at least one game a season with a big-time football school, an Auburn, Georgia,

Mississippi, or Tennessee. The gate receipts from a game with one of the SEC powerhouses went a long way toward balancing the athletic budget at Chattanooga. These David and Goliath contests usually ended predictably: "We lost some of the finest games ever played in the South," quipped Moore. But not always. On November 8, 1958, more than 40,000 spectators at Neyland Stadium in Knoxville watched Chattanooga defeat the Tennessee Volunteers by a score of 14-6. When the whistle sounded, jubilant fans from Chattanooga charged the end zones, fought briefly with Tennessee fans for possession of the goal posts; and then both groups joined in fighting police and security forces that had been ordered to drive them off the field. Back in the locker room, the Chattanooga players heard a "tremendous commotion," said starting end Harold Wilkes. Upon investigation, they saw the mob of fans doing battle with over 100 policemen armed with truncheons, tear gas grenades, and a high-pressure fire hose. Paddy wagons were on the scene; flames leapt up from a torched police cruiser. The battle went on for almost an hour.[26] "It was the damnedest riot you ever saw," said Wilkes.

In the fall of 1958, David Lockmiller was offered the presidency of Ohio Wesleyan University. He accepted the post because, he explained to an associate, "Having been here 17 years and having reached the age of 52, it seemed proper to depart with everything moving along splendidly, including the football victory over the University of Tennessee.... Ohio Wesleyan is a larger and older school with a national patronage. It provides a new challenge.... The last president, Arthur Fleming, is now in Eisenhower's Cabinet."[27]

The process of selecting a new president was handled by a few of the most senior members of the board. Lupton Patten, immediate past chairman of the board, and his fellow members of the executive committee, including recently elected board chairman William E. Brock, Jr., exercised broad discretion in the matter. They saw no reason to involve the full board in their deliberations or to interview a candidate from the University of North Carolina whose merits they had been urged to consider by several of the younger trustees.[28]

Instead of looking to a Chapel Hill for the next president, the executive committee turned inward and settled on a favorite son from Athens, Tennessee. He was LeRoy A. "Cordy" Martin, a 57-year-old Methodist clergyman who had headed Tennessee Wesleyan College since 1950. Martin was well known to the older trustees as an alumnus of Chattanooga (1924), as the son of a former trustee, and as the brother of alumnus and trustee Edwin O. Martin, who had supported David Lockmiller for the presidency in 1942 and was a good friend of Lupton Patten. The full board, acting on the executive committee's recommendation, elected LeRoy Martin president of the university on January 31, 1959.

LeRoy Martin possessed the qualities it took to succeed at the helm of a small, denominational college like Tennessee Wesleyan. Kind-hearted, genial, effective with an audience, he disarmed potential critics. "You couldn't help liking him," said a professor at Chattanooga. He was "a man who alienated no one," wrote a reporter for the local *Times*.[29]

During Martin's first year in office, a local philanthropist, who "desired to remain anonymous," funded the creation of an award like none other on campus. The philanthropist was Cartter Lupton, son of John T. Lupton and heir to his Coca-Cola bottling empire. Lupton carefully specified how his gift was to be used. It would establish the Alexander and Charlotte Guerry Professorships as a lasting tribute to the achievements of the university's seventh president and his wife. The Guerry Professorships would pay honor as well as stipends to those faculty members who had distinguished themselves in teaching, community service, scholarship, or a combination of the three. A Guerry Professorship soon came to be regarded as the highest accolade that the university could bestow upon a faculty member. The first four recipients, named in 1961, were Irvine W. Grote (chemistry), Edwin S. Lindsey (English), Paul L. Palmer (education and psychology), and Maxwell A. Smith (modern languages).

Among other highlights of the Martin years were additions to the physical plant, principally Cadek Hall in 1961 and the $2 million Maclellan Gymnasium in 1965. Maclellan Gymnasium, with a seating capacity of 3,500, allowed varsity basketball to be played on campus rather than, as had been the custom, at local high schools; and it permitted convocations of the entire student body for the first time since World War II. The student body itself doubled in size during Martin's years in office. Enrollment, after hovering at 1,000 through the 1950s, shot up to 1,760 in 1964 and reached 2,092 the next year. Between 1958 and 1964, the faculty grew from 60 to 90 members, and the annual budget increased from $1 million to $2.3 million.

There also were additions to the curriculum, including graduate programs leading to the master's degree in education, business administration, and science. Chapel attendance was made voluntary except for freshmen; in 1963, the library finally opened its stacks to students, and the teaching load for most professors was reduced from 15 to 12 hours in 1965.

All those developments, however, were of minor import compared with two actions taken by the board of trustees. As President Martin observed in his report of 1964-65: "Twenty years from now when the One-Hundredth Anniversary of the University is observed, the historian will probably refer to two highly significant decisions made by the Board during the 1960s." And indeed he will.

The first of those decisions required the trustees to take hold of the sharp moral and political issues raised by the civil rights movement. For nearly a decade, events had been nudging the trustees ever closer to a vote on color-blind admissions. During 1954 and 1955, the U.S. Supreme Court's historic rulings in *Brown vs. Board of Education of Topeka* had ended federal acceptance of separate public schools for blacks and whites and mandated the desegregation "with all deliberate speed" of public schools and gathering places, common carriers, and state-supported institutions of higher education. While private colleges and universities were not directly affected, the *Brown* rulings did, by implication, nullify state laws requiring segregation in higher education and all but guaranteed that private schools would come under increased pressure to integrate.

Massive white resistance to the *Brown* rulings swept the South during the late 1950s and early 1960s. Some counties closed their public systems rather than integrate them, and compulsory attendance laws were repealed in various school districts. A black student seeking admission to the University of Mississippi in 1958 was arrested on a charge of disturbing the peace and remanded to a state mental hospital for a lunacy hearing. Mob violence at several schools brought the dispatch of federal troops to the region for the first time since Reconstruction. Paratroopers returned nine black students to the Little Rock Central High School in September 1957, and the army secured James Meredith's enrollment at Ole Miss in September 1962.[30]

Segregationist sentiment remained strong, but it was no match for the federal government's new-found resolve to enforce the constitutional guarantee of "equal protection under the law." Further, the courage displayed by young black demonstrators began to challenge the consciences of those whites who casually, often unthinkingly, accepted the Jim Crow laws of that day. In 1963, the televised spectacle of police dogs attacking peaceable demonstrators on the streets of Birmingham convinced many of those disengaged whites that there was something morally rotten about the segregationist position.

In 1961, the state-supported universities of Tennessee began to admit blacks not just to graduate but also to undergraduate programs. Private institutions soon fell in line with the trend toward color-blind admissions. By 1962, Emory, Vanderbilt, Sewanee, Tulane, Tusculum, Scarritt, Madison, and even Maryville had officially committed themselves to biracial education.[31] At both Vanderbilt and Sewanee, desegregation had come about in the glare of publicity and only after damaging struggles in which faculty members resigned when their respective boards refused black admissions.[32] It was that sort of internal strife that President Martin and the executive committee fervently wanted to avoid at the University of Chattanooga. Although Martin supported and worked for a policy of open admissions, he was hesitant to push the matter until reasonably confident that desegregation could be accomplished "with dignity and with general acceptance by the faculty, students, and community."[33]

In the meantime, though, the consequences of continued inaction were growing more serious. The university stood little chance of winning foundation support or federal grants if it continued to reject black applicants. It also faced the possible loss of its tax-exempt status and imminent loss of its R.O.T.C. program. In addition, the local school system was moving toward integration; this put pressure on the university, engendering the feeling on campus that, recalled one professor, "we should at least be in advance of the city schools."[34]

It was against this backdrop that the board, meeting in special session on February 25, 1963, authorized "temporary" and "limited" integration of graduate programs during the summer session. Over the next two and one-half years, the university gradually lifted all racial restrictions on enrollment. On May 24, 1964, the board voted to admit "qualified students without regard to race," beginning with graduate students that summer and with undergraduates in the fall of 1965.[35] That year, Horace Traylor became the first black to receive a degree (master of education) from the University of Chattanooga.

As the trustees faced up to the race issue, they also were preparing to unveil a long-range plan that, in many respects, was a good deal more remarkable than their decision to desegregate. The plan had taken form during 16 months of meetings attended by a select group of trustees, faculty, and administrators who comprised the "Committee on Institutional Direction." Its chairman was John T. "Jack" Lupton II, son of Cartter Lupton and a board member since 1956. Its charge was to pin down the university's "role and purpose," pointing the way ahead.

Some members of the committee felt that the university had allowed its local constituency to dictate its role and purpose. Almost

90 percent of the students lived within a 50-mile radius of Chattanooga, and their overwhelming interest was in the technical and pre-professional offerings on campus. Undergraduate and graduate programs in those areas had multiplied many fold since 1945, while the liberal arts college – once the *only* college and still depicted in promotional literature as the main academic unit – was primarily engaged in offering the general education courses required of undergraduates. This bothered several members of the committee. It seemed to them that the potential of the liberal arts college had gone undeveloped in the years since World War II. They made much of the university's failure to qualify for a chapter of Phi Beta Kappa in the 1950s. Echoing their concern, the local *Times* asked in an editorial how Chattanooga could justify charging $600 a year tuition when Vanderbilt with its Phi Beta Kappa chapter charged only $750 a year.[36]

Of course, Vanderbilt could charge $750 a year because it attracted droves of upper-income students from across the South and beyond. Chattanooga enjoyed no such latitude in pricing, and a chapter of Phi Beta Kappa would not have been much of a selling point with the local crop of predominately lower-income and middle-income high school graduates that the university looked to each year to fill its freshman class. This dependence on the local market concerned many of the committee members, particularly when they reflected on the likelihood that the State of Tennessee would soon extend the benefits of low-priced higher education to the Chattanooga area.

The idea of establishing a state college in Chattanooga had occurred to more than one governor of Tennessee, but the proposed college had always gone to another city: Middle Tennessee State to

Murfreesboro in 1911, East Tennesseee State to Johnson City the same year, Tennessee Technological to Cookeville in 1915, and Austin Peay to Clarksville in 1927. There matters had stood until 1957, when the Educational Survey Subcommittee of the Tennessee Legislative Council issued the results of its two-year study of schooling in Tennessee, commissioned by Governor Frank Clement. According to the Subcommittee's report, citizens of the Chattanooga-Hamilton County area lacked the opportunities for public higher education afforded to their fellow Tennesseans. In a statewide analysis of the number of students per-1,000 population attending state institutions of higher education, the Subcommittee found that Hamilton County ranked last among the 95 counties of Tennessee. The report showed a ratio of 12 students per-1,000-population for the state at large, as against six students per-1,000-population in Hamilton County. Based on that statistical comparison, the Subcommittee concluded that a four-year state college should be established in Chattanooga "as soon as possible" and projected that such an institution would draw an enrollment of 4,400 students by school year 1964-1965.[37]

That conclusion aroused the interest of Chattanoogans. Representatives of the Chamber of Commerce and other individuals began importuning Governor Clement to choose their city as the site of a state college. In 1963, they were given a vocational school, Chattanooga State Technical Institute. They renewed their efforts two years later when a junior college came up for grabs, but it went to the nearby city of Cleveland. That was not necessarily a misfortune for the Chattanoogans; the selection of Cleveland probably worked to their advantage in the long run, since it left the door open for a four-year college in their city.

The University of Chattanooga, with its tuition charges more than double those of the state-supported schools, now faced the prospect of strong competition in the territory it had long had to itself. A four-year state college would pose a "serious threat" to the university's "welfare," concluded an internal study of 1965.[38] Few doubted that "the state would move into Chattanooga," said Provost August Eberle, "and therefore the university was going to have to do something other than what it was doing."

Under those circumstances, the Committee on Institutional Direction developed a long-range plan to recast the university in the image of a Davidson or a Washington and Lee, transforming it into an elite institution no longer dependent on a purely local constituency or vulnerable to the placement of a state college in its backyard. This blueprint for the future, adopted by the board in March 1965, called for the university to achieve "national stature" as an urban institution committed to "general education and the liberal arts." It pledged the university to "strive to attain a faculty equal in teaching competence and scholarship to those in nationally recognized colleges, to diversify its student body by providing additional residence halls, to create an imaginative overall campus plan, and to improve vastly the library facilities." [39]

The board expected to bring about those sweeping changes in the span of 10 years. It could be done, said Board Chairman William E. Brock, Jr., who assured all concerned that the trustees were "determined to translate [the plan] into action." They had set themselves a herculean task, to transform a respectable area college into an institution of "national stature." They would have to raise millions in capital, amounts far exceeding the modest sums gathered in recent campaigns. They would also have to come to terms with the hard fact that, in making the University of Chattanooga more like an "undergraduate Emory," they would lose the good gray institution they liked so well. It could not rise to national prominence and also remain a corporate citizen as upstanding and predictable as the Community Chest or the Y.M.C.A. By recruiting more faculty and students of top rank from a national pool, the university would become more pluralistic and cosmopolitan, more open to a wide variety of beliefs, to innovative research and teaching, including scholarship which clashed with the beliefs and values of Chattanooga's commercial-civic elite. Was the board ready for that?

Hardly had the trustees committed themselves to the long-range plan when they took a step that cast doubt on their willingness to tolerate a diverse range of opinion on campus. They had announced their intention to recruit and retain high quality faculty and staff, yet they acted otherwise in the case of August Eberle, who had served with distinction as provost since 1957. There were faculty members who regarded him as "*de facto* head of the university" during the administration of President LeRoy Martin. President Martin himself described Eberle as "a man who does the work of three with imagination, integrity and reliability." The Chattanooga *Times* praised Eberle as "an educator of impressive stature, an administrator of proved ability, and a citizen of wide concerns." But his personality and beliefs rubbed the board the wrong way, and several influential members of the executive committee had grown to dislike him every bit as much as he had grown to dislike them. He did not show them the deference they thought proper; they bridled when he challenged their thinking on academic questions or declined to grant the little favors some of them requested for relatives and friends. He wanted to take higher education closer to the people, while they planned to make the university more appealing to a select clientele. And his civic activities were not exactly the sort that the trustees deemed appropriate for a high-ranking official of the university; as president of the local Community Action Program, Eberle had been outspoken in promoting welfare benefits for the have-nots of Chattanooga.

In late June 1965, the executive committee denied Eberle a merit raise, without linking the denial to any specific deficiency in his performance as provost. Eberle, interpreting the action as a blunt invitation to get with the program or get out, thereupon handed in his resignation. His defiant move, and the circumstances surrounding it, became front-page news in the local *Times*. In statements to the press, he emphasized that his decision had been prompted not so much by the salary level granted or denied him as by the executive committee's overall involvement in administrative decisions.

"Decisions concerning individual faculty members should be made by the administrators, and members of the board should make only basic policy decisions," he said. "However, I know in my case, as in the case of others, board members actually have been involved in making decisions on individuals.... If things keep moving in the same direction as they have been moving [at the university], I don't think it would be too many years before board members would insist on interviewing prospective faculty members."

Distressed by the loss of a valued colleague, a delegation from the faculty visited Board Chairman Brock in an effort to have Eberle reinstated, but it was too late for that. Eberle would be remembered by his peers as one of the university's "most approachable administrators;" and, in 1966, the year after his departure, the students dedicated the yearbook to him.[40]

Throughout the controversy, President Martin remained above the fray, alienating no one. He seemed perfectly happy to follow the lead set by members of the executive committee. The burdens of decision-making had always weighed heavily on him. He preferred to play a passive, ceremonial role. And that was exactly what the executive committee had in mind for him. In September 1965, the board announced that Martin would continue in office pending the selection of a new president, at which time he would step down to the long vacant post of chancellor.

The leading candidate for president emerged before he himself knew he was being considered for the job. His name had been proposed by Trustee John T. "Jack" Lupton II who called him "the best teacher I ever had." Several of the other trustees had also studied history under him at Baylor School in the years just before World War II. Since then, William Henry Masterson had taken a Ph.D. at the University of Pennsylvania and joined the faculty of Rice University in Houston, Texas. A brilliant academician, Masterson had served as the first dean of humanities at Rice. In addition to his teaching and administrative duties there, he had served as editor of the *Journal of Southern History* and was the author of *William Blount* (LSU Press, 1954), a well-received biography of Tennessee's first territorial governor and first U.S. Senator.

Masterson had settled into a comfortable and productive career at Rice, which boasted the largest endowment of any private university in the South. He relished life in Texas, where successive generations of his family had lived since the 1830s. Agreeably situated at the age of 51, he was not searching for new worlds to conquer when, as he recalled, "Jack [Lupton] *appeared* at Rice one day."[41] The chance Lupton offered him, to preside over an academic renaissance, surprised and then intrigued Masterson. Following their conversation in Houston, Masterson visited Chattanooga and met with the trustees and faculty. In a short while, he decided to exchange the snug harbor of Rice for the uncertain waters of Chattanooga; and on February 18, 1966, the board elected William Masterson president of the university.

After taking up residence on campus in July, President Masterson began the work of translating the board's policy statement into the kind of language that inspired and moved people to action. An eloquent speaker, he unflaggingly called for a commitment to quality in undergraduate education. "Real centers of undergraduate learning geared to meet the challenges of our society and our day are in woefully short supply," he told the faculty in September. There was no excuse for run-of-the-mill programs, he said, reciting "the dreary litany of the mediocre: 'We have no money' – that is, poverty excuses apathy; 'We serve the community' – that is, we do not dare to lead it; 'We have a poor class of students' – that is, we are too lazy to teach and too dull to inspire; 'Our neighborhood is bad' – but so was Copernicus' and Peter Abelard's and so is Chicago's and CCNY's. " Henceforth, he told the faculty, "we must here strive to provide a generation of new leadership for this region and the nation – a leadership that is learned and humane as well as proficient and adaptable."

During his first months in office, Masterson carried his message to dozens of local civic organizations. In his address to the Rotary Club on October 27, he succinctly described the university's goals and the rationale behind them. "The university has had to make a choice either to become a state school or to maintain its traditional private character. In 1965, the trustees made their choice…. The university will join that small and distinguished group of non-denominational universities, not more than five or six, perhaps, in the whole South, who are determined to remain limited in size, whose primary emphasis in function is undergraduate, whose specialty is effective instruction in depth, whose concern is for the individual – to educate him humanely…. We shall be the University capstone of Chattanooga's already established tradition of fine private schools, such as Baylor, McCallie, and GPS. Our compeers will be Davidson, Sewanee, Southwestern [now Rhodes], and Washington and Lee."

President Masterson pursued those long-range objectives with a sense of urgency, for he fully expected that a state college would be established in Chattanooga within four to seven years. In the interim, the university needed "money – lots of money" to strengthen its program and plant, he told the Brainerd Kiwanis Club in December 1966. "I don't want to push the panic button," he said, then added: "I've got about five years. Wish me luck."

7
The Transfer

If private capital has only the wish to keep government out and not the will to keep it out, the financial status... of independent universities and colleges... will deteriorate to such a point that money must come from any source available to meet the commitments to their faculties, the expectations of the young, and the demands of society....

If philanthropy fails, government will step in.

– Henry W. Wriston, president, Brown University (1950)

In December 1967, the University of Chattanooga launched the largest fund-raising drive in its history. Named "Bold Venture," the campaign sought $9 million for a new science building and library, extensive renovations on campus, and recruitment of faculty, staff, and students. It was the "first giant step" toward making the university a "compelling alternative to state-controlled instruction," said President Masterson, and he urged patrons to respond with "vitality and resolution before time overtakes us."

Though large in comparison with earlier campaigns, Bold Venture's $9 million goal seemed like "a drop in the bucket" to the chairman of economics and business, Professor Arthur Vieth, who told a civic club that the university actually needed "$18 million or

$25 million or maybe $50 million" to finance its ambitious long-range plan.[1]

Certainly, Bold Venture would have been seen as more desperate than bold had patrons known how far expenditures were running ahead of revenues. At a special meeting of the board on June 5, 1967, the participants learned that the $3.7 million budget for 1967-1968 showed a deficit of $633,000 and that continued shortfalls through 1970-1971 were likely to result in a cumulative deficit of $1.8 million for the four-year period. Jack Lupton, chairman of the finance committee, advised his fellow trustees that the projected deficit of $1.8 million would have to be recovered from capital raised through Bold Venture.

The extent to which aspirations exceeded funding was not common knowledge outside the boardroom, though the faculty did grasp the situation in a general way. Said one professor: "We all knew that the university had financial difficulties. That was apparent every time we needed a piece of chalk. You almost had to check it out."[2] But better times were ahead, Masterson told them, for "the trustees will proceed under any circumstances with the [long-range plan], and the state institution under any form in which it comes will be an escape valve for us in furnishing a site for those activities that we do not wish to undertake."[3]

Masterson pressed ahead with plans to raise academic standards and develop the commuter campus into a residential campus. Dormitory accommodations expanded with the purchase of Fortwood Apartments in 1967 and the opening of Stagmaier Hall in January 1968. A special fund provided by Cartter Lupton enabled Masterson to leaven the existing faculty with a group of young, first-rate teachers and scholars from some of the nation's leading graduate programs. For the 1968-1969 year alone, he hired nine new faculty members, two of whom, Ziad Keilany and Paul Ramsey, would later be named to Guerry Professorships.

Masterson also brought about the physical unification of a campus that had long been split in half by the busy thoroughfare of Oak Street. The "Ding-ee, Ding-ee, Ding-ee" of rumbling streetcars, which in earlier decades punctuated class sessions every 15 minutes, had now given way to the roar of automobiles whizzing along Oak Street. "It was a major nuisance and danger," said one professor, while another remarked philosophically that the thunder of engines and stench of exhaust fumes helped his students appreciate why Blake, Wordsworth and the other romantic poets had recoiled from the Industrial Revolution.[4]

Traffic had always flowed through the heart of campus, and because nothing had ever been done about it, many people assumed that nothing could be done about it. They assumed wrong, as Masterson discovered when he took the matter up with Mayor Ralph Kelley and other elected officials. Their response was agreeably forthright. On April 2, 1968, the Chattanooga City Commission voted to close the portion of Oak Street running through campus, as well as a segment of Baldwin Street that bisected the grounds. In place of the public motorways, landscaped walkways soon graced the center of campus.

In April 1968, the University of Chattanooga abruptly veered away from the plan to become a "compelling alternative to state-controlled instruction." Support formed around an utterly different plan, which had been hammered out before anyone other than a few insiders realized what was going on. No more than a handful of the trustees, joined at times by President Masterson, took part in the round of off-the-record discussions culminating in a vote by the board on a motion to turn over operations to state education officials. The board's opposition to the transfer seemed rock solid at first, but it crumbled under the force of internal problems and outside pressures.

Chief among those outside pressures was the State of Tennessee's design for higher education in Chattanooga. The case for a state campus had been advanced skillfully by the local Chamber of Commerce. A special committee of the Chamber, headed by attorney Robert Kirk Walker, documented the need with an array of facts, figures, and arguments that were widely circulated in the local press during 1966 and 1967. The Walker Committee focused attention on the fact that Chattanooga was the only large metropolitan area in Tennessee not having a state college where residents could obtain instruction at public-school rates. Walker, an astute politician and future mayor of Chattanooga, concentrated on mobilizing broad-based support for a state college, while staying out of the partisan contention over which of the state's two rival educational bodies, the Board of Education or the University of Tennessee, should have control over such a college. That was an issue best left to Governor Buford Ellington, said Walker, noting that "when the Governor decided which way it was to go, that was the way we wanted it to go all along."[5]

The State Board of Education, which exercised authority over grades 1 through 12 and over the regional universities such as Memphis State (now the University of Memphis) and East Tennessee State, had recently been given dominion over the burgeoning network of junior, or "community," colleges; and that, according to sources close to Governor Ellington, was a big factor in Ellington's decision to award the Chattanooga territory to the University of Tennessee (UT).[6] A land-grant institution founded as Blount College in 1794, UT offered the greatest variety of undergraduate and graduate programs of any public university in the state. Its main campus in Knoxville enrolled some 21,000 students in 1967, many of them working toward advanced degrees in such fields as agriculture, architecture, arts and sciences, business, education, engineering, law, and veterinary medicine. Additional campuses included the medical units in Memphis, the Space Institute in Tullahoma, and the four-year undergraduate college in Martin.

In the decades since World War II, the University of Tennessee had experienced phenomenal growth, particularly during the presidency of Andrew D. "Andy" Holt. Immensely popular, Holt was the folksy guru of higher education in Tennessee, champion of every citizen's right to collegiate instruction, an indefatigable speaker who had been dispensing his homespun wisdom with self-deprecating humor to more than 200 PTAs, 4-H Clubs, American Legions, graduating classes, and other groups each year for the past 20 years.[7]

The years of public adulation had neither bloated Holt's ego nor blinded him to his own limitations as an administrator; he delegated authority widely and well, adhering to the maxim: "Surround yourself with people who are smarter than you are...[and] give them a chance to spread their wings."[8] His principal lieutenant was Edward J. Boling, who had been named vice president of development in 1961, after serving as state budget director in the Clement administration (1954-1958) and state commissioner of finance and administration in Governor Ellington's cabinet.[9]

Close ties existed between UT and the executive branch of state government. The governor served automatically as chairman of the UT board and appointed its members. There also was a fair amount of cross-fertilization between the governor's staff and the UT staff. Ed Boling had left Ellington's cabinet for Andy Holt's in 1961 and would later succeed Holt as president of UT. Joseph E. Johnson, executive assistant to Ellington in 1962, became executive assistant to Holt in 1963 and would be elected president of UT in 1991. William Snodgrass, state comptroller of the treasury, had been on a leave of absence from UT for some 14 years as of 1966, and S.B. "Bo" Roberts would return to UT in 1970 after a four-year leave of absence during which he had been executive administrator to Governor Ellington.[10]

During 1967, Holt and Boling made UT's interest in Chattanooga known to Robert Kirk Walker and other local advocates of a state college for the community. As Boling put it: "We worked night and day to convince the people down in Chattanooga that what they really wanted was the University of Tennessee.... We reacted to what they wanted but we helped the community want us."[11]

By early summer of 1967, Holt and Boling were ready to approach the Tennessee Higher Education Commission (THEC), a coordinating agency created that year by the legislature upon Governor Ellington's request. At a meeting of the UT board, with Governor Ellington presiding as chairman, the trustees formally requested authority to initiate studies of the "requirements and costs for the orderly establishment of a diversified Branch of the University to be known as the University of Tennessee at Chattanooga." THEC approved the request, and, by January 1968, the University of Tennessee had assembled an elaborate planning document for the proposed branch campus.[12] Holt and Boling meant to "go all out" to secure a campus in Chattanooga, and nothing of consequence stood in their path. "We had the people [in Chattanooga] with us," Boling recalled. "We had the governor with us, we had everything that we needed."[13]

A cautionary note, however, was struck by UT trustee Ben Douglas, who pointed out that hardly any thought was being given to the plan's impact on the University of Chattanooga. "If we aren't careful," Douglas warned, "there is going to be a funeral down there."[14]

Events were moving headlong in the one direction least expected and least welcomed by officials at the University of Chattanooga. They had braced themselves for the arrival of "a community college or some state college," not for "the University of Tennessee itself."[15] Unprepared to cross swords with UT, they tried to reach a live-and-let-live agreement with it. As late as February 1968, President Masterson and the trustees still hoped to work out an alliance with UT and the state of Tennessee. From the state, they asked for tuition grants that would roughly equalize the cost of attending public and private universities in Tennessee. From UT, they sought "rational cooperation," "curricular collaboration," and a "contractual agreement" whereby the University of Chattanooga and the proposed University of Tennessee at Chattanooga would agree to offer complementary rather than competing programs of study.[16] They might as well have asked for the moon.

The appeals for a cooperative arrangement went unheeded in Knoxville and Nashville, but Andy Holt assured Bill Masterson that UT's intent was "to supplement," not supplant, the University of Chattanooga.[17] Less encouraging was the stance taken by the

Tennessee Higher Education Commission. In February 1968, after reviewing a report on higher education in Chattanooga prepared by the Southern Regional Education Board, members of THEC quietly began to promote the idea of merging the University of Chattanooga into UT.[18]

The one member of THEC who could sell or kill that idea was Chattanooga banker Scott L. "Scotty" Probasco, Jr. Probasco was uniquely positioned to act as an intermediary, for he served not only on THEC but also as a third-generation trustee of the University of Chattanooga, as a boardmember of the Benwood Foundation which was among the university's two or three largest benefactors, as Governor Ellington's top financial backer in Hamilton County, and as a member of the UT Development Council. He was also, in the words of a *Times* columnist, "the only man in Tennessee with as much enthusiasm as University of Tennessee President Andrew Holt."[19]

Scotty Probasco, at age 39, was exuberant, effervescent, a born optimist who punctuated his sentences with exclamations of "Great Work!" He had opposed any move to bring the University of Chattanooga under state control, and he continued to do so right up to February 26, 1968, when he voted with the eight other members of THEC to recommend the "immediate" establishment of a $15 million branch of UT in Chattanooga. After the vote, over lunch at Nashville's Capitol Park Inn, one of Probasco's fellow commissioners, John M. Jones of Greeneville, chided him, suggesting that by holding out for an independent University of Chattanooga while simultaneously calling for a comprehensive branch of UT, Probasco was pursuing mutually exclusive objectives to the detriment of both institutions and the citizens of Chattanooga. How could Probasco deny,

Jones asked, that "the University of Chattanooga, with its limited resources, would be far better off in serving the people by merging with UT"? [20]

The question hit home. Reflecting on it, Probasco found that his real interest was in seeing the university expand its role in Chattanooga rather than evolve as planned into a neo-Davidson for academically superior students from all over the country. That, he concluded, "was not our destiny… not what we were established to be. My interest in that was superseded by my interest in the community."[21] The more he thought about the situation, the more convinced he became that it would be "nothing but a basic ego trip for big foundations and companies and individuals supportive of UC to try to keep this thing alive in the face of something that could come in here and do it much, much cheaper."[22]

Back in Chattanooga, Probasco talked the matter over with a few close associates, including Jack Lupton, and soon grew determined to bring the university and UT to the bargaining table. The main problem was how to get the Chattanooga trustees to the table. By and large, they were likely to react to such an idea much as the trustees of Probasco's *alma mater*, Dartmouth, would have reacted had one of their number proposed a merger with the University of New Hampshire. But Probasco knew the pressure points, knew how to proceed by indirection, how to work the backchannels; and there were at least two internal factors operating to his advantage.

First, the trustees had not come up with the means to underwrite the development of an independent University of Chattanooga; enrollment had tapered off in 1967, tuition costs would have to be raised still higher, deficits loomed all the way to

1971, and – worst of all – the Bold Venture campaign had bogged down barely more than halfway to its $9 million goal.[23] The trustees had a financial albatross around their necks.

Second, relatively few of the trustees were alumni; the vast majority on the board, including its most influential members, came from the commercial-civic elite of Chattanooga, and for them the university was not *alma mater* but civic asset. As one of the trustees who was a graduate explained: "[Most of] the trustees had an *acquired* interest in the University of Chattanooga... not an emotional, old school tie... [but rather] a sense of civic pride that didn't carry with it the enthusiasm that [would have existed] if we had had more trustees who were graduates."[24] Indeed, most of the board's leaders already owed their fiercest loyalties, both as alumni and trustees, to one or the other of Chattanooga's rival preparatory schools, Baylor or McCallie.

In Knoxville, officials at UT knew exactly what they wanted from Chattanooga. The concept of merger appealed to Andy Holt. Acquiring a ready-made faculty and campus would not only accelerate the opening of UT-Chattanooga but also satisfy Holt's desire to avoid unpleasantries or open conflict with the board at Chattanooga.[25] Under no circumstances, though, did Holt intend to negotiate in the glare of publicity. In 1951, he had suffered through highly-publicized and fruitless merger talks with Memphis State which had split the UT board, and he was on guard against a repeat performance at Chattanooga.[26] "We do not proposition them," he instructed staff members. His position toward Chattanooga was "We would prefer to merge with you if a merger makes sense to you at all";[27] and he was prepared to walk away at the first insinuation from

Chattanooga that UT was the aggressor, intent on gobbling up a small, struggling institution.

Within days of the THEC meeting of February 26, Holt and Ed Boling accepted an invitation to meet with five representatives of the UC Board at the Lookout Mountain home of Chairman Bill Brock, Jr. In addition to Brock, the Chattanoogans consisted of Scotty Probasco, Jack Lupton, Bill Masterson, and Robert L. Maclellan, vice-chairman of the university board and CEO of Provident Life and Accident Insurance Company. During the course of this sometimes stormy session, Holt and Boling mostly sat in amazed silence while the four Chattanooga trustees argued the university's future.[28] When Probasco pitched the idea of a merger, Brock and Maclellan reacted with anguished incredulity. Maclellan kept rubbing his hands together, Probasco remembered, and saying, "Oh, no, Scotty, not the *university*," while Brock's face "got longer and longer" until Probasco thought "it was going to hit the floor."[29]

Brock's face probably reached its maximum elongation when Lupton and Probasco frankly confessed their unwillingness to spend the foreseeable future trying to cover deficits incurred by operating Chattanooga in competition with UT. The University at Chattanooga would be stronger and more useful as a part of UT than it could ever be on its own, they insisted. Those sentiments – coming from the two young men who were in line to assume future board leadership – carried the day. Brock and Maclellan, both in their 60s, reluctantly agreed to go along with a merger. Holt and Boling could almost hear the ice breaking; they returned to Knoxville with the distinct impression that Chattanooga was ready to do business.[30]

To effect a merger, the Chattanoogans had to make haste, since UT was moving ahead with plans to build its own campus in Chattanooga; and, once land was acquired, an agreement would no longer be possible.[31] The clock began ticking loudly on March 13, 1968, when Governor Ellington signed into law an act of the General Assembly which established The University of Tennessee at Chattanooga, with an initial outlay of $5 million for site acquisition and construction.

Nine days later, the executive committee – composed of Brock, Maclellan, Probasco, and Lupton as well as J. Burton Frierson, Jr., William G. Raoul, H. Clay Evans Johnson and others – asked one of its members to find out whether Governor Ellington would object to a merger. After a quick trip to Nashville, Probasco reported that Ellington had given the go-ahead.[32] The executive committee thereupon authorized negotiations aimed at transferring the university's "facilities" to UT.

The bargaining took place in Knoxville at Holt's residence and in hotel rooms a discreet distance from the campus. Time and again the talks threatened to break down, but inevitably Holt would say, "Oh, come on. Let's sit down and talk it over."[33] His ingratiating, aw-shucks manner smoothed many a ruffled feather. "Andy Holt was a magnificent arm-twister with Bill Brock," remarked a Chattanooga trustee.[34] Holt had "a great relationship with those people," Boling recalled. "There were several times when they would say, 'It's got to be this way or we're out,' when I would probably have said, 'Forget it. We don't have to have you anyhow. We can go another way'…. We worked out some things that I don't think I would have gone along with if it had been my decision."[35]

University Hall, affectionately called "Old Main," fronted McCallie Avenue and sat in the approximate center of today's Quadrangle. Completed in the spring of 1886 at an estimated cost of $40,000, Old Main housed science laboratories, a chapel, 39 dormitory rooms, administrative offices, classrooms, a library, a dining hall and kitchen, boiler rooms, meetings rooms, and apartments for the president and faculty members.

Faculty and staff in 1889. The Reverend Edward S. Lewis, president and dean (1886-1890) stands at center in the back row, and to his left are the Reverend Wesley W. Hooper and the Reverend John J. Manker.

Alas! poor Yorick: the anatomy laboratory at Chattanooga Medical College, one of the proprietary schools affiliated with U.S. Grant University from 1889 to 1910.

John Fletcher Spence, chancellor of
U.S. Grant University (1889-1891)
and president (1891-1893).

Wesley W. Hooper, dean,
college of arts
and sciences
(1904-1918).

John A. Patten Memorial chapel was dedicated on May 30, 1919. This photograph was taken in June 1919 and features the first commencement processional into the chapel.

One of the last photos taken of Old Main and other early campus buildings. Old Main was torn down in 1917. When the building was slated for demolition in 1915, a student wrote:

Old noble mass,

A far landmark for those who pass…

Today you stand for progress wide;

Tomorrow swept before its tide you fall…

A group of faculty and staff in 1920.
(Standing left to right): Lonnie Norton Ward,
David W. Cornelius, Nita Tansey (later Mrs. Irvine W. Grote),
Nathaniel E. Griffin, Wyman R. Green, Mary Alice Allen, Earl K. Kline,
Katie Pearl Jones, and John Hockings.
Middle row, from left: Wesley W. Hooper, John W. Edwards, Edith E. Ware,
Frank Hooper, Mary Clyde Farrior, Carlos E. Conant, and Henry H. Young.
Front row, from left: student assistants Jack Saunders, Irvine W. Grote,
Bill Jarratt, and Wilbur Reynolds.

Strike Up The Band:
UC's brass band in formation on the quadrangle, 1930.

Dignitaries outside Patten Chapel when a LL.D. Degree was conferred upon Adolph S. Ochs, publisher of the Chattanooga *Times* (1878-1896) and of the New York *Times* (1896-1935). From left to right: Arlo Brown, John H. Finley, Frank F. Hooper, Adolph Ochs, Williams S. Bovard, and Bishop W. P. Thirkield.

Chamberlain Field, with Old Main in the background

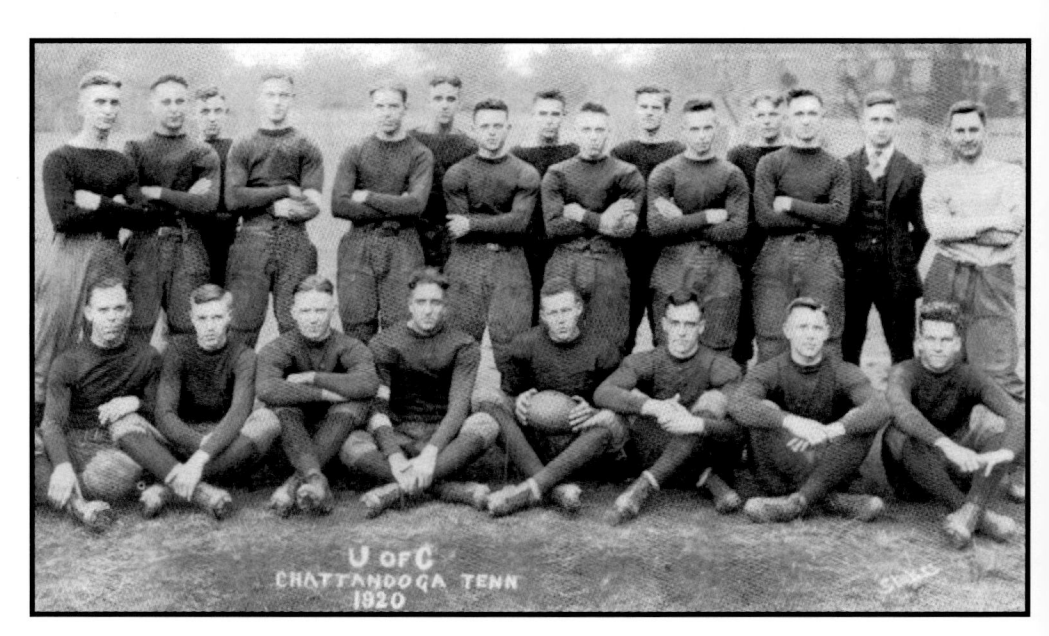

The football team of 1920.

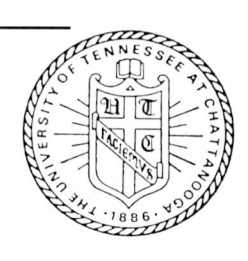

Arlo Ayres Brown,
president of the University
of Chattanooga
(1921-1929).

John H. Race (1862-1954), president of the university from 1897 to 1914. "One could not think of 'Old Main' without seeing Dr. Race, seated in his accustomed chair, his right arm extended, resting on his knee, with his eyeglasses balanced at the end of his index finger, and perhaps cautioning the assembled student body not to spend four years at UC and go home resembling the empty boxcars he could see thru the window in the freight yards (Clarence Gates '14)."

Alexander Guerry,
president of the University of
Chattanooga
(1929-1938).

David A. Lockmiller,
president of the
University of
Chattanooga
(1942-1959).

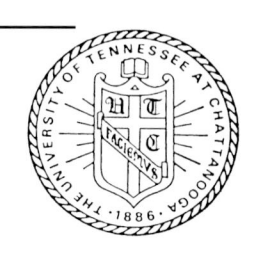

SELECT YOUR COLLEGE CAREFULLY

Chattanooga has the following advantages:
    I. Highest possible educational rating.
        1. A member of the Association of Colleges and Secondary Schools of the Southern States.
        2. On the list of colleges approved by the Association of American Universities.
        3. Its credits are accepted anywhere in the world.
    II. Highest ideals of scholarships and Christian service.
    III. Faculty of exceptional ability and training.
    IV. Equipment modern and adequate, often recommended by visitors as ideal.
    V. Wholesome student activities, religious, social and athletic. Student body represents seventeen states and two foreign countries.
    VI. Environment of rare beauty and historical interest.

1920's advertisement for the University.

Bird's eye view of the campus as it was in the 1930s.

Stanley F. "Jack" Bretske, UC comptroller and vice president (1924-1963).

Edwin S. Lindsey, faculty member (1924-1968), Guerry Professor of English and chairman of the department.

THE UNIVERSITY
in Wartime

Army Air Force cadets, pictured here on the cover of a 1943 brochure, on the front quadrangle overlooking McCallie Avenue.

1943: Graduates of UC's first CTD unit get ready to shove off.

Students honing their skills in secretarial science, one of several vocational offerings developed during the 1940s.

A group of faculty and staff, mid-1940s. Front row (from left): Godfrey Tietze, Eleanor McGilliard, Dorothy Hackett Ward, Rollo A. Kilburn, David Lockmiller, Maxwell Smith, Edwin Lindsey, Ruth Perry, and Wilbur Butts.
Middle row (from left): James Livingood, Terrel Tatum, Robert Anacker, Isa McIlwraith, Irvine Grote, Betty Blocker, Paul Palmer, Anna Manson, and Arthur Plettner,
Back row (from left): Frank Prescott, Georgia Bell, Harold Strobel, Robert Woods, Winston Massey, Willard Anspach, J. Oscar Miller, William Swan, Harold Cadek, Isobel Griscom, and Gilbert Govan.

Andrew C. "Scrappy" Moore, head football coach (1931-1967).

LeRoy A. Martin, president of UC (1959-1966).

Halfback Joe Ambercrombie makes historic catch in 14-6 win over UT.

UC's 1958 upset victory over the Volunteers in Knoxville.

Photos reprinted with permission of *Chattanooga Times*.

August W. Eberle, provost and dean of applied sciences (1957-1965).

James W. Livingood, faculty member (1937-1975), Guerry Professor of history and chairman of the department; dean of arts and sciences (1957-1969).

Fifteen months after the decision to desegregate summer graduate courses, the UC board adopted a color-blind admissions policy, beginning with graduate students that summer and with undergraduates in the fall of 1965.

Jane W. Harbaugh,
faculty member (1957-),
Guerry Professor of history and
chairman of the department;
dean of arts and sciences
(1969-1975);
vice chancellor for academic affairs
(1975-1982);
and associate provost
(1982-).

George C. Connor,
faculty member (1959-1985),
Guerry Professor of English and
chairman of the department.

Dorothy Hackett Ward, faculty
member (1938-1975),
Guerry Professor of theatre
and speech and chairman of the
department.

George A. Cress,
faculty member
(1951-1991)
Guerry Professor of
art and chairman of the department.

A Student/Faculty/Alumni Center, located on Oak Street, was dedicated on November 25, 1958. The facility was later named the Alexander Guerry Center in memory of UC's seventh president.

Members of the UC board in 1965 included (seated, from left): Scott L. Probasco, Jr.; John T. Lupton II; W. E. Brock, Jr.; Raymond B. Witt, Jr., and John L. Hutcheson, Jr. Standing (from left): Summerfield K. Johnston, LeRoy A. Martin, and Donald H. Overmyer.

The combined UC and Chattanooga public libraries were housed in this building on McCallie at Douglas from 1940 until 1974.

Dorothy Hackett Ward and a group of her drama students during the 1960s.

William Henry Masterson, the last president of UC (1966-1969) and the first chancellor of UTC (1969-1973); faculty member (1973-1979) and Guerry Professor of history.

James E. Drinnon, Jr., chancellor of UTC (1973-1981).

Irvine W. Grote,
faculty member (1931-1969),
Guerry Professor of chemistry and
chairman of the department.

Grote Hall was dedicated as the new science and engineering building in April 1970. The building was named honoring Irvine Grote, distinguished inventor, collector, research chemist, world traveler, and UC faculty member.

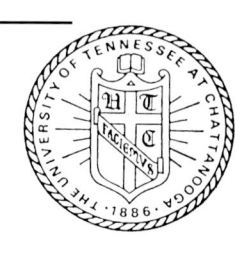

Andrew D. Holt,
president of UT
(1959-1970)

During the 1970s, more than $22 million went into the construction of five major buildings on campus, including the UTC Lupton Library, dedicated in 1974 and named in honor of Mr. and Mrs. T. Cartter Lupton in 1985.

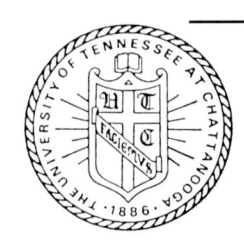

The University Center, on Vine Street at Baldwin, opened in September 1974.

A campus walkway leading from Vine Street up "Cardiac Hill" to Oak Street and old campus.

The Student Village opened in 1975 and was among the first apartment-style student housing in the nation. With kitchens, living areas, and baths along with bedrooms, the apartments became a model for student residences across the country. The complex was renamed the Edward and Carolyn Boling Apartments in 1988 to honor the retiring UT president and his wife.

During the 1970s, UTC saw a dramatic increase in enrollment and added many professional programs, especially those involving technology.

UTC's $15 million arena, popularly known as the "Roundhouse," opened in September 1982. It gave area residents a panoply of entertainment options, drawing thousands of spectators yearly to circuses, rodeos, ice shows, tractor pulls, and performances by concert artists ranging from Alabama and Itzhak Perlman to Metallica and Kenny Rogers.

An aerial view of the UTC campus in the late 1980s.

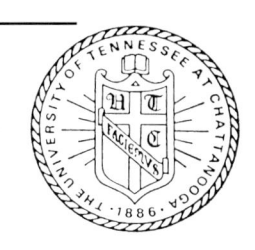

WUTC began broadcasting in 1982. The station features jazz and blues music along with National Public Radio programming.

Chancellor Fred Obear addresses the audience during an announcement ceremony for several of UTC's Chairs of Excellence. Tennessee Governor Lamar Alexander and UT President Ed Boling (forefront) observe.

In 1999, UTC announced establishment of its tenth endowed chair.

The $59.8 million endowment held by the University of Chattanooga Foundation in 1995 was managed by a board of trustees whose members included (seated, from left): James B. Irvine, Jr.; James D. Kennedy, Jr.; Thomas O. Duff, Jr.; Mervin Pregulman; Joseph E. Johnson; and Daniel K. Frierson. Standing (from left): James L. Hill; John P. Guerry; JoAnn Cline; Clifford L. Hendrix, Jr.; Paul J. Kinser; Paul M. Starnes; Susan F. Davenport; Robert J. Sudderth, Jr.; Peter T. Cooper; Frederick W. Obear; John R. Anderson; Phil B. Whitaker; James L. Jackson; and W. A. Bryan Patten.

UTC Chancellor Emeritus Fred Obear and Scotty Probasco. Probasco has served the University in various capacities, including as a trustee of the University of Tennessee and as a trustee and officer of the University of Chattanooga Foundation.

By the late 1990s, UTC had an enrollment of more than 8,600 bachelor's and master's degree students. Graduates could receive degrees from one of five colleges: Arts and Sciences, Business Adminstration, Education and Applied Professional Studies, Engineering and Computer Science, and Health and Human Services.

The UTC Challenger Center opened in January 1995. One of an international network, the center offers math and science training to elementary students and adults through simulated space missions.

Frederick W. Obear,
chancellor of UTC
(1981-1997).

Bill W. Stacy,
chancellor of UTC
(1997 -   ).

By mid-April, the talks had progressed to the point of an "agreement in principle," entered into by five representatives from Chattanooga and four from UT. Those from Chattanooga were trustees W. E. Brock, Jr., Robert L. Maclellan, J. Burton Frierson, Jr., William G. Raoul, and President William Masterson. The delegates from Knoxville were President Andrew Holt and trustees Jerome Taylor, William E. Miller, and Herbert Walters.[36]

They shook hands on the framework for a merger, nailing down the guidelines for its consummation:

- The University of Chattanooga would become The University of Tennessee at Chattanooga (UTC), governed by the UT board in all policy and fiscal matters, and administered by a chancellor who reported directly to the president of UT. The transfer would take place on July 1, 1969, if all the details could be completed by then. Bill Masterson would assume the post of chancellor.
- Full-time employees of Chattanooga would suffer no loss in compensation, tenure, academic freedom, or retirement benefits as a result of the transfer.
- UT would seek state appropriations and other financial resources for UTC "on the same basis as [for] other units of the university, so that for equivalent programs equal resources would be made available on the Chattanooga campus as on the Knoxville campus and other campuses of UT."
- Admission and retention standards would not be lowered below those at other campuses of UT. (At that

time, the University of Chattanooga required of entering freshmen an ACT score of 16 and a 2.6 high school average, while UT required an ACT score of 17 *or* a 2.0 high school average.)
- The "identity and individuality" of Chattanooga's athletic program would be preserved. (Protection was later extended to other traditional features at Chattanooga: the names of buildings, chairs, professorships, school songs, and the blue and gold colors of the school.)[37]
- UT would pay $1 million for Chattanooga's 36-acre campus and other physical assets, as well as assume responsibility for operations projected to generate deficits on the order of $600,000 a year for the next three years.
- The $1 million payment from UT would go to a private foundation to be organized and maintained by the Chattanooga trustees; its governing board would also have charge of the $5.3 million endowment and the capital netted through Bold Venture. The foundation thus would retain the university's entire productive capital, managing and using it solely to "enrich the educational program" at UTC, with all funding decisions being subject to approval by the UT board.[38]

The proposed foundation – a rarity in the annals of private-public school mergers – gave what might otherwise have been regarded as a sell-out the aspect of a "joint venture," a "unique combination of private and public resources." It sweetened the deal for Chattanooga, allowing the trustees to turn over the operating assets and headaches, while hanging on to the ready capital and, through it, exercising some measure of influence over UTC. They were not skipping out, just stepping into new roles. Their plan was to become guardians, perpetuating the values and ideals of the University of Chattanooga through a foundation embedded in UTC.

That foundation would, in fact, be the corporate successor to the University of Chattanooga. Chartered as the University of Chattanooga Foundation, Inc. on June 30, 1969, it was formed by amending the university's charter of 1889. In place of the University of Chattanooga and its educational objectives, the charter amendment substituted the University of Chattanooga Foundation, defining its purpose as "the support of higher education through special programs and projects of The University of Tennessee at Chattanooga in order to enrich its educational program over and above the level possible with normal operating and capital funds available to the University of Tennessee." Further, grants from the foundation would go to support "unique and innovative means and methods designed to effect a continuing movement toward academic excellence" at UTC. Grant requests were to come "primarily from the Chancellor of UTC and his staff." All funding decisions were to be made by the foundation's trustees, but none of the funds entrusted to them could be disbursed "without prior approval of the President of UT and the Board of Trustees of UT."[39]

This "prior approval" clause, which in effect gave veto power to UT, was not to everyone's liking. The foundation's architects in Chattanooga had hoped to make their creation a freestanding entity. In April 1968, they had predicted that its board would be empowered to allocate funds on its own authority to UTC or even to other institutions.[40] Without that leeway, argued counsel for Chattanooga, the foundation might become a "rubber stamp... of insignificant stature," a mere processor of grant requests from UTC.[41] It was a good try on the part of Chattanooga, but no one at Knoxville, not even Andy Holt, could work up any enthusiasm for the idea of an autonomous foundation. "That was just never going to happen," said the assistant counsel for UT.[42] And it never did.

The agreement in principle with Knoxville remained a closely guarded secret until April 24, 1968. That afternoon, at a called meeting of the Chattanooga board, Brock, Probasco, and others on the executive committee laid it out for the full board. A sharp exchange of opinion ensued as several of the trustees complained of the lack of prior consultation and expressed their opposition to the proposed transfer.

James Irvine, Jr. asked if perhaps he had missed some recent meetings, since, as far as he could tell, the board was considering the "mechanics of a merger" without having discussed its merits. Everett Allen questioned whether those who advocated the transfer would withdraw their support from the university unless they had their way in the matter.

"Why are we changing direction?" asked another trustee. In response, Burton Frierson outlined the university's "substantial and serious" financial problems, and H. Clay Evans Johnson suggested that the money needed to operate in competition with UT would not be forthcoming.

After some two hours of give and take, a majority of the trustees favored or leaned toward approval of the agreement with UT, but a determined minority continued to speak against it. Shortly before adjournment, Chairman Brock announced that the board would reconvene the next day for a vote on the issue.

The meeting that next day – Thursday, April 25, 1968 – convened at the President's house on the corner of Oak and Douglas. There were plenty of chairs to go around, since 11 of the 48 trustees were otherwise engaged on this landmark occasion for the University of Chattanooga.[43]

The session opened with protests from various trustees over the "short notice" given to reach a decision on so momentous a question. They accused the executive committee of trying to "steamroll the meeting" and complained of being "taken for a ride." Unfortunately for them, they were members of a board where decisions came from the top down. The line between steamrolling and leadership had blurred long ago; major policy changes had been initiated by the executive committee and ratified by the full board ever since the 1920s. For good or ill, the board as a whole was dependent on the labor, judgment, and financial support of the seven men who composed its executive committee.

That point was stated explicitly by James Irvine. As he put it to the other trustees, "Those to whom the major responsibility [has] been delegated [are] entitled to special consideration from the full board." In deference to their judgment, and given the majority sentiment, Irvine declared himself in favor of the transfer and offered his thoughts on wording a motion to that effect.

Max Finley then spoke up to ask for a time out. He wanted a chance to "absorb all the facts and possibilities" before making up his mind. An adjournment until the following week could do no harm, he suggested, and might bring the board into closer harmony. That suggestion prompted Chairman Brock to relate the gist of a conversation the previous evening with Andy Holt. Holt had telephoned him, "unhappy" with the lack of conclusive action from Chattanooga. His own board had endorsed the agreement in principle, and he was not about to start haggling with the Chattanooga board. Holt was, Brock told the trustees, "pushing for a clear-cut decision."

Time was running out for Chattanooga.

At that point, Robert L. Maclellan introduced a motion to proceed with the transfer in accordance with the agreement in principle. Don Overmyer requested a roll call vote. There being no objection to that procedure, the roll was called and the motion carried by a margin of 22 to 5, with Chairman Brock not voting and with Raymond B. Witt, Jr., Don Overmyer, Creed Bates, Jr., Everett Allen, and George Awad voting against the measure. Awad, a recent addition to the board, suggested that the vote be made unanimous, but the other dissenters flatly refused to join in a show of unity.[44]

Community reaction to the decision was largely favorable, most citizens viewing it as "the wise and economical thing to do."[45] The Chattanooga *News-Free Press*, a faithful mirror of local opinion, hailed the advent of UTC as the "greatest single progressive step in our [city's] modern history."[46] The response from Chattanooga alumni and patrons was less enthusiastic. Donors canceled about $400,000 in pledges to Bold Venture soon after the board action, and officials feared losing the "loyalty of longstanding contributors."[47] Many of them were not overjoyed to be gathered into the bosom of UT. Among them was Raymond Witt, Jr., alumnus and trustee. Years later, when asked why he had voted against the transfer, Witt replied: "UC was my university. It had never been a football school, and Knoxville's only claim to fame was its football team. I didn't want any part of that."[48]

Representatives from Chattanooga and Knoxville spent the better part of a year laboring over the details of a final agreement. Early on in the process, a sobering legal question arose for the Chattanooga trustees. Their authority to make the transfer was open to challenge from an unexpected quarter. Although the university at Chattanooga had severed its last denominational ties in 1935, its charter still contained a reversionary clause, dating from 1889, which stipulated that all assets and property would "revert to the... Methodist Episcopal Church" should the trustees fail to maintain "a University of Christian Learning."

Were church officials likely to invoke that clause? Probably not, counsel advised, but no one could say what might happen in "this kind of situation."[49] Rather than hope for the best, Chattanooga negotiated an agreement with the United Methodist Church, which surrendered any claim it might have had to the university's assets in exchange for certain relatively minor concessions.[50] As a further safeguard, Chattanooga filed a friendly suit in Hamilton County Chancery Court, seeking a declaratory judgment on the board's authority to carry out the agreement with UT. That authority was upheld by Chancellor Ray Brock, Jr., who decreed on June 18, 1969, that the actions contemplated by the Chattanooga trustees were consistent with their fiduciary responsibilities.[51]

Attorneys for Chattanooga and Knoxville drew up the instrument of merger, which was then scrutinized, argued over, and modified several times until, in its seventh or eighth draft, the wording proved acceptable to both sides. The resulting "Agreement of Merger and Plan of Transition" adhered closely to the terms of the gentlemen's agreement reached earlier by Andy Holt, Bill Brock, and their colleagues. It did, however, contain one new twist: a provision obviously meant to allay the last-minute anxieties of Brock and others, who feared that UTC would be relegated to a supporting role as a catchment for the overflowing undergraduate population at Knoxville and as a feeder for the doctoral programs there. A different, more inviting, future was implied by the provision, which read: "The parties agree that the UTC salary schedule must be such as to attract the calibre of faculty necessary to support a doctoral program... it being intended that UTC become a doctoral-granting institution as soon as practicable."[52] On the strength of that declared intention, the Chattanoogans expected to see the institution develop along the lines of a comprehensive university.

The Agreement was executed without fanfare by Andy Holt and Bill Brock on March 4, 1969. Three months later, on June 19, the UT board assembled in Knoxville and, with a crowd of "educational and governmental dignitaries" looking on, ratified the Agreement. On hand was Scotty Probasco, who had brought along the property titles to the University of Chattanooga and a few words to say over them. "In speaking for all the people of Chattanooga," Probasco said as he handed the deeds to Holt, "I think this occasion marks the city's proudest day."

It also was the occasion when, to the general amazement of those present, Andy Holt announced his retirement, effective August 31, 1970. It had been widely thought that Holt would stay on till his 70th birthday in 1974, and he had indicated as much himself from time to time.[53] His decision came as a "total surprise," even to Ed Boling. And it was an unpleasant surprise for the Chattanoogans; Holt had been instrumental in making the merger happen, and they had counted on him to help make it work.

For Chattanooga, Holt's impending retirement added to the

uncertainties already created by an administrative restructuring at Knoxville. On July 1, 1968, the board had endorsed plans to reorganize UT as a "System," with a central directorate removed from hands-on control of the constituent campuses. That System, headed by the president in Knoxville, was designed to bring greater efficiency, coordination, and unity of purpose to the university's ungainly assortment of campuses, stretching from Memphis to Knoxville and soon to include Chattanooga. Though intended to clarify lines of authority, the reorganization intensified the problem – common to most large organizations – of determining who actually was responsible for any particular decision.[54] Did the responsibility belong to the individual campus or to the System or did it fall into the great in-between where System and campus intersected? There were few definite answers for Chattanooga, other than that it had best adapt itself to the System's evolution.

On July 1, 1969, in accordance with the instrument of merger, the 83-year-old University of Chattanooga became The University of Tennessee at Chattanooga. No heads rolled, and no sweeping changes went into effect. The faculty remained intact, reinforced by 55 new members hired in expectation of increased enrollment. Bill Masterson, the last president of UC, became the first chancellor of UTC, and his administrative team was largely the same as before the merger. The people were the same but, as they soon discovered, the agenda now included a much wider range of public service obligations, the first of which was to absorb the programs of a struggling local school, Chattanooga City College.

Founded as Zion College in 1949, Chattanooga City was a junior college which had a predominantly black student body and operated a remedial, or "compensatory," program for students who possessed a high school diploma but not the basic skills to enter college. Located on Fortwood Street, six blocks east of UTC, City College had facilities valued at $337,000, a full-time faculty of 16, an enrollment of 234 students, and not a prayer of surviving alongside UTC.

Its president, the Reverend Horace J. Traylor, had been seeking to have it included in the deal between UT and UC. To "exclude" City College "would be a mistake," he had told Andy Holt, Bill Masterson, and Robert Kirk Walker.[55] The local Chamber of Commerce had endorsed Traylor's proposal, and both Holt and Masterson were "exploring the possibility" of taking City College into UTC; but the required state funds – $300,000 – had not been appropriated by early April 1969, nearly a year after Traylor's initial overtures to UT.

At that point, Chattanooga Mayor A.L. Bender went to Governor Ellington and explained that more was at stake than just the welfare of one small school. The previous summer, black ghettoes in cities across the nation had gone up in flames; and Mayor Bender, reminding Ellington of the "problems... with growing black militancy" in Chattanooga, told him that the city was in "critical need" of the funds to complete the transaction right away.[56] Shortly thereafter, Ellington saw to it that funds were made available; and, on August 27, 1969, Chattanooga City College was acquired by UT and absorbed into UTC.

When UTC's fall semester opened in 1969, tuition costs for in-state residents amounted to $315, a sharp reduction from the

$950 charged at UC the previous year. The price-cut made the institution affordable to a great many more of the working-class students who were its mainstay. That fall they registered in numbers never seen at UC, pushing enrollment up to 3,200 students, as compared with 2,000 the year before. Those figures were "concrete proof of the need for UTC," said Andy Holt, and he forecast an enrollment of 10,000 by 1980.[57]

As enrollment boomed, so did construction on campus. In recalling that era of hardhats and backhoes, one alumnus remarked that, from the day he entered UTC in 1969 till the day he graduated in 1973, "the campus was a perpetual construction site."[58] Between 1970 and 1974, three major additions went up on campus. The first was Grote Hall, a $2.4 million science and engineering building dedicated in 1970 and named for Irvine W. Grote, inventor, world traveler, and head of the UC chemistry department from 1941 to 1964. On the other side of Vine Street, cater-corner to Grote Hall, a new library building began to rise in 1972. Finished in 1974 at a cost of $5.4 million, the 116,000-square-foot structure was later named in honor of Mr. and Mrs. T. Cartter Lupton, whose benefactions had made possible many academic initiatives on campus. Completing the trio of new buildings was the $3.6 million University Center. Located at Vine and Baldwin, it opened in September 1974. By then, there were 4,500 students enrolled at UTC.

Those were years of rapid growth and difficult adjustments for Chattanooga no less than for Knoxville. The Holt era had ended on August 31, 1970, when Edward J. Boling took office as president of the UT System. President Boling's leadership style and focus were decidedly different from his predecessor's. Andy Holt had been the strong father figure whom nobody wanted to let down, while Ed

Boling was the hard-nosed businessman whom nobody wanted to displease. More the actuary than the academician, more at ease with legislative delegations than with faculty committees, Boling was competent, tenacious, and plainspoken. "You never had to figure out where you were with Ed or where he stood," said one of his closest colleagues.[59]

Holt had inspired devotion; Boling would command respect. His own strengths, management and organization, were the same strengths he intended to impart to the UT System.[60] One of his first actions as president was to wire the campuses to a Management by Objectives (MBO) program, a formal method of planning and measuring individual performance, which was then the going thing in corporate America.

The push for system-wide efficiency and orderliness gave birth to elaborate mechanisms for planning, measuring, and grading everyone's performance. Paperwork multiplied, and procedural questions took on a logic of their own. Small matters acquired weighty significance, as when members of the UT board objected to the blue-and-gold colors displayed by Chattanooga, complaining that since the UT orange-and-white was good enough for all the other campuses then it ought to be good enough for UTC as well.[61]

The administrators at Chattanooga often felt overwhelmed by it all, victims of what one called Knoxville's "mania for standardization."[62] They tried to adjust to the increased level of supervision and surveillance, but their efforts were half-hearted and unsuccessful. As one of them described it: "At times everybody seemed to get mad at once.... The demands for accountability aroused otherwise mild tempers. Because we suspected we would be swamped by size, we were constantly looking for such instances and found probably more than were real."[63]

System officials began to have strong misgivings about the administrators in Chattanooga. "You could almost feel them pulling in the opposite direction we wanted to go," said President Boling.[64] Though Boling named no names, it was hardly a secret that Chancellor Masterson was disenchanted with the course of events. In early February 1969, he had accepted the presidency of Rice University, only to resign four days later in the midst of protests by Rice students and faculty over the board's failure to consult with them beforehand.[65] Though Andy Holt had welcomed him back to UTC, he did not seem too pleased to be back. "Something went out of Masterson during the Rice episode," said one of his staff.[66] After his return, Masterson "didn't talk about the future much anymore," a faculty member recalled.[67] An aristocrat of intellect who held to the view that democracy was "irrelevant to the idea of a university's purpose," Masterson had fallen among publicans and cost accountants.[68]

By background and temperament, he was ill-equipped to handle the administrative complexities and the "interminable political considerations"[69] that went with the job of chancellor. The pressures of office soon began to tell on him, affecting his judgment and his sense of propriety.[70] By spring 1972, Chancellor Masterson had used up much of his credibility, not just with Knoxville but also with members of his own staff, segments of the UTC faculty, and a number of local civic leaders.

System officials intervened during summer 1972. President Boling, in a July 14 letter, officially expressed a "lack of confidence" in Chancellor Masterson and notified him that a "management study team" from Knoxville had been deputized to "study and reorganize"

UTC.[71] Heading the team was James E. Drinnon, Jr., an attorney and former F.B.I. agent, who had joined the UT legal staff in 1965 and become executive assistant to Boling in 1972. Drinnon's assignment was to work with Masterson "in the general administration of UTC," which, in practice, meant that many decisions once left up to the chancellor now had to be approved by Drinnon. Even grant requests to the UC Foundation required Drinnon's "concurrence."[72]

During spring 1973, various civic leaders in Chattanooga, including UT trustee Paul Kinser, urged Boling to make a change in leadership at UTC.[73] Rumors of an impending change were picked up and reported by a local newspaper,[74] and senior officials at Knoxville quietly began looking around for someone who could be moved into the chancellorship on short notice.[75] Finally, in early June, Boling asked for Masterson's resignation and received it, effective July 1, 1973. After stepping down as chancellor, Masterson would take a one-year sabbatical, sponsored by the UC Foundation and then return to UTC as a full professor of history, continuing in that position until his retirement in 1979.

The process of selecting Masterson's successor would, Boling announced, involve a year-long search. Meanwhile, to serve as UTC's interim chancellor, Boling appointed UT vice president Jim Drinnon. Thirty-four years old at the time, Drinnon was, in his own words, "strong willed," "aggressive," and "just too young" to doubt his ability to fix whatever needed fixing at UTC. Drinnon knew the campus better than anyone else at Knoxville, and he left Knoxville with a "clear mandate" from Boling to act as the System's troubleshooter in Chattanooga.[76]

8
Growing Up in the System

We are looking for a man of fine appearance, of commanding presence, one who will impress the public; he must be a fine speaker at public assemblies; he must be a great scholar and a great teacher; he must be a man of winning manners; he must have tact so that he can get along with and govern the faculty; he must be popular with the students; he must also be a man of business training, a man of affairs; he must be a great administrator.... [But,] gentlemen, there is no such man.

– Rutherford B. Hayes, to the other trustees of Ohio State University as they prepared to select a new president (early 1890s)

As interim chancellor, Jim Drinnon brought to UTC the skills of a first-rate manager, a burning determination to succeed, and an insider's knowledge of the UT system. "Jim knew which buttons to push," an official at Knoxville observed. "He understood the history and the legal background and knew how to operate as a part of state government."[1] He immediately tightened up the administrative controls on campus, introducing zero-base budgeting, a five-year plan, and stricter methods of evaluating individual performance.

Not given to small talk and collegiality, Drinnon took charge in an unambiguous, if brusque, manner. "What do you do around here?" he would often ask administrators upon meeting them for the first time. Ten or 12 of them, including the chief academic officer, Floyd "Mike" Brownley, soon parted company with UTC. Key members of the new administrative team formed by Drinnon consisted of Charles M. Temple, executive vice chancellor; Jane W. Harbaugh, vice-chancellor for academic affairs; Charles M. Hyder, dean of professional studies; and Bert C. Bach, executive dean of faculty.

Though at first viewed as a hatchet man from Knoxville, Jim Drinnon soon came to be seen in a more favorable light by many of the faculty and staff. They began to regard him as "fair," "knowledgeable," and "decisive."[2] Drinnon could make things happen, which was more than they had seen others do in a long while. Changes in direction had occurred with dizzying frequency over the past seven years: the good gray university of the 1940s and 1950s had gone in search of the academic promised land in 1966, only to enter the UT fold three years later and struggle since then to regain its bearings. After the years of drift and disarray, there were many on campus who welcomed Drinnon's rough-and-ready pragmatism, his knack for the art of the possible. At their request, he agreed to stay in Chattanooga instead of going back to Knoxville; and, in August 1974, President Boling named Drinnon chancellor of UTC.

During his first two years in office, Drinnon made his own personal transition from UT to UTC, leaving few doubts where his primary allegiance belonged. He stopped going to football games in Knoxville and turned down an insistent offer to become general counsel to the UT board.[3] A holdover from the Masterson administration noticed that Drinnon grew "more sympathetic to what we had been doing at UC."[4] And to Ed Boling it seemed that his protege became "less loyal" to UT.[5] Certainly, Drinnon meant to be his own man: he would mend fences with Knoxville but not impose its agenda, bring stability to the campus but not kill its individuality or his own. In the view of a top campus official, Chancellor Drinnon "was fighting for autonomy, not only for UTC but for himself."[6]

UTC continued to expand at a fast clip through the 1970s. The campus more than doubled in size, increasing from 35 to 79 acres, and some $22 million went into the construction of five major buildings: the University Library and the University Center in 1974, the Village Apartments in 1975 [renamed the Boling Apartments in 1988], Holt Hall in 1976, and the Fine Arts Center in 1980. The faculty grew from 190 to 260 members, with 68 percent having a doctoral or terminal degree, as compared with 34 percent in 1969. During that same period, the library's holdings increased from 157,000 to 664,000 volumes; and the University of Chattanooga Foundation provided a total of $4.5 million in funds for scholarships, distinguished professorships, and special programs not usually found on the campus of a state-supported institution.

Grants from the UC Foundation, together with $500,000 from Chattanooga's Lyndhurst Foundation, underwrote the Brock Scholars program in 1979. A notable addition to academic life on campus, this interdisciplinary honors program, originated by UTC Professor Peter Consacro and others, would attract exceptionally bright students by offering them not only scholarships but also the sort of high-powered instruction and challenging intellectual environment more often associated with an Emory or a Duke than with a state university in Tennessee.

The UC Foundation, through its support for the honors program and similar undertakings, encouraged a private-school tone on campus, even as budgetary decisions in Nashville and Knoxville dictated a public-school approach. UTC had come into being during the go-go years of state higher education, when new campuses were popping up like Jack-in-the-Boxes, when "dollars for higher education flowed as freely as they had ever flowed" in Tennessee.[7] Since then, however, state appropriations had barely kept pace with the double-digit inflation of the 1970s. Yearly expenditures at UTC jumped from $6.5 million to $18.2 million between 1969 and 1979, while state appropriations increased from $2.9 million to just $9.1 million. Born during the free-spending 1960s, UTC came of age during a succession of lean decades for higher education in Tennessee.

As state appropriations tapered off, their allocation became subject to a funding formula devised and applied by the Tennessee Higher Education Commission. Based primarily on student headcount and the extent of a school's graduate programs, THEC's formula rewarded graduate-level expansion, large enrollments, and the development of undergraduate programs that filled the classrooms. The result was that, no matter how high the quality or innate value of a curricular offering, it earned few state dollars if students elected to stay away from it; marketability was the key. As Chancellor Drinnon observed in 1974, "Money for higher education in Tennessee tends to follow student interest rather than lead it... for the funding formulae finance only those curricular programs actually generating credit hours."[8]

Given the THEC slant, Drinnon decided to pull out the stops, to go after size and numbers and make UTC the "fastest growing campus" in Tennessee. The emphasis would be on "quantity," remarked a veteran administrator,[9] and, in pursuit of quantity, the institution acquired many of the trappings and features of a commercial enterprise. A marketing campaign was organized to attract the "average student." Entrance requirements were, in many cases, waived for the sake of growth in headcount.[10] Salesmanship grew in importance: "The students are our customers," Drinnon would tell staff members. "We need to provide them with service."[11] To better serve its student-customers, UTC gave them a heaping new selection of the pre-professional offerings that most of them desired. Between 1969 and 1979, the selection expanded to include 35 additional degree programs – nine at the master's level – which prepared graduates for careers in such fields as communications, computer science, engineering management, environmental studies, and criminal justice.

Aggressive salesmanship enabled the Drinnon administration to pump enrollment up to nearly 7,500 students by 1980. To achieve those results in a time of fiscal austerity, resources had to be shifted from "low growth" to "high growth" areas, a move which heightened inter-departmental friction and rivalry. For example, the creation of so many new degree programs concentrated in applied sciences necessitated budget cutbacks in arts and sciences, which nettled members of that college and remained a sore point 20 years later.[12] Charges that one or another program had been "robbed" to pay for some other program were heard frequently.

The drive for growth, as the faculty understood it, would pay off in due course, yielding handsome increases in state funding for UTC. The underlying assumption, recalled one professor, was that "if we got the programs and increased our enrollment, the money truck would soon follow."[13] That prospect was not without its charms on a campus where faculty salaries were lower than those paid at nearly all comparable institutions in the Southeast.[14] And so the faculty waited, holding themselves in readiness for the promised event, until disillusionment set in, and they began to crack jokes about the "money truck," feeling more and more like characters in *Waiting for Godot*.[15]

When the money truck finally did arrive, it was not at all what the faculty had expected. In 1980, ground was broken for the UTC Arena (popularly known as the "Roundhouse"), a 211,000 square-foot sports-and-entertainment complex. Its cost – a whopping $15 million – was borne jointly by UTC, Hamilton County, the City of Chattanooga, and the State of Tennessee. Opened in September 1982, the Arena gave area residents a panoply of entertainment options, drawing thousands of spectators yearly to circuses, rodeos, ice shows, tractor pulls, and performances by concert artists ranging from Alabama and Itzhak Perlman to Metallica and Kenny Rogers.

Lining up the $15 million in capital for the Arena was a remarkable accomplishment, but it earned Drinnon faint praise on campus. The costly venture into public entertainment, so blatant an embodiment of the administration's commitment to growth through mass marketing, caused many of the faculty to question Drinnon's priorities, to lament the "intense commercialization of the institution,"[16] and to speculate that UTC was in danger of becoming "a glorified four-year community college."[17] Professors who once had welcomed Drinnon's forceful leadership now considered him "arrogant" and "impatient."[18]

To his credit, Jim Drinnon had imparted a sense of direction to

UTC at a point in the mid-1970s when it was floundering badly, and he had also managed to keep some blue-and-gold in a color scheme that, in other hands, might well have become starkly orange-and-white. By winter 1979, however, Drinnon had, he confessed, "lost some enthusiasm," felt he probably had done all he could do at UTC,[19] and was "ready to leave academia... no matter what."[20] At that time, his personal life had become the object of public scrutiny as he went through a marital breakup that set tongues wagging on and off campus. To Ed Boling's way of thinking, the situation undermined Drinnon's effectiveness as chancellor of UTC. In November 1980, Boling asked for his resignation, and Drinnon promptly submitted it, effective January 1, 1981.[21] After leaving the UT System, Drinnon served as general manager of the 1982 World's Fair, then practiced law for 11 years before acquiring a retail store in Knoxville.

Charles M. Temple, executive vice-chancellor since 1974, filled in as chancellor while a search for Drinnon's successor got underway in January 1981. Conducting the search was a 16-member "advisory committee" appointed by President Boling and chaired by John W. Prados, UT vice-president for academic affairs. As with earlier instances of filling a vacant chancellorship, Boling would make the final selection from a list of five or six top candidates identified by the advisory committee.[22]

The UTC faculty council, though not involved directly in the selection process, wasted no time in making its preferences known, suggesting to the advisory committee that it look for a candidate who displayed a veritable galaxy of talents and attainments. Among them were "an earned research doctorate...

significant experience as a full-time teacher at the university level... an established record in research [and scholarship]... experience as a university administrator with line responsibility at the level of dean or above... demonstrated ability to work effectively with community leaders, legislative delegations, alumni, and accrediting agencies... an understand[ing of] the innovative teaching and scholarly role of UTC in the UT system... [and] experience in private fund raising."

Whether a mere mortal could meet all those specifications was arguable. When the entire list of criteria was presented to the full council, one of its members declared: "But God is busy!"[23]

After evaluating more than 150 candidates for the post, the advisory committee narrowed the field to six finalists, two of them officials at Knoxville.[24] Handicappers gave them the inside track, because President Boling almost invariably picked someone from Knoxville to head the campuses.[25] But Boling settled on one of the other finalists, a 45-year-old educator turned administrator who had no connections whatsoever with either Knoxville or Chattanooga. His overall suitability for UTC was, Boling concluded, "virtually impossible" to beat.[26] He was Frederick W. Obear.

A native of Massachusetts, Fred Obear held a Ph.D. in chemistry from the University of New Hampshire, where he had served as a graduate teaching assistant before joining the faculty of Oakland University (then Michigan State University – Oakland) at Rochester, Michigan, in 1960. There, he had scaled the academic ladder, rising through the ranks from assistant professor to provost by 1970. His tenure saw the addition of three doctoral programs to the curriculum and creation of Oakland's school of nursing, its honors college, and its evening college.

Upon assuming the chancellorship in July 1981, Fred Obear

began to encourage changes in UTC's internal as well as external relations. His approach to governance was more collegial than managerial. Whenever possible, he preferred to orchestrate the contributions of others and, if possible, anticipate and by careful planning avert sharp conflict. He laid stress on open discussion in which divergent views could find expression, wanting to "build trust so a sense of community could be developed on campus."[27] Gracious and urbane in manner, Obear was outgoing, sensitive to the needs of others, and noted for his ever-ready smile. More than any previous chancellor, he emphasized the process of decision-making as much or more than he emphasized precise and preset goals.

UTC's self-image had deteriorated in the 1970s; many members of the university community now felt a sense of powerlessness, a sense that, as a Guerry professor remarked in 1983, "the forces... determining UTC's future are largely off campus."[28] Obear worked to counteract that perception and restore faith in UTC's ability to determine its own destiny. His challenge was nothing less than to pull the institution together, reconciling as far as possible each of the disparate elements and interests – faculty, alumni, students, the local commercial-civic elite, Knoxville, THEC – and imparting to all a sense of shared mission and purpose.

The spirit of unity was not so easy to invoke in the early 1980s, when state funding sank to a new low that reinforced the every-man-for-himself attitude on state campuses from Memphis to Knoxville. For three straight years, 1981-1983, the actual state appropriations for UTC were substantially reduced by impoundments levied because tax revenues fell short of projections. In 1983, faculty salaries at UTC were still below those paid at UT Knoxville and far below those paid at most other state universities in the South.[29]

The impoundments of 1981-1983 betokened what lay ahead. Higher education had lost its once strong claim on tax dollars, not only in Nashville but also in statehouses around the country. The states' share of higher education expenditures had peaked at 57 percent in 1974 and was steadily going down, to 45 percent by 1994. As state funding declined, tuition costs rose, and university officials increasingly turned to the private sector for assistance. "Publicly-aided institutions that aspire to excellence are not going to achieve that with just public aid," said Obear in 1983.[30]

Mindful of the need to drum up private support, Obear threw himself into the business of re-invigorating the town-gown relationship. He showed up all over Chattanooga, at ribbon-cuttings and charitable events, public forums and festivals, at the podium of any civic group that invited him to give a talk. "Fred Obear is the only guy in Chattanooga who attends more functions than I do," Mayor Gene Roberts would say in the 1980s.[31] "I splattered myself across this community," Obear recalled.[32] In the process, he rekindled the enthusiasm of many long-time patrons and expanded UTC's circle of friends. Their support was evident in 1988, when UTC's Centennial campaign, launched three years earlier, netted a total of $21 million in gifts and pledges against a goal of $15 million.

Obear intended to quicken not only "external confidence" but also "internal trust." The forced resignations of two chancellors within the span of eight years had dampened the mood on campus, leading many of the faculty to ask, "Where are we going? What will we be when we grow up?"[33] To answer those questions, Obear assembled a planning council whose charge was to define, as one member recalled, "who we are, what we are, what we are doing, and what overall institutional direction we should be taking."[34]

Out of this and other initiatives, UTC began to define itself as a "metropolitan university." That label had been popularized by a group of educators who held distinctive views on the role of municipal universities in late 20th-century America. Central to their thinking was the idea that metropolitan universities took outreach to the limit, establishing well-nigh symbiotic relationships with their communities, so that "you couldn't tell where the campus ended and the city began."[35]

As Obear explained it: "The metropolitan label was intended to convey more than a description of geography; it also represented an educational philosophy. Such institutions were campuses of *access* as well as quality, serving a greater proportion of commuting, part-time [and] adult... students than their residential campus counterparts.... They were incredible resources for their communities, wielding, for example, enormous economic benefits; but they also drew heavily on the resources of the regions in which they were located to enrich the traditional curricular offerings through field experiences, internships, work-study programs, cooperative educational opportunities and the like."

Another distinquishing feature of such campuses, Obear observed, was their encouragement of partnerships. "I frequently said that we were inventing a new math in which we constantly proved that 1 + 1 equaled more than 2! This was a way of emphasizing that by joining forces with other entities – K-12 schools, museums, social service agencies, businesses, foundations – the 'whole' indeed became greater than the sum of its parts."

Certainly, the metropolitan strategy put the university back in touch with its historical strengths. As Obear remarked: "Given the University's beginnings – its creation catalyzed by local citizens who thought it important to establish a university in Chattanoga and fought to keep it here – strengthening the ties between the campus and the community as reflected in the metropolitan university model seemed a natural move to make. We had our roots in such an active town-gown connection, a working partnership designed to advance an institution interactive from the start – and we served a largely regional student population. As the current jargon goes, 'This was a no brainer.' "[36]

Working with Obear in outreach was Ron Area, vice-chancellor for development. Other key members of Obear's team included David Larson, vice chancellor for administration and finance; Charles Renneisen, vice chancellor for student affairs and dean of students; and Sandra Packard, provost and vice-chancellor for academic affairs.

Relations with Knoxville remained on an even keel, though Chattanooga did raise some awkward questions about a provision in the Merger Agreement of 1969. In it, the parties had agreed that "the UTC salary schedule must be such as to attract the calibre of faculty necessary to support a doctoral program… it being intended that UTC become a doctoral-granting institution as soon as practicable." Nothing of the sort had happened. Faculty salaries had not risen to the level of those at Knoxville, and UTC in 1984 was no closer to mounting a doctoral program than it had been in 1969, largely because both THEC and the Boling administration opposed the spread of such programs beyond Knoxville.[37]

Those programs had become valuable assets since World War II. They often generated enormous streams of revenue, not only drawing millions in grants and research contracts ($137 million for UT Knoxville in 1989) but also qualifying a school for the highest per-student allocations given under the THEC guidelines. For each student enrolled, a school received a set dollar amount, the amount depending on where the school ranked in THEC's system of classification. At the top level was UT Knoxville, a comprehensive research institution, and near the bottom was UT-Chattanooga, primarily an undergraduate institution.

THEC's policies and the stance of System officials had, in effect, imposed ceilings on compensation and curricular development not envisioned in the UC-UT Merger Agreement of 1969. The repeated failure over a period of 15 years to win approval for even one doctoral program was a source of growing frustration among those on campus and in the community who felt that UTC had ended up playing second fiddle to UT's main campus in Knoxville. That feeling was expressed forcefully by Eric Schonblom, president of UTC's faculty council in 1984. In a letter to Ed Boling that May, Schonblom wrote: "I don't quarrel with the THEC policy of limiting doctoral programs in Tennessee…. What I do find disturbing is the notion that 'proliferation of degree programs' always takes place away from Knoxville, and that it is taken for granted that if a degree is given at Knoxville then the 'duplicate' program is the one on the other campus. A real commitment to make UTC a 'major' campus after 1969 would have seen the shifting of certain doctoral programs from Knoxville to Chattanooga."[38]

In 1984, Chancellor Obear raised the issue with System officials. Their response, formulated by Vice President John W. Prados, was that circumstances had changed so much since 1969 that it was unrealistic for Chattanooga to insist on compliance with each and every term of the Merger Agreement. As Prados wrote to Obear:

"The decision to place UTC in a different [salary] category than UTK... was made by THEC, which was not a party to the merger agreement.... At the time the merger agreement was written, public higher education in Tennessee was expanding dramatically.... Shortly after the merger, the climate changed... [to] one of contraction.... It would be wholly irresponsible to talk about development of doctoral programs at UTC now or in the foreseeable future. I do not view this as a violation of the agreement. 'As soon as practicable' appeared reasonably imminent at the time the agreement was drafted; it now appears to lie far in the future." [39]

The last word on the subject was pronounced by Ed Boling, who suggested to Obear that UTC had best leave well enough alone. "I believe we have made UTC a first-class campus," Boling advised Obear. "And, in doing so, we have given it quite a bit of autonomy. If by insisting on the contract, UTC must change its rules and live by UTK's, such is okay with me." [40] As late as 1999, 30 years after the merger, UTC officials were still searching for the green light to initiate at least one doctoral program in Chattanooga.

Hard times returned for UTC in the early 1990s, when budgetary decisions in Nashville led to three years of back-to-back salary freezes. State appropriations for Chattanooga fell by some 12 percent between 1990 and 1993, making it ever more difficult to recruit and retain outstanding faculty. During that time of belt-tightening on campus, Chancellor Obear taught a freshman seminar.

He also continued to make vital connections between UTC and the Chattanooga area, an accomplishment that many saw as the hallmark of his administration. Looking back on the Obear years in 1999, Margaret Kelley, vice-chancellor for development, remarked:

"When Fred came here in 1981, he was a Yankee invading a traditional, southern town. Its relationship with the university had been forged by an impressive group of trustees of the University of Chattanooga, and the relationship continued through the establishment of the University of Chattanooga Foundation with many of those same people serving as stewards of the university's critically important endowment funds. With his always intact dignity, his careful planning and attention to detail, and his respect for people of all sorts, Fred was able to preserve that base of support and expand it. His attention to local alumni, his careful selection of a wide cross-section of community representatives for membership on the Chancellor's Roundtable (started by Jim Drinnon), and his welcoming of all segments of the community into the affairs and activities of UTC opened up the gates to any and all who were interested in enhancing what he considered Chattanooga's single most important institution, its university."[41]

Even after more than a decade in office, Obear remained the conciliator, adept at balancing multiple constituencies. Nimble and resourceful, he would serve under three UT presidents: Edward Boling, Lamar Alexander, and Joseph Johnson. More than either of his two predecessors in office, Obear understood that the chancellor was nothing if not a wise servant to many masters. As he once remarked, "The main power of the chancellor is… the power of persuasion."[42]

In 1996, after 15 years of wielding the power of persuasion expertly, Fred Obear announced his retirement as chancellor. During his tenure, UTC had advanced on several fronts. Notably, the earlier hue and cry for student headcount gave way to a more selective approach to growth, which took enrollment from 7,500 students in

1981 to 8,500 in 1996. As the focus shifted away from growth for the sake of growth, admission standards rose steadily until, in 1996, the GPAs and test scores of entering freshmen were the highest in the history of UTC and third highest among state institutions in Tennessee.

Moreover, undergraduate and graduate degree programs continued to expand in numbers, especially in the health sciences with the addition of a physical therapy major and a master's degree in nursing. Fully endowed chairs, initially funded at $1 million, grew from one to 10 during Obear's tenure and enriched UTC's college of arts and sciences as well as its professional schools and colleges, and a Center of Excellence in Computer Applications – one of the first 14 centers in Tennessee and one of the first five to achieve the "mature Center of Excellence" status – was established. As a side benefit of the well-received, biennial Conference on Southern Literature, the campus became the home of the prestigious Fellowship of Southern Writers. With support from the Getty Trust and later the Annenberg Foundation, combined with local private and foundation gifts, the Southeast Center for Education in the Arts, one of only six national centers, became a reality. At about the same time, a Challenger Center (the first of its kind to be located on a college campus, the first with a teaching and a learning component, and the first in Tennessee) was opened.

Over the same period, the endowment held by the University of Chattanooga Foundation more than quadrupled, from $14.4 million to $66.3 million, thereby placing UTC among the nation's top 20 public universities in the ratio of endowment funds per student. The campus grew from 79 to 105 acres, and the 21st Century campaign exceeded its goal of $20 million by raising $24 million as of 1996.

That year, *U.S. News and World Report* ranked UTC third in the "best buy" category for regional universities in the South.

An exhaustive search for Obear's successor ended in June 1997 with the election of Bill W. Stacy as chancellor of UTC. A native of Bristol, Tennessee, Stacy had served as president of Southeast Missouri State University during the 1980s and then as founding president of California State University-San Marcos, where he had started off in 1989 with no students, faculty, curriculum, or campus. "He'll hit the ground running," predicted his good friend Fred Obear.

Upon assuming office in August 1997, Bill Stacy became the 14th individual to head the university at Chattanooga. Since its beginning in 1886, the university has undergone changes that its founders could scarcely have imagined. It has weathered depression and wars, the sectional and sectarian conflicts of the 1890s, financial malnourishment in mid-century, and the popular demand for brand names and one-stop shopping in higher education.

Through it all, the university has drawn strength from its roots in the Chattanooga country. Whether called UTC or UC or U.S. Grant, whether governed by a board at Knoxville or Chattanooga or Cincinnati, the institution has been – first and foremost – the university at Chattanooga. The UT System, private capital, and Methodism have each had a hand in carving the institution's distinctive features. And yet the process of definition goes on.

NOTES AND SOURCES

Chapter 1. **The Methodist University**

1. "...great central university" (John M. Walden, University of Chattanooga Board Minutes, 1908), "for the white population" (Resolution of the General Conference, Methodist Episcopal Church, North 1880), "in that territory lying east of the Mississippi River," (Resolution of the Holston Conference, Methodist Episcopal Church, North, 1882).
2. William Gibbs McAdoo, in C. Vann Woodward, *Origins of the New South* (1951).
3. Chattanooga *Times*, March 3, 1883 (letter to the editor from "G.C.C."); Gilbert Govan and James Livingood, *The University of Chattanooga* (1947), pp. 35-38.
4. W.B. Hesseltine, "Methodism and Reconstruction in Tennessee" (1931), p. 60.
5. LeRoy A. Martin, *A History of Tennessee Wesleyan College* (1957), p. 21.
6. Merton E. Coulter, *William G. Brownlow: Fighting Parson of the Southern Highlands* (1937), pp. 300-301.
7. Ralph E. Morrow, *Northern Methodism and Reconstruction* (1956), p. 153.
8. Ibid., p. 115.
9. Ibid., p. 120.
10. Ibid., p. 220.

11. Isaac P. Martin, *History of Methodism in the Holston Conference* (1945), pp. 195-201.
12. Ibid., p. 87.
13. John A. Patten, Jr., "The Stone Church Celebration," Chattanooga *Times*, May 12, 1935.
14. John M. Walden, University of Chattanooga Board Minutes, June 1908.
15. John M. Newcomb, in Linda Walker, *UTC: A Pictorial Review* (1986), p. 9.
16. A group of 28 men incorporated Chattanooga University in 1886 and served as its first board of trustees. The officers were: Bishop John Morgan Walden (board president), Hiram S. Chamberlain and Julius F. Loomis (vice-presidents), Reverend Thomas C. Carter (secretary), and Dr. J.H. Van Deman (treasurer). Members of the executive committee included Reverend Richard S. Rust, Henry Clay Beck, John Wesley Adams, Dr. John R. Rathmell, Reverend T.C. Warner, David E. Rees, Creed F. Bates, Andrew Jackson Gahagan, and Samuel D. Wester. The other trustees were John T. Wilder, David M. Key, David Woodworth, Jr., Reverend John J. Manker, William Rule, Reverend John W. Mann, J.B. Hoxsie, Alvin Hawkins, Reverend W.H. Rogers, Reverend John W. Ramsey, Reverend E.H. Vaughn, Reverend James Mitchell, Reverend J.L. Freeman, and Reverend J.D. Roberson.
17. Full texts of the Chattanooga University charter and the "Agreement" can be found in LeRoy Martin, pp. 60-69.
18. The course of study for B.A. candidates was two years each of Latin and Greek, two years of French or German, one year of natural science (chemistry, physics, geology, and astronomy

each required for one quarter), three quarters of English literature, two quarters of the history of philosophy, two of psychology, and one each in rhetoric, logic, ethics, art criticism, history of civilization, and political economy, with three quarters of religion completing the course of study.

Chapter 2. A Double-Faced Somewhat

1. William Wilson to John W. Hamilton, editor New York *Independent*, December 1886.
2. The *Athenian*, undated clipping, circa January 1887.
3. Caulkins, Carter, and Johnson each gave a detailed written account of the exchange. Their accounts are substantially in agreement, except that Carter has Caulkins saying "No, sir," when Johnson extends his hand. See Chattanooga *Times* January 3 and 4, 1887, and the *Holston Methodist* (Church South), January 1887.
4. *New York Independent*, January 6, 1887.
5. Dwight Culver, *Negro Segregation in the Methodist Church* (1953), pp. 57-59.
6. John W. Hamilton, *New York Independent*, September 22, 1887.
7. "Vindicate the character": *Methodist Times*, London, Spring 1887. "The shame": John W. Hamilton, *New York Independent*, November 18, 1886.
8. "Double-faced somewhat": See Edward S. Lewis, "What About Chattanooga University?" *Methodist Advocate*, September 7, 1887.
9. Ibid.
10. Chattanooga *Times*, July 5, 1887.
11. Chattanooga *Times*, June 5, 1890.

12. The name *Grant Memorial University*, which the Athens school adopted in 1886, was chosen by John Spence as a memorial to President Ulysses Simpson Grant, who had died in July 1885. The name also served as a promotional device in Spence's efforts to solicit contributions from Grant's supporters in the North. See LeRoy Martin, p. 49.
13. Govan-Livingood, *The University of Chattanooga*, p. 67.
14. Chattanooga *Times*, May 29, 1980.
15. Govan-Livingood, p. 75.

Chapter 3. Grit and Grace

1. John H. Race to Gilbert E. Govan, August 29, 1945 (UTC archives).
2. "Grant University – John H. Race – Chattanooga University," Typescript of March 22, 1935 (author unknown) UTC archives; and Chattanooga *Times*, October 16, 1954.
3. U.S. Grant University Board Minutes, May 16, 1899.
4. John W. Hamilton to John H. Race, June 1, 1899 (UTC archives).
5. Dr. E.A. Cobleigh to John Race, January 22, 1902. The use of cadavers for instructional purposes was a touchy matter. After the medical school moved into the west wing of Old Main in 1896, Dr. Cobleigh wrote Race to inquire "whether it will be allowed us to use a cadaver in the University building for the purpose of classwork in operative surgery. This is not dissection, not night work, but is the using of a dead body for actual performance of surgical operations by members of the class…. [A table] will be used with a cover to shut down and lock so

the subject can be easily rolled into a closet between 'Acts'... While skeptical regarding the actual dissection work being legitimate in the Building, I am free to consider this as perfectly legitimate, and it ought to be unobjectionable."

6. U.S. Grant University Board Minutes, May 31, 1901; and "Annual Report of the College of Liberal Arts... Grant University, Athens, Tennessee, 1904-1905" (UTC archives).

7. Most trustees and professors at Athens believed that their school – and not its affiliate in Chattanooga – was the one true school of the Church North in East Tennessee. That view was stated in 1912 by Professor David Bolton of Athens, who maintained that the removal of the liberal arts college to Chattanooga in 1904 had "depriv[ed] the Methodists... in the South of an Institution meeting their demands for the education of their sons and daughters. Today Methodists in the South have no University in the South which they patronize as they once did the University of Athens." In "John Fletcher Spence," typescript (UTC archives).

8. John H. Race to Gilbert Govan, August 29, 1945 (UTC archives).

9. Jonathan Daniels, *A Southerner Discovers the South* (1938).

10. In a petition addressed to the board of U.S. Grant University in 1905, trustee G.F. Lockmiller, Dean W. A. Wright, and 14 other friends of the Athens school refer to the "colossal folly of any policy that leaves Athens without her collegiate rank." They also suggest that the two schools are basically incompatible, observing: "... there is not and never has been that mutual sympathy and cooperation between the allied schools absolutely essential to unity of administration." (UTC archives).

11. Ibid.
12. The words quoted are attributed to Dean W.A. Wright and Professor David Bolton in Martin, *A History of Tennessee Wesleyan College*, p. 107.
13. Govan and Livingood, *The University of Chattanooga* (1947), p. 103.
14. For the academic year 1906-1907, the liberal arts faculty consisted of Wesley W. Hooper, dean of the college and professor of ethics and economics; Walter Hullihen (the one member of the faculty with a Ph.D.), professor of Latin and Greek; Anna A. Fisher, professor of English; John S. Fletcher, professor of history and politics; Charles H. Winder, professor of physics and chemistry; Frank F. Hooper, professor of mathematics; Maude L. Winchester, instructor in French and German; Mary Shuton, instructor in biology and geology; Elizabeth Hullihen, assistant instructor in languages. Their individual salaries for the year ranged from the $1,500 paid Dean W.W. Hooper to the $450 paid Assistant Instructor Elizabeth Hullihen.
15. Govan and Livingood, *The University of Chattanooga*, p. 225.
16. University of Chattanooga Faculty Minutes, December 5, 1910 (UTC archives).
17. C. Vann Woodward, *Origins of the New South* (1951), p. 437.
18. University of Chattanooga Board Minutes, June 11, 1907.
19. The report was signed by Bishop William F. Anderson, Francis Martin, Z.W. Wheland, and the Reverend John Pearson. University of Chattanooga Board Minutes, June 5, 1911.
20. James Kirkland, "Higher Education in the South," in *The South in the Building of the Nation* vol. 5, pp. 234-235; and Paul

Conkin, *Gone with the Ivy* (1985), pp. 109-110.
21. The words quoted are taken from a 1914 report of the General Education Board, which reads in part: "The states have not generally shown themselves competent to deal with higher education on a nonpartisan, impersonal, and comprehensive basis… Rival religious bodies have invaded fields fully – or more than fully – occupied already; misguided individuals have founded a new college instead of strengthening an old one." Cited in Frederick Rudolph, *The American College and University* (1968), p. 433.
22. Ibid., p. 432.

Chapter 4. **Modern Times**

1. Ernest C. Wareing, associate editor *Western Christian Advocate* (Cincinnati) to Fred W. Hixson, June 4, 1915 (UTC archives).
2. President Hixson frequently sought instructions from the board, even on relatively minor issues which he and his staff might have resolved on their own. In his 1915 report to the board, for example, he directed the board's attention to the fact that Chamberlain Field was being used less by university students than by boys from the town, who "take short cuts, climb over fences if they can, if not they go through them. Swing on gates, carve their names, leave water faucets open, put toilets out of commission and do various other uncalled-for things." He then asks for guidance from the board: "Should we ask the city to instruct its officers to keep all boys off our grounds or should we ask it to make a monthly appropriation for their care and the inevitable waste and breakage, or should we charge a small

admission fee of everyone who enters the grounds to cover these expenses?"

3. Jerome C. Hixson, "Chattanooga (1914-1920)," Typescript memoir of 1982 (UTC archives); See also John Wilson, *The Patten Chronicle*, p. 46, p. 54, and p. 57.
4. Ibid.
5. Jerome Hixson, "Chattanooga," p. 9.
6. "Self-Study of the University of Chattanooga, 1925," Typescript (UTC archives).
7. W.R. Pouder (Johnson City, Tennessee) to Fred Hixson, November 27, 1915 (UTC archives).
8. Ibid. And see Arlo A. Brown to C.H. Rogers, registrar of the East Tennessee Middle School, January 22, 1923 (UTC archives).
9. Dorothy Hackett Ward, interview with the author, June 26, 1996.
10. Frank W. Prescott, interview with George C. Connor, December 3, 1980.
11. Jerome Hixson, "Chattanooga."
12. Arlo A. Brown, "A Bird's Eye View of the History of the University of Chattanooga," Speech delivered at UC on April 20, 1936 (UTC archives).
13. Edwin S. Lindsey, interview with George Connor, 1980.
14. Paul Palmer, University Dean, in "Annual Report to the President 1927-1928," University of Chattanooga Board Minutes.
15. University of Chattanooga Board Minutes, June 7, 1927 and June 5, 1933.
16. John Longwith, *Building to Last* (1984), p. 53.

Chapter 5. **Not Just Another Mill Town**

1. John Longwith, *Castle on a Cliff*, (1994) pp. 36-39. "Mr. and Mrs. Guerry saved Baylor [School]," wrote George Bradford, perhaps the most respected teacher at Baylor during the Guerry years. As Bradford recalled: "[The Guerrys] came in Baylor's time of distress [1913]. Summers would find him in Knoxville or Birmingham trying to find boys for his school. He never lost faith, never thought of quitting. He taught Latin and English, thoroughly, as he did everything else.... In the struggling days of Baylor he did the coaching of the athletic teams.... He was the school disciplinarian.... He did much of the office work. He wrote the catalogue, made other teachers put their grades in the book, kept an eye on the yard and house servants, smoothed over trouble in the kitchen, and so ran Baylor that never a check was late, never a bill unpaid.... He became a part of every activity... [and] always Mrs. [Charlotte] Guerry was with him." (George Bradford, "Alex Guerry," Chattanooga *Times*, October 20, 1948.)
2. The words quoted are the concluding sentence in the last address by Alex Guerry, "Subsidized Intercollegiate Athletics," which he delivered to the Rotary Club of Knoxville, Tennessee, on October 19, 1948, a few hours before his death.
3. George Hazard, Jr., *When We Came to the Ridge: Part One of the History of the McCallie School* (1991), p. 68.
4. Moultrie Guerry, et al., *Men Who Made Sewanee* (1981), p. 121.
5. The account of Alex Guerry's years at Baylor School is taken largely from Longwith, *Castle on a Cliff* (1994), pp. 36-39 and 41-73.

6. Alexander Guerry, "Sewanee's Intercollegiate Athletic Policy," *Sewanee Alumni News*, circa 1947. Guerry died in October 1948 while on a speaking trip to Knoxville, the capital of Big Orange country, where he told the Rotary Club:

   Many universities in the South and in the whole country make their students and the public feel that one of the institution's most important objectives is to have a winning football team even though the football team is made up of players secured by compensation for their athletic ability… Furthermore, there is no question of the fact that many coaches in the strongest, largest, and best known institutions of higher learning receive much larger salaries than the finest teachers… This is evidence, clear and indisputable, that the colleges and universities consider a capable coach who can produce winning teams more important and more valuable than those men who are the foundation of the existence and purpose of an institution of learning. To give its students a sense of values is one of the main and one of the essential objectives of education and of an educational institution. When, however, a college or university places such undue emphasis upon the importance of a winning subsidized team as compared with its apparent emphasis upon the real qualities of an educational institution… the result is a distortion of values. The actual result is that colleges and universities are destroying a sense of values for their students and the public.

7. Raymond B. Witt, Jr., interview with the author, April 29, 1996.

8. Longwith, *Building to Last* (1984), p. 72.
9. Ibid., pp. 73-86
10. In June 1934, the finance committee of the board adopted a new investment policy designed to protect the remaining endowment corpus. Under the new rules, deposit and investment accounts were to be split among three local banks, investments were to be diversified rather than concentrated in one type of asset, and funds were not to be placed in securities in which members of the finance committee had a direct or indirect financial stake.
11. University of Chattanooga Board Minutes, June 1, 1936.
12. James W. Livingood, interview with the author, May 16, 1996.
13. Edwin S. Lindsey, interview with George Connor, 1980.
14. David A. Lockmiller, interview with George Connor, May 21, 1981.
15. George C. Connor, interview with Rickie Pierce, July 14, 1982.

Chapter 6. **Bounds of Place and Time**

1. David A. Lockmiller to Edwin O. Martin, May 14, 1942.
2. David A. Lockmiller, interview with the author, September 18, 1997.
3. Natalie Schlack, interview with the author, June 11, 1996.
4. James W. Livingood, "Remarks at the Unveiling of the Portrait of Dr. David Alexander Lockmiller on April 23, 1969."
5. David Lockmiller, interview with the author, May 6, 1996.
6. "Your Twenty Acres of Diamonds," University of Chattanooga brochure, 1955.

7. David Lockmiller, *Scholars on Parade* (1993), p. 155.
8. "University of Chattanooga Self-Evaluation Report, Submitted to the Southern Association of Colleges and Secondary Schools, November 1959," p. 9.
9. Dorothy Hackett Ward, interview with the author, June 26, 1996.
10. Grace MacGaw, interview with George Connor, June 4, 1982.
11. Jane Worth Harbaugh, interview with the author, June 18, 1996.
12. President Lockmiller traveled extensively, both in the states and abroad, from 1949 through 1956. In 1949, a grant from the American-Scandinavian Foundation enabled him to tour the major universities of Norway, Sweden, Denmark, and Finland. During a 10-week sabbatical in 1953, he visited numerous universities and civic organizations in Japan, Formosa, Hong Kong, Thailand, and India as an "educational specialist" for the U.S. Department of State. In 1956, he toured the main universities of Great Britain under a grant from the Rockefeller Foundation. ("Data Concerning David A. Lockmiller, President, University of Chattanooga," Typescript, UTC archives.)
13. August W. Eberle, interview with George Connor, October 15, 1982. The "Self-Evaluation Report" (op. cit., p. 7) also mentions the discrepancy between Chattanooga's stated purposes and programs and its actual purposes and programs. As the report notes, the "curriculum has been broadened to serve the changing professional and vocational needs of the region. The present [statement of purpose and school catalog] rightly give emphasis to liberal and cultural objectives. It does not, however, completely reflect the role of the University as it serves to meet the educational needs of the Chattanooga area."
14. The "Self-Evaluation Report" of 1959 (op. cit.) contained

numerous recommendations, including these: "That a democratic system of budget development be established at the departmental level," and "That, wherever practicable, heads of departments be allowed the privilege of making recommendations for salary increases of department members."

15. David Lockmiller, interview with the author, May 6, 1996.
16. Raymond B. Witt, Jr., interview with the author, April 29, 1996.
17. Dorothy Hackett Ward, interview with the author, June 26, 1996.
18. David Lockmiller, interview with the author, May 10, 1996.
19. University of Chattanooga, "Greater Chattanooga and Its University... Dynamic Partners," 1959, p. 14.
20. George A. Cress, interview with the author, June 18, 1996.
21. Lin G. Parker, "The Measure of the Man Is Found in Those Who Know Him," Chattanooga *News-Free Press*, May 11, 1988.
22. George Connor, interview with Rickie Pierce, July 14, 1982. In November 1980, in his remarks at the dedication of the Dorothy Hackett Ward Theatre on campus, Connor reminisced:

> There was never a more demanding, hard-hearted, tyrannical director than Dorothy Hackett Ward. She laid out for us the highest possible standards for our work, and when we failed to reach those standards – and I am afraid to say that was rather often – she called the failure to our attention in polite but vigorous language. It was the custom in the final rehearsal for her to summon the cast after each act for a critique. Critique! Now there is a euphemism if there ever was one. "Excoriation" would have been a better word, or even "blood-letting." I still remember vividly from

April 1941 one such "critique" at the dress rehearsal for *Romeo and Juliet*, the first of many Shakespearean plays which Mrs. Ward did in her long University tenure. On that occasion she regaled us with rather a long catalog of our sins and ended by saying indignantly, 'And furthermore this scene took 78 seconds longer tonight than it took last night.' This point was met with a stunned silence, broken after a moment by a young man, unhappily one of those who did not return from World War II, who said, 'Well, is that good or bad?'

23. U.C. "Self-Evaluation Report" of 1959, op. cit., pp. 69-71; and Robert W. Fenix to William H. Masterson, January 26, 1966.
24. The "Football" entry in the *Encyclopedia of Southern Culture* (1989), mentions Scrappy Moore in a paragraph listing "many other outstanding football coaches," such as Wallace Butts, John Vaught, and Ralph "Shug" Jordan. It goes on to say: "Among southern teams that were not affiliated with major conferences, Pie Vann [Southern Mississippi], A.C. "Scrappy" Moore [University of Chattanooga] and Bill Peterson [Florida State] had outstanding winning records."
25. Harold Wilkes, interview with the author, July 17, 1996.
26. George Short, "Chattanooga Conquers Tennessee 14-6 Fans Riot After Game," Chattanooga *Times*, November 9, 1958.
27. David A. Lockmiller to R.A. Kilburn, November 12, 1958. Lockmiller's tenure at Ohio Wesleyan was brief (1959-1961). At the end of his first year there, students and faculty leaders claimed he had "arbitrarily interfered with promotions, merit raises and personnel matters"; several professors resigned in protest against his administration. In 1961, the board of

trustees accepted his resignation as president of Ohio Wesleyan (typescript of Associated Press dispatch, Delaware Ohio, "OWU Students Press for Lockmiller Ouster," circa 1961).
28. Raymond B. Witt, Jr., interview with the author, April 29, 1996. The candidate from UNC was brought to the executive committee's attention by Witt, J. Burton Frierson, and Cartter Lupton.
29. Linda Hawkins, "Dr. Martin: Lover of Life, Books and Conversation," Chattanooga *Times*, August 13, 1971.
30. *Encyclopedia of Southern Culture*, pp. 248-249; Lucas, *American Higher Education*, pp. 240-242.
31. Conkin, *Gone with the Ivy*, p. 576; *Encyclopedia of Southern Culture*, p. 282.
32. Conkin, *Gone with the Ivy*, p. 541, pp. 543-580.
33. Tom Griscom, "Dr. LeRoy Martin's 'Striking' Contributions Recalled in Presentation to UTC of Portrait," Chattanooga *News-Free Press*, August 15, 1971.
34. Jane Harbaugh, interview with the author, July 23, 1996.
35. The open admissions policy displeased traditionalists at the university and in the community. While the Chattanooga *Times* praised the new policy, the Chattanooga *News-Free Press* expressed the traditionalists' "regret" in an editorial on the subject. The *News-Free Press* editorial, May 27, 1964, reads: "Decision Regretted"
> With publicly supported schools under broad and unconstitutional attack by racial agitators and the Supreme Court, it is unfortunate that the privately supported University of Chattanooga has chosen to integrate its facilities and thus deprive students of this area of an alternative to racial mixing.
>
> As an independent and private college, the University of Chattanooga has been free, so far, from the excesses of the

judicial dictators. Its independent administration has had the right to make its own decisions. Last summer, "temporary" and "limited" integration was approved by trustees after consideration of a number of factors, including Federal grants. It seemed evident that the temporary integration of last summer was only a forecast of the choice that was made yesterday to integrate graduate study immediately and the entire university at the beginning of the fall term of 1965.

The trustees of the university have the right to make the decision they have made, but many supporters of the university and citizens of this area regret the unnecessary policy that has been adopted.

36. LeRoy A. Martin to David Lockmiller, March 30, 1961. In this letter, Martin requests information about the earlier application to Phi Beta Kappa, explaining: "I, of course, had no intention of initiating another application to Phi Beta Kappa. One of our younger and more influential trustees has been insisting that the University secure this recognition. The Chattanooga *Times* has also become officially interested in the matter and wants to know why the University does not have a chapter…"
37. "Faculty Committee Report: The Impact of the Proposed Junior College on the University of Chattanooga," typescript, circa 1965 (UTC archives).
38. "Faculty Committee Report" (op. cit.), p. 9.
39. University of Chattanooga, "A Policy Statement of Role and Purpose," March 9, 1965.
40. This account of the circumstances surrounding Eberle's resignation is based on the following sources: Lee Weigel, "Dr.

August Eberle Quits as Provost at University," Chattanooga *Times*, July 1, 1965; Eberle, "The Policy Board and the Professor," speech delivered at the Jewish Community Center under the auspices of the Adult Education Council, August 1, 1965 (text reprinted in Chattanooga *Times*, August 2, 1965); Eberle to George Connor, October 21, 1985; George Cress, interview with the author, July 30, 1996; George Connor, interview with the author, December 26, 1998; August Eberle, interview with George Connor, October 15, 1982; Jane Harbaugh, interview with the author, June 18, 1996; Ruth S. Holmberg, interview with the author, June 19, 1996; Grace MacGaw, interview with George Connor, June 4, 1982; and Dorothy Hackett Ward, interview with the author, June 18, 1996.

Eberle's resignation prompted an editorial in the local *Times* (July 3, 1965). Titled "The Larger Issues," it reads:

> Both campus and community suffer a heavy blow in the resignation of Dr. August W. Eberle as provost of the University of Chattanooga. He is an educator of impressive stature, an administrator of proved ability, a citizen of wide concerns. He possesses integrity of purpose and energy of person; he has used both to bring higher education closer to the people, and people closer together in effective community action.
>
> The abruptness of Dr. Eberle's notice of resignation served to bring what might have been an internal problem for the university forcibly to the attention of the public at large. Its substance, however, is properly a cause for community concern if its implications are correctly read.
>
> The issues involved transcend the salary level granted or

denied a single staff member. They touch on the role of the university trustee which must be that of policy-maker, not administrator.

This is a hard area for most people to understand, and one which is easy for others to misinterpret. A single paragraph from conclusions reached by trustees of the Carnegie Foundation for the Advancement of Teaching is pertinent:

'Non-academic people misunderstand the role of college or university trustees because they are accustomed to organizations in which power, authority, and influence flow from the top down. They conceive of the board as the pinnacle of a power hierarchy. In the board room, they imagine, are the buttons that must be pressed if action is to be initiated anywhere in the institution. Nothing could be further from the truth. The heart of the university community is the men and women who carry forward the university's central tasks of teaching and research. All of the university's machinery is, or should be, designed to facilitate the performance of those tasks and to heighten the effectiveness of those men and women. Good trustees never forget that basic responsibility.'

These are high standards to contemplate, hard goals to reach. They are necessary, here or anywhere a program of educational excellence is conceived and carried out.
41. William Henry Masterson, interview with George Connor, September 5, 1981. Early in his first year as president, Masterson prepared a succinct analysis of the university's past development and future course as he saw it. (Masterson to Roy F. Nichols, October 18, 1966). This insightful analysis reads in part:

[The university] has all of its life been an urban school which although private has been called on to perform the functions of a state school. Its finances have therefore been limited…. The main pressure on it has simply been to 'provide for the community.'

The trustees decided a couple of years ago that they wanted to make it academically more respectable – in fact to make it academically very respectable along the rather unusual lines of a private, non-sectarian, small, undergraduate, urban institution. The trustees are in brief the power structure not only of this city but of this general area who closely resemble the late Nineteenth Century 50 tycoons without whose agreement nothing significant could happen. They own or control everything worth having in the area but they are men of education and strong social consciousness. My coming here was a bid by them (I taught the younger ones at the Baylor Prep School here before coming to Pennsylvania) to implement the plans mentioned. We are in the process of transforming the school from its general purpose-public institution past to the desideratum I have mentioned.

This has all been complicated by the recent push for a state school in the area which will be carried out, but which does not affect the trustees' decision to proceed with their own plans here….

The city is enormously proud of this school and there are an astonishing number of people devoted to it. Whether they are devoted to what it was or to what it will be remains to be seen…. Most of the trustees send their children elsewhere, but since the University is there they do not wish it to look bad or to fail and one or two are personally devoted.

Chapter 7. **The Transfer**

1. Arthur Vieth, speech delivered to the Rotary Club, January 4, 1968 (Chattanooga *Times*, January 5, 1968).
2. Arlie Herron, interview with the author, June 10, 1996.
3. William Masterson, speech to the faculty, September 6, 1966. In a letter to State Senator Thomas A. Harris (April 22, 1968) Masterson wrote: "When I first arrived [in Chattanooga] in July 1966, the matter of the state institution coming at some future date was under some discussion, and I repeatedly obtained from the Board of Trustees a reaffirmation of their decision to proceed according to previously announced policies, a reaffirmation signified by our launching the largest financial drive [Bold Venture] in our history."
4. Arlie Herron, interview with the author, June 10, 1996.
5. Robert Kirk Walker, interview with the author, July 23, 1996. In his report of June 28, 1967 to the Chamber of Commerce, Walker presented the following conclusions:

    For over half a century, the need for and the form of a state college for this community has been debated and studied…. Every study… has demonstrated conclusively an imperative need for a liberal arts college…. With each passing year at least 500 to 1,000… deserving young men and women from this community who want – who desperately need higher education – find that they must push their skiff out into life's main stream deprived of the opportunity that only a local state college will provide. The bulk of this group of potential college students cannot afford to pay the tuition that private institutions must of necessity charge. Similarly, they cannot economically afford to go away to another state college whether it be in Knoxville, Cookeville, Murfreesboro or elsewhere. The tuition, room and board as a boarding student at Tennessee Tech, U.T., or Middle Tennessee State University would presently be within the range of $900 to $1,100 per year and the annual tuition costs at the University of Chattanooga presently are $850. This needy and deserving group cannot afford to follow either course; however, with the $200 to $300 tuition costs charged by a state college, [this group would be able to attend college], live at home and perhaps have a part-time job.

Also active in the campaign to bring a state college to Chattanooga was the Hamilton County Chapter of the University of Tennessee Alumni Association, whose officers included Ray L. Brock, Jr., Edward M. Fisher, Lawrence D. Levine, Claude Jack Powell, Sam H. Powell, and Godwin Williams, Jr. During 1967 they enlisted the support of Chattanooga businessman Paul J. Kinser, who had managed Governor Ellington's 1966 campaign in Hamilton County. During private interviews with Governor Ellington in 1967, Kinser advocated the establishment in Chattanooga of a branch campus of the University of Tennessee. For details, see Lawrence D. Levine, "Bringing the University of Tennessee to, Chattanooga," typescript (UTC archives).

6. Edward J. Boling, interview with James Montgomery, October 11, 1970; Joseph E. Johnson, interview with the author, August 22, 1996. Boling, during an interview with the author (August 1, 1996), remarked: "[Commissioner of Education Howard] Warf couldn't get past Ellington.... Ellington gave him the junior colleges and we got Chattanooga."
7. Susan Harris McCue, "Life History of Andrew David Holt: An Interpretive Biography of One of Tennessee's Leading Educators" (dissertation, University of Tennessee, 1995).
8. James Montgomery, et. al., *To Foster Knowledge: A History of the University of Tennessee 1794-1970* (1984), p. 256.
9. In 1960, when Andy Holt asked Boling to become vice-president of development at U.T., Boling was state finance commissioner for Governor Buford Ellington, who had, Boling recalled, promised him the presidency of one of the "state board colleges, probably Austin Peay." When Boling accepted Holt's offer instead, Ellington was amazed; "Buford thought it was the silliest thing I'd ever done," said Boling, who explained that he had accepted Holt's offer because "I'd rather be a vice president at UT than be president of one of the state colleges" (Boling, interview with the author, August 1, 1996).
10. Edward J. Boling, interview with James Montgomery, October 11, 1970.
11. Edward Boling, interview with James Montgomery, October 11, 1970. See also Andrew Holt to Robert Kirk Walker, August 1, 1967, August 19, 1967, August 31, 1967, and September 11, 1967; and Holt to Sam Powell, June 27, 1967 (UTC archives).
12. "The Proposed University of Tennessee at Chattanooga," mimeograph, Office of Institutional Research, University of

Tennessee Knoxville, January 1968.

13. Boling, interview with James Montgomery, October 11, 1970.
14. Fred Travis, "Trustees Take First Step On A 'UT of Chattanooga,'" Chattanooga *Times*, June 16, 1967.
15. William H. Masterson to William W. Jellema, October 24, 1968 (UTC archives).
16. University of Chattanooga board minutes, June 5, 1967; William Masterson to Thomas O. Duff, Jr., July 12, 1967; and Masterson to Andrew Holt, July 18, 1967.

    As to the feasibility of state tuition grants to students attending private colleges in Tennessee, the Southern Regional Education Board (SREB) concluded in a study focusing on higher education in Chattanooga: "Even though it may have merit, the political climate in the state at this time does not seem favorable to legislative adoption of the scholarship plan" (Southern Regional Education Board, "Report of the Committee to Study the Need for a State-Supported Institution in the Chattanooga, Tennessee Area," February 1968).

    A similar conclusion had been set forth on September 29, 1966, at the first meeting of the Walker Committee of the Chattanooga Chamber. According to the minutes, none of the committeemen took exception to the idea advanced by one of them that "any work done on tuition support will destroy" the chances of securing a state college for Chattanooga.

17. On one occasion, responding to rumors that the University of Chattanooga was a takeover target for UT, Holt declared: "Any speculation that the University of Tennessee's Board of Trustees or administration is considering the possibility of absorbing the University of Chattanooga as a branch… is in

complete error…. Our [aim is to respond] to the expressed desire of the people of Chattanooga for a publicly aided program of higher education which would meet the needs of the Chattanooga area and would supplement the programs now in existence at the University of Chattanooga and other institutions in the region" ("Holt Denies UT To Take Over UC," Chattanooga *Times*, November 3, 1966).

18. The study by the Southern Regional Education Board was commissioned by THEC in mid-December 1967 and the report submitted on February 1, 1968. The consultants who conducted the study were Prince Woodard, director, Virginia Council on Higher Education; Paul Reynolds, dean, Wilmington College; A.J. Brumbaugh, consultant, SREB, and E.F. Schietinger, associate director for research, SREB.

    Among the SREB's "Conclusions and Recommendations" was the suggestion "that the University of Chattanooga become a state-supported institution; that it broaden its programs to include post-high school, liberal, professional and graduate education." This suggestion, however, "would have merit" only if it "were the direction in which the trustees and administration [of UC] were disposed to move."
    There followed a discussion of the university's position:
    By action of the trustees, on recommendation of the administration and faculty, the University of Chattanooga is positively committed to retaining its status as a private institution, dedicated to 'upgrading the quality of all programs, eliminating those activities which could not be feasibly brought to high standards, and adding new studies in areas of public service only when such augmentation does

not impede the improvement of quality. All planning is to be directed toward a full-time student body of 2,250 which represents an increase of 25% over the 1967-68 enrollment.' In pursuing this policy, the University of Chattanooga desires to continue to be a potent influence in the cultural life of the community. It seems clear to the committee that in pursuit of this commendable policy, the University of Chattanooga cannot serve the broad educational needs of all post-high school youth of the area, the majority of whom probably could not qualify for admission either on academic or financial grounds. It must be recognized, however, that currently 83% of the University of Chattanooga students come from the metropolitan area. It is estimated that a period of time will be required to make the transition from what the University now is to what it wishes to become (A.J. Brumbaugh, et. al., "Report of the Committee to Study the Need for a State-Supported Institution in the Chattanooga, Tennessee Area," SREB, February 1, 1968).

19. Martin Ochs, "Probasco's, and UTC's, 59 Days," Chattanooga *Times*, May 23, 1968.
20. John M. Jones to Charles F. Brakebill, December 26, 1994 (UTC archives); Ed Boling, interview with James Montgomery, October 11, 1970; and Scott L. Probasco, Jr., quoted in Chattanooga *Times*, April 27, 1995.

   THEC consisted of nine members, all appointed by the governor, three from each of the state's grand divisions (East, Middle, West), and a professional staff headed by an executive director (John K. Folger). In addition to Scott Probasco, Jr., the members in February 1968 were John M. Jones, Greeneville newspaper publisher; E. Bruce Fisher, Knoxville attorney; John R. Long, Springfield attorney; Mrs. Richard M. Hawkins, Clarksville PTA leader; Al Clark Mifflin, Jr., Murfreesboro banker; Roland H. Myers, Memphis physician; C.A. Kirkendoll, president of Lane College in Jackson; and Walter P. Armstrong, Memphis attorney. According to the THEC resolution of February 26, 1968, a UT branch in Chattanooga was needed in order to serve several groups of students. These included: 1) students in Hamilton County who had the potential for collegiate work but did not attend college; 2) students from southeastern Tennessee who desired to attend a public institution near home, including graduates of Cleveland State Community College; and 3) students who, in the near future, could not be accommodated on the Knoxville campus because a cap would soon be placed on undergraduate enrollment there.

21. Martin Ochs, op. cit.
22. Mike Pare, "Probasco Says Private Support Boosted UTC in 1969 Merger," Chattanooga *Free Press*, December 21, 1994.
23. University of Chattanooga Board minutes, April 24, 1968. One group of 113 solicitors, headed by Trustee Thomas A. Lupton, had collected pledges of only $75,000 since the campaign's inception in December 1967. Bold Venture was conceived as the first in a series of major fundraising drives, and so its lackluster showing dampened hopes of securing the even larger sums needed to sustain and develop the University of Chattanooga. "The lack of response from the alumni," Masterson told the trustees on April 24, 1968, had "shaken his confidence in the last few months."
24. Raymond B. Witt, Jr., interview with George Connor, August

31, 1981. In a similar vein, President Masterson observed: "The city is enormously proud of this school.... Most of the trustees send their children elsewhere, but since the University is theirs they do not wish it to look bad or to fail and one or two of them are personally devoted (Masterson to Roy F. Nichols, October 18, 1966).

25. Edward Boling, interview with the author, August 1, 1996.

26. Harold Read, UT vice-president for finance in 1968, said: "See, we had a bad experience... with Memphis State University, and we – being the [UT] administrators – were doing everything we could do to see that that experience didn't take place again, where the media found out about what you were doing before you even have discussions on the subject... and it's whipped before it even starts" (cited in McCue, op. cit., p. 245). See also Montgomery, op. cit., pp. 245-248.

27. Montgomery, op. cit., p. 282.

28. Edward Boling, interview with James Montgomery, op. cit.

29. Scott Probasco, Jr., quoted in Chattanooga *Times*, April 27, 1995.

30. Edward Boling, op. cit. As to the consensus reached by the Chattanooga trustees during that meeting, Jack Lupton commented: "The general conclusion was that we couldn't turn the opportunity down and if we did, we were dead in the water" (Jack Lupton to the author, January 18, 1999).

31. Looking back on events, President Masterson commented: "It is important to recognize that our decision [to merge with UT] was reached under the pressure of time. Once the legislature had authorized the establishment of a UT campus and once the suggestion was made that UC should be that campus,

there was relatively little time to come to a decision" (William Masterson to William W. Jellema, October 24, 1968).

32. Scott Probasco, Jr. to Governor Buford Ellington, January 17, 1969 (UTC archives).
33. Boling, interview with Montgomery, op. cit.
34. Raymond B. Witt, Jr., interview with the author, July 16, 1996.
35. Boling, interview with Montgomery, op. cit.
36. University of Chattanooga Board minutes, April 25, 1968.
37. UC – UT, "Agreement and Plan of Transition," March 4, 1969, sections VII and XX. (The Agreement is reprinted in full in Appendix F herein.)
38. This treatment of the "agreement in principle" of mid-April 1968 is based on UC Board minutes, April 25, 1968; and "Guidelines for Consummation of UC – UT Merger," *UC Today*, May 1968.
39. "Amendment to Charter of Incorporation of University of Chattanooga," June 3, 1969.
40. University of Chattanooga Board minutes, April 24, 1968.
41. Raymond B. Witt, Jr. (secretary and counsel, UC Board) to John C. Baugh (general counsel, UT), June 17, 1968 and June 26, 1968; Baugh to Witt, June 21, 1968 (UTC archives).
42. James E. Drinnon, Jr., interview with the author, July 9, 1996.
43. Not present at the April 25 meeting were trustees Gordon L. Davenport, Thomas O. Duff, Jr., Joseph H. Davenport, Jr., Ruth S. (Golden) Holmberg, Alexander Guerry, Jr. (son of the university's seventh president); John L. Hutcheson, Jr., Edwin O. Martin, Richard L. Moore, Jr., Gordon P. Street, E. Hornsby Wasson, and Earl W. Winger.
44. University of Chattanooga Board minutes, April 24-25, 1968.

45. William Masterson to William Jellema, op. cit.
46. "The UC and UTC Decision," Chattanooga *News Free-Press*, April 26, 1968.
47. Masterson to Jellema, op. cit.
48. Raymond B. Witt, Jr., interview with the author, July 16, 1996.
49. Raymond Witt, Jr. (legal counsel, UC) to William E. Brock, Jr., May 2, 1968 (UTC archives).
50. Andrew Holt to Reber Boult (legal counsel, United Methodist Church), January 28, 1969. In exchange for a quitclaim from the United Methodist Church, the University of Tennessee agreed to the following points: 1) UC would deed the John A. Patten Chapel and the land on which it was located to the United Methodist Church which would, in turn, deed it to UTC on condition that it be maintained in perpetuity as an "appropriate" chapel for "non-sectarian" religious programs on campus; 2) A permanent plaque would be placed in the chapel recording the fact that the chapel was given to the institution by the Church and also stating the role played by the Church in the history of the institution; 3) UTC would establish a Distinguished Professorship of Religious Studies and supplement its occupant's regular salary by a minimum of $5,000 to be provided by the University of Chattanooga Foundation; and 4) A representative of the Church would be elected by its Board of Education to serve on the board of the UC Foundation.
51. *University of Chattanooga et al. v. Board of Trustees of the United Methodist Church et al.* in Chancery Court of Hamilton County, Tennessee, Part I. The final decree reads in part:

> ...the Court finds that the evaluation by the Board of Trustees of the University of Chattanooga of the circum-

stances in which said Board found itself in 1967 and 1968 justified and supported the decision of the Board of Trustees to transfer operational control of the University of Chattanooga and certain of its educational assets to the University of Tennessee upon the assumption by the University of Tennessee of the responsibility for providing annual operating expenses to support and expand educational facilities at the University of Chattanooga.... This Court finds that the Trustees of the University of Chattanooga named in this decree, being cognizant of the problems facing the University of Chattanooga if it attempted to continue as a private institution, properly acted as a Board, and each trustee properly acted in his individual capacity to discharge his and its fiduciary responsibility under the University's Charter of Incorporation (as amended).

52. UC – UTC, "Agreement of Merger and Plan of Transition," March 4, 1969. (The full text of this document appears as Appendix F herein).

53. For example, in a letter to William Masterson (November 7, 1966), Holt wrote: "I would like to have your solemn promise that you will remain as President of the University of Chattanooga for at least nine years. This is how long I shall remain at the University of Tennessee provided our Board of Trustees does not dispose of my service earlier."

54. Montgomery, et al., op. cit., pp. 282-284; "Historical Vignette: The Creation of the UT System," *Context* (UT publication), April 2, 1992.

55. "A Recommendation," from Chattanooga City College, July

16, 1968, typescript; Robert Kirk Walker, "Report to the Executive Committee of the Greater Chattanooga Chamber of Commerce," July 26, 1968; Andrew D. Holt to Robert Kirk Walker, August 7, 1968; William Masterson to Robert Kirk Walker, August 23, 1968 (UTC archives).

56. A.L. Bender to Buford Ellington, April 14, 1969 (UTC archives); J.B. Collins, "Bender Hopeful on Merger in '69 of UTC-City College," Chattanooga *News-Free Press*, April 18 1969; "Agreement of Merger," between UT and Chattanooga City College, August 27, 1969 (UTC archives).

57. Andrew Holt, speech delivered at the first convocation of UTC, September 24, 1969.

58. Douglas Hale, interview with the author, June 7, 1996.

59. Joseph E. Johnson, interview with Milton Klein, May 21, 1990 (UT archives, Knoxville).

60. Ibid.

61. Ed Boling, interview with Montgomery, op. cit.

62. David Parker, interview with the author, May 15, 1996.

63. Jane W. Harbaugh, "Dream No Little Dreams," UTC commencement speech, December 17, 1994.

64. Ronnie Moore, "Local Legislators Say Drinnon Most Likely Interim Head," Chattanooga *News-Free Press*, June 8, 1973.

65. William Masterson to Martin Ochs, February 21, 1969; University of Chattanooga faculty minutes, February 28, 1969; "Dr. W.H. Masterson, 68, Dies in Accident; Ex-UTC Chancellor," Chattanooga *Times*, March 3, 1983.

66. George Connor, interview with the author, June 7, 1996.

67. Arlie Herron, interview with the author, June 10, 1996.

68. William Masterson, "From Shadows and Symbols into Truth,"

address to the Alpha Society (UTC), April 20, 1979.
69. William Masterson, interview with George Connor, September 5, 1981.
70. J. Burton Frierson, Jr. to Edward Boling, July 24, 1972; James Drinnon, interview with the author, July 9, 1996; George Connor, interview with the author, June 7, 1996; Reed Sanderlin, interview with the author, August 7, 1996.
71. James Drinnon to William Masterson, July 19, 1972; Masterson to Drinnon, August 7, 1972.
72. Ibid.
73. See, for example, Z. Cartter Patten to Edward Boling, May 8, 1973, in the "Boling Papers," UT archives, Knoxville.
74. Chattanooga *News-Free Press*, April 30, 1973, June 4, 1973, and June 5, 1973.
75. Joseph E. Johnson, confidential memorandum to Ed Boling, March 13, 1973 (UT archives).
76. James Drinnon, interview with the author, July 9, 1996.

Chapter 8. **Growing Up in the System**

1. Joseph E. Johnson, interview with the author, August 22, 1996.
2. "knowledgeable and decisive": Grace MacGaw, interview with George Connor, June 4, 1982; "fair": George Cress, interview with the author, June 18, 1996. See also Ziad Keilany, interview with the author, June 7, 1996. Jane Harbaugh, in an interview of July 16, 1996, said: "Drinnon was… open about fiscal matters…. You could argue with him…. There was a certain orderliness and thinking through of consequences…. His critique [of what UTC needed] then was very productive."

3. James E. Drinnon, Jr., interview with the author, July 9, 1996.
4. David Parker, interview with the author, May 15, 1996.
5. Edward J. Boling, interview with the author, August 1, 1996.
6. Jane W. Harbaugh, interview with the author, July 23, 1996.
7. John W. Prados, interview with the author, July 5, 1996; Prados to Frederick W. Obear, April 5, 1984; and "Community Colleges," in *Tennessee Encyclopedia of History and Culture* (1998).
8. James Drinnon, Jr., "Annual Report to the Trustees of the University of Chattanooga Foundation," May 1974.
9. Grace MacGaw, interview with George Connor, June 4, 1981. See also Patricia P. Bytnar, interview with the author, July 23, 1996.
10. UTC application to Phi Beta Kappa, 1977; George Keller, "Keller Report" to the administration of UTC, 1984 (UTC archives); Natalie Schlack, interview with George Connor, January 29, 1982; and Charles Renneisen, interview with the author, July 22, 1996.
11. James Drinnon, Jr., interview with the author, July 9, 1996.
12. James A. Ward, interview with the author, July 15, 1996.
13. Patricia P. Bytnar, interview with the author, July 23, 1996.
14. Lamar Alexander, "Report Card, the University of Tennessee; Progress: 1985-1990" (UT publication).
15. Bytnar, op. cit.
16. Grace MacGaw, op. cit.
17. George Cress, interview with George Connor, October 26, 1981.
18. Ziad Keilany, interview with the author, June 24, 1996.
19. Jim Drinnon, interview with George Connor, December 19, 1980.

20. Jim Drinnon, interview with the author, July 9, 1996.
21. Edward Boling, interview with the author, August 1, 1996; and Jim Drinnon, interview with the author, July 9, 1996.
22. Ed Boling, memorandum to UTC faculty and staff, December 10, 1980. In addition to John Prados, the advisory committee consisted of Claude Bond, retired assistant superintendent of Chattanooga City schools; Walker Breland, UTC associate professor; Karla Brown, UTC student; Lee Dyer, UTC student; Robert Fritz, UTC physical plant employee; William Hales, Jr., UTC professor; Charles M. Hyder, UTC executive dean of graduate studies and research; Joseph E. Kelly, UTC student; James E. Moon, UTC professor; Barbara Norwood, UTC assistant professor; Eric Schonblom, UTC associate professor; John C. Stophel, Chattanooga attorney; Ann S. Tinnon, director of financial aid at UTC; Thomas G. Waddell, UTC associate professor; Patricia Walker, UTC associate professor; and Betty Whaley, president of the UT National Alumni Association. Ed Boling also involved Paul J. Kinser and Scott L. Probasco, Jr. in the latter stages of the selection process.
23. Robert C. Fulton, memorandum to the UTC Faculty Council, January 14, 1981.
24. Besides Frederick Obear, the finalists were Bert C. Bach, UTC executive dean of faculty; Garrett Briggs, associate dean of liberal arts, UT Knoxville; Leroy Keith, Jr., executive vice president, University of the District of Columbia; Robert H. Maier, vice chancellor for academic affairs, East Carolina University; and C. Warren Neel, dean of business administration, UT Knoxville (Charles Temple, memorandum to UTC faculty and staff, March 18, 1981).

25. Frederick Obear, interview with the author, June 12, 1996.
26. Ed Boling to the Hamilton County delegates of the Tennessee General Assembly, May 8, 1981.
27. Frederick Obear, in "Thoughts Upon Retiring," *Tennessee Alumnus*, spring 1997.
28. Benjamin H. Gross, interview with George Connor, August 26, 1997.
29. David Larson, "The University of Tennessee at Chattanooga: Planning for Excellence," August 1983 (UTC internal study); and Joseph E. Johnson to Frederick Obear, September 15, 1988.
30. Frederick Obear, interview with George Connor, July 19, 1983.
31. Gene Roberts, interview with the author, June 16, 1996.
32. Frederick Obear, interview with the author, June 12, 1996.
33. Pat Bytnar, interview with the author, July 23, 1996.
34. Margaret Kelley to the author, October 5, 1999.
35. Frederick Obear to the author, September 27, 1999.
36. Ibid.
37. Ed Boling, interview with James Montgomery, October 11, 1970; Boling, interview with the author, August 1, 1996; Elmer Ellis to Andy Holt, May 1, 1968 (UT archives); Joseph E. Johnson to Frederick Obear, September 15, 1988; Johnson to Lamar Alexander, June 27, 1988; Frederick Obear, interview with the author, June 12, 1996; and John W. Prados, interview with the author, July 5, 1996.
38. J. Eric Schonblom to Edward Boling, May 21, 1984.
39. John Prados to Frederick Obear, April 15, 1984.
40. Edward Boling to Frederick Obear, August 15, 1984.
41. Margaret Kelley to the author, October 5, 1999.
42. Frederick Obear, in *Tennessee Alumnus*, op. cit.

Selected Bibliography

Armstrong, Zella. *The History of Hamilton County and Chattanooga Tennessee.* 2 vols. Chattanooga: Lookout Publishing Company, 1931 and 1940.

Boling, Edward J. Interview by Milton Klein, November 5, 1990. Transcript of tape recording, Office of the Historian, University of Tennessee.

———. Papers. Office of the Historian, University of Tennessee.

Bradford, George L. "Alex Guerry." Chattanooga *Times*, October 20, 1948.

Byrum, C. Stephen. *A History of the Chattanooga District of the United Methodist Church.* Chattanooga: Paidia Productions, 1988.

Conkin, Paul K. *Gone with the Ivy: A Biography of Vanderbilt University.* Knoxville: University of Tennessee Press, 1985.

Coulter, E. Merton. *William G. Brownlow: Fighting Parson of the Southern Highlands.* Chapel Hill: University of North Carolina Press, 1937.

Culver, Dwight W. *Negro Segregation in the Methodist Church.* New Haven: Yale University Press, 1953.

Dabney, Charles W. *Universal Education in the South.* Chapel Hill: University of North Carolina Press, 1936.

Dykeman, Wilma. *Tennessee; A History.* Newport, Tennessee: Wakestone Books, 1993.

Eberle, Elizabeth Ann. "A History of Post-Civil War Methodist Episcopal Academies Affiliated with the Universities at Athens and Chattanooga." M.A. thesis, University of Chattanooga, August 1963.

Eller, Ronald. *Miners, Millhands, and Mountaineers: Industrialization of the Appalachian South 1890-1930*. Knoxville: University of Tennessee Press, 1982.

Federal Writers' Project of the W.P.A. *The W.P.A. Guide to Tennessee*. New York: Viking, 1939.

Flexner, Stuart Berg, and Anne H. Soukhanov. *Speaking Freely: A Guided Tour of American English from Plymouth Rock to Silicon Valley*. New York: Oxford University Press, 1997.

Gitlin, Todd. *The Sixties: Years of Hope, Days of Rage*. New York: Bantam Books, 1993.

Govan, Gilbert E., and James W. Livingood. *The Chattanooga Country, 1540-1962: From Tomahawks to TVA*. Chapel Hill: University of North Carolina Press, 1963.

———. *The University of Chattanooga: Sixty Years*. Chattanooga: University of Chattanooga, 1947.

Guerry, Moultrie, and A.B. and Elizabeth Chitty. *Men Who Made Sewanee*. Sewanee, Tennessee: University of the South Press, 1981.

Hesseltine, W.B. "Methodism and Reconstruction in Tennessee." *East Tennessee Historical Society Publications* 3, January 1931.

Hixson, Jerome C. "Chattanooga (1914-1920)" Manuscript, University of Tennessee at Chattanooga, 1982.

Hofstadter, Richard *Anti-Intellectualism in American Life*. New York: Random House, 1962.

Holt, Andrew D. Papers. Office of the Historian, University of Tennessee.

———. "The University of Tennessee: Dynamic Spirit of the Volunteer State." Newcomen Society Address, Knoxville, Tennessee, November 18, 1966.

James, William. "The Ph.D. Octopus." In *Memories and Studies*. New York: Longmans, Green, and Co., 1911.

Jencks, Christopher, and David Riesman. *The Academic Revolution*. Chicago: University of Chicago Press, 1968.

Johnson, Daniel M., and David A. Bell, ed. *Metropolitan Universities: An Emerging Model in Higher Education*. Denton, Texas: University of North Texas Press, 1995.

Johnson, Joseph E. Interview by Milton Klein, May 21, 1990. Office of the Historian, University of Tennessee.

Josephson, Matthew. *The Robber Barons*. New York: Harcourt, Brace and Company, 1932.

Leuchtenberg, William E. *The Perils of Prosperity, 1914-1932*. Chicago: University of Chicago Press, 1958.

Lockmiller, David A. *Scholars on Parade: Colleges and Universities, Academic Degrees, Caps and Gowns, Hood Colors, Regalia*. Chapel Hill: University of North Carolina Press, 1993.

Longwith, John. *Building to Last: The Story of the American National Bank and Trust Company*. Chattanooga: American National Bank, 1984.

———. *Castle on a Cliff: A History of Baylor School*. Chattanooga: Baylor School, 1994.

Lucas, Christopher J. *American Higher Education: A History*. New York: St. Martin's, 1994.

Manker, John J. "Chattanooga University: A Historical Sketch." n.p., October 19, 1886.

Marsden, George M. *The Soul of the American University: From Protestant Establishment to Established Nonbelief*. Oxford: Oxford University Press, 1994.

Martin, Isaac Patton. *History of Methodism in the Holston Conference*. Knoxville: Methodist Historical Society, 1945.

Martin, LeRoy A. *A History of Tennessee Wesleyan College, 1857-1957*. n.p., 1957.

Masterson, William H. Interview by George Connor, September 5, 1981, Tape recording, UTC.

McCue, Susan Harris. "Life History of Andrew David Holt: An Interpretive Biography of One of Tennessee's Leading Educators." Dissertation, University of Tennessee, October 1995.

McGuffey, Charles D. *Standard History of Chattanooga, Tennessee*. Knoxville: Crew and Dorey, 1911.

Mitchell, Samuel C., ed. *The South in the Building of the Nation*. vol. 10. Richmond: Southern Historical Publication Society, 1909.

Montgomery, James R., Stanley J. Folmsbee, and Lee S. Greene. *To Foster Knowledge: A History of the University of Tennessee, 1794-1970*. Knoxville: University of Tennessee Press, 1984.

Morrow, Ralph E. *Northern Methodism and Reconstruction*. East Lansing: Michigan State University Press, 1956.

Piatt, Albert E. "The University of Chattanooga – The University of Tennessee at Chattanooga, From Private to Public: Three Decades of Change." Manuscript, 1993, University of Tennessee at Chattanooga.

Price, R.N. *Holston Methodism: From its Origin to the Present Time*. vol. 5. Nashville: Publishing House of the Methodist Episcopal Church South, 1913.

Rudolph, Frederick. *The American College and University: A History*. New York: Knopf, 1968.

Sweet, William Warren. *Methodism in American History*. New York: Methodist Book Concern, 1933.

Tanner, Mary Poston, and Frederick W. Obear, "Realizing the Potential of Educational Technologies: A Challenge to Metropolitan Universities." *Metropolitan Universities*, Summer 1995.

University of Chattanooga. Minutes of the Board of Trustees, 1907-1969.

———. "Self-Evaluation Report to the Southern Association of Colleges and Secondary Schools, November 1959."

University of Tennessee at Chattanooga. "The Direct and Indirect Economic Impact of The University of Tennessee at Chattanooga on the Chattanooga Area, 1991-1992."

———. "Fact Book, 1995-1996." Internal publication by the Office of Planning, Evaluation, and Institutional Research.

———. "Targets of Opportunity: A Report to President-Elect Lamar Alexander, May 1988."

U.S. Grant University. Minutes of the Board of Trustees, 1897-1907. (All earlier minute books were destroyed by fire in the 1890s.)

Veysey, Laurence R. *The Emergence of the American University*. Chicago: University of Chicago Press, 1965.

Walker, Linda. *UTC: A Pictorial Review*. n.p., 1986.

West, Carroll Van, ed., *Tennessee Encyclopedia of History and Culture*. Nashville: Tennessee Historical Society, 1998.

Wilson, Charles Regan, and William Ferris, ed. *Encyclopedia of Southern Culture*, "Education" section. Chapel Hill: University of North Carolina Press, 1989.

Wilson, John. *The Patten Chronicle*. Chattanooga: Roy McDonald, n.d.

Wolff, Robert Paul. *The Ideal of the American University*. Boston: Little, Beacon, 1969.

Woodward, C. Vann. *Origins of the New South: 1877-1913*. Baton Rouge: Louisiana State University Press, 1951.

———. *Reunion and Reaction: The Compromise of 1877 and the End of Reconstruction*. Boston: Little, Brown and Company, 1951.

APPENDIX A

Chronology

1883   (May) The Freedmen's Aid Society of the Methodist Episcopal Church, North selected Chattanooga as the location for a "great central university" of the church.
(July) A 13-acre site on McCallie Avenue acquired for the proposed school at a cost of $31,000.

1884   (February 6) Groundbreaking ceremonies for "Old Main," a four-story building (completed in spring 1886) on McCallie Avenue between Douglas and Baldwin Streets.

1886   (July 8) Chattanooga University incorporated for "the general diffusion of knowledge, with powers to confer degrees, etc." The incorporators and first trustees were Bishop John Walden (board president), Hiram S. Chamberlain and Julius F. Loomis (vice-presidents), Thomas C. Carter (secretary), Dr. J.H. Van Deman (treasurer), John Wesley Adams, Creed F. Bates, Henry Clay Beck, J.L. Freeman, Andrew J. Gahagan, Alvin Hawkins, J.B. Hoxsie, David M. Key, John J. Manker, John W. Mann, James Mitchell, John W. Ramsey, Dr. John Rathmell, David E. Rees,

	J.D. Roberson, W.H. Rogers, Richard S. Rust, E.H. Vaughn, T.C. Warner, Samuel D. Wester, John T. Wilder, and David Woodworth, Jr. (September 15) Chattanooga University opened with an enrollment of 118 students and a staff of eight teachers, including Dean and Acting President Edward S. Lewis.
1889	(April 27) Chattanooga University consolidated with Grant Memorial University (formerly East Tennessee Wesleyan) at Athens.
(May 2) John F. Spence, head of the Athens school, elected president of the newly-consolidated university.
(June 5) Hiram S. Chamberlain elected president of the board.
(October 28) Name changed to U.S. Grant University. By terms of the charter, Chattanooga to offer college, preparatory, and professional programs, while Athens operates a theology school and develops vocational programs.
(September 23) A medical school, loosely affiliated with the university, opened on the Chattanooga campus.
1891	(June 7) Bishop Isaac W. Joyce replaced John Spence as head of the university.
1892	(June 7) College of liberal arts moved from Chattanooga to Athens. School of theology moved to Athens; Reverend John T. Newcomb, dean.

1893	Academic department discontinued at Chattanooga and all preparatory work consolidated at Athens.
1896	Bishop Joyce resigned as head of the university.
1897	(fall) John H. Race (1862-1954) elected president.
1898	(fall) A law school, loosely affiliated with the university, opened on the Chattanooga campus.
1902	(spring) John Race resigned as president but reassumed that post at the behest of the board of bishops of the Methodist Episcopal Church, North.
1904	(August 15) Chancery Court in McMinn County issued a temporary injunction preventing Race and the university board from exercising any control over the branch school in Athens. (September 29) Ruling of the McMinn County Chancellor reversed on appeal. (October 5) The college of liberal arts reopened at Chattanooga, with Wesley Hooper dean. Degrees offered: A.B., B.S., and Litt. B. Enrollment of 49 students in 1904-1905 and 88 in 1905-1906.
1905	(fall) First full schedule of intercollegiate football games: University of Tennessee defeated 5-0.
1905-1906	Successful drive to raise the university's first $200,000 in endowment; leading donors were Daniel K. Pearsons of Chicago ($50,000) and industrialist Andrew Carnegie of New York ($30,000).

1906	Students produced first issue of the *University Echo*.
1907	(June 18) By charter amendment, U.S. Grant University re-named the University of Chattanooga; the branch at Athens designated as the Athens School of the University of Chattanooga.
1908	(fall) Chamberlain Field opened.
1909	(May 21) Methodist Episcopal Church, North deeded all property to the local board of trustees. (June) In gratitude to John Race, local citizens raised $20,000 to build an on-campus residence for the university president.
1910	University joined the Association of Colleges and Secondary Schools of the Southern States as 21st collegiate member.(December 6) Faculty suspended intercollegiate competition in football during the 1911 season.
1911	First issue of college annual *The Moccasin*.
1912	(November 1) Two-year $500,000 financial campaign succeeded in raising the $350,000 necessary to secure a $150,000 gift from the Rockefeller-funded General Education Board.
1913	(June) John H. Race resigned as president. University joined the Southern Intercollegiate Athletic Association.
1914	(April 28) Fred Whitlo Hixson elected president. The board of trustees included: John Wesley

Adams, Bishop William F. Anderson, J.E. Annis, J.W. Bayless, Henry Clay Beck, William E. Brock, Hiram S. Chamberlain, R.B. Davenport, H. Clay Evans, Ross Faxon, Herman Ferger, John W. Fisher, J.A. Fowler, G.T. Francisco, J.A. Grigsby, Bishop T.S. Henderson, President Fred Hixson, George F. Lockmiller, John J. Manker, Francis Martin, John A. Patten, John Pearson, Harry S. Probasco, John Race, T.C. Thompson, J.D. Walsh, and Z.W. Wheland.

(June 14) Ground broken for gymnasium at corner of Oak and Baldwin Streets; cornerstone laid October 22, 1914.

1915 (September 9) Construction begun on Administration Building (re-named Founders Hall in 1950) as well as adjoining classroom building (named John H. Race Hall in 1950). Cornerstone laid April 26, 1916. President Hixson designed university emblem consisting of a shield bearing the motto *Faciemus* (we shall accomplish).

1917 (June) Construction begun on Science Hall (re-named Wesley W. Hooper Hall in 1950) and the John A. Patten Memorial Chapel.

(November) First classes held in new building; workers started demolishing Old Main.

1918 (May 17) Alpha, a scholastic honor society, organized.

(October 1) Unit of the Student Army Training

	Corps arrived on campus. War in Europe ended November 11; the unit disbanded December 7.
1919	(May 17) John A. Patten Memorial Chapel dedicated.
	(September) Frank F. Hooper succeeded Wesley Hooper as dean of the college.
1920	(January) Students permitted to hold dances off campus.
	(July 2) President Fred Hixson resigned to accept the presidency of Allegheny College in Pennsylvania. Dean Frank Hooper served as acting president.
	Enrollment of 180 undergraduates for academic year 1919-1920.
1921	(July 1) Election of Arlo Ayres Brown as president.
	(November 1) $850,000 campaign launched with W.E. Brock as chairman; goal reached May 4, 1922.
1923	(June) Program in business leading to the Bachelor of Business Administration degree offered.
1925	(June 26) Branch at Athens granted independence and re-chartered as Tennessee Wesleyan College.
	Summer school sessions, discontinued during World War I, re-established.
1926	(fall) Paul L. Palmer succeeded Frank Hooper as dean of the college. The faculty consisted of

Thomas P. Abernathy, Paul Bales, Ellen M. Coolidge, David W. Cornelius, John W. Edwards, Edith Gill, Wyman R. Green, Isobel Griscom, Frank F. Hooper, Claudius O. Johnson, Earl K. Kline, George A. Leatherman, Edwin S. Lindsey, Mary H. MacKinlay, James S. McLemore, A.C. "Scrappy" Moore, Blynn Owen, Paul L. Palmer, Ruth C. Perry, Clyde W. Phelps, John W. Prince, William C. Redd, Mrs. L.M. Russell, Margaret Smith Colby, Maxwell A. Smith, Louis F. Snow, Terrell L. Tatum, Frank Thomas, and Godfrey Tietze.

1927 (fall) Local contributions of more than $60,000 financed construction of Oak Street Stadium with a seating capacity of 5,000.

1927-1928 Enrollment of 392 undergraduates; 159 students in the summer sessions.

1928 (fall) Major in music established. Opening of the Little Theatre.

Latin or Greek dropped as requirement for the A.B. degree.

The board of trustees consisted of Z.W. Wheland (chairman, 1921-1932), Henry Clay Beck (1928-1933), William E. Brock (1913-1950), Arlo A. Brown (1921-1929), William A. Burnette (1928-1932), Morrow Chamberlain (1916-1959), John S. Fletcher (1917-1961), J.A. Grigsby (1914-1944), W.K. Harris (1916-1939), Ken Hicks (1924-1933), C.H. Hutson (1916-1929), Bishop

Frederick Keeney (1928-1936), Paul J. Kruesi (1928-1955), G.F. Lockmiller (1914-1939), John Thomas Lupton (1909-1912; 1917-1934), J.M. Melear (1921-1954), R.M. Millard (1926-1930), Stacy E. Nelson (1925-1961), Bishop Thomas Nicholson (1916-1929), Manker D. Patten (1926-1940), George H. Patten (1922-1942), Mrs. John A. Patten (1916-1929), Z.C. Patten (1917-1948), Scott L. Probasco (1921-1955), R.P. Purse (1920-1935), John H. Race (1898-1954), S.R. Read (1922-1942), Bishop E.G. Richardson (1921-1929), M.S. Roberts (1919-1941), Bishop H. Lester Smith (1928-1932), Bishop W.P. Thirkield (1899-1907; 1924-1928), T.C. Thompson (1909-1937), W.B. Townsend (1922-1934), F. L. Underwood (1920-1942), and C.N. Woodworth, (1917-1928).

1929 President Arlo Brown resigned to accept presidency of Drew Theological Seminary.
(June 5) Alexander Guerry elected president of the university; Guerry was the first layman, non-Methodist, and southerner to hold that office.
(fall) Student commons under Oak Street Stadium opened with a cafeteria and club rooms.

1930 (April) First of three biennial public affairs institutes brought nationally-known thinkers to campus for addresses and roundtable discussions on major issues of the day.
(September) Evening college organized; faculty

	lectures and music programs broadcast over local radio station WDOD.
	(November) Chattanooga Art Association opened gallery on campus.
	Left the Southern Intercollegiate Athletic Association.
1931	Andrew Cecil "Scrappy" Moore appointed head football coach, a position he would hold until 1967.
1932	(June) Morrow Chamberlain elected president of the board upon resignation of Z.W. Wheland.
1933	(March) The university's $1 million endowment impaired when the First National-Chattanooga National Bank went into receivership.
	(fall) First homecoming day for alumni.
1934	(April) Tennessee Valley Institute convened on campus to discuss the economic and social impact of TVA.
	(fall) Formation of Chattanooga Symphony Orchestra under sponsorship of the university. First annual sustaining fund drive.
1935	(February) University charter amended to remove provision that two-thirds of trustees be members of the Methodist Episcopal Church, North.
	(June) Cooperative arrangement between university and Cadek Conservatory led to granting of Bachelor of Music degree.
1936	(spring) Comprehensive examinations in major

	field required of seniors.
	(April 17-25) University celebrated its semicentennial.
	Julliard Professorship of Music established.
1937	(December 17) Alexander Guerry resigned to become vice-chancellor, the University of the South.
1938	(June 21) Archie M. Palmer elected president.
1939	(December) Joint university-public library opened in new building constructed with aid from the U.S. Public Works Administration. Dedicated April 6, 1940; named John Storrs Fletcher Library in 1961.
	Civil Air Pilot Training Program started; discontinued February 1943.
1942	(May) President Archie Palmer resigned to take post with the Food Administration division of the U.S. Office of Price Administration.
	(August) David A. Lockmiller elected president.
1943	(February 19) Contract with War Department to house, feed, and instruct a College Training Detachment of the Army Air Corps. 1,234 cadets trained before contract ended June 30, 1944.
	Intercollegiate athletics suspended for duration of the war.
	(June) Judy Smith became first women elected president of the student body.
	(September) Comptroller Stanley F. "Jack"

| | Bretske elected vice president.
Two-year programs in home economics and secretarial science offered. |
|------|---|
| 1944 | (September) Agreement with the School of Nursing of Baroness Erlanger and T.C. Thompson Children's Hospital to begin training pre-clinical nurses in basic sciences.
(fall) City of Chattanooga deeded Clarence T. Jones Observatory to university. |
| 1945 | (September) Industrial Research Institute opened on campus. |
| 1946 | (June) Sixtieth Commencement included memorial service for the 62 alumni killed in the war; 1,250 alumni had served in the armed forces.
(September) Revised curriculum with a core program of required survey courses. Interdepartmental majors introduced. New majors established in art, dramatics and speech, health and physical education, home economics, psychology and religion, geography, and psychology.
(November) Management of intercollegiate athletics turned over to the Athletic Association of the University of Chattanooga, composed of local citizens.
Joined the Association of Urban Universities and the Association of University Evening Colleges. |

1947	Official flag and seal of the university adopted. (May) Publication of *The University of Chattanooga: Sixty Years*, by Gilbert E. Govan and James W. Livingood. (November 8) Dedication of Bretske Dining Hall and the Alumni Memorial Gateway. Major in general engineering established.
1948	Cadek Conservatory merged into the university. (fall) M.A. program in education offered. Patten House bequeathed to the University upon the death of Z.C. Patten. Exterior renovations began in 1991 and interior work began in 1994. Upon completion in 1996, the Alumni Affairs Office and the Faculty Club were housed in the facility.
1949	(April 10) Dedication of Annie Merner Pfeiffer Hall, a women's dormitory. (September) Industrial management, industrial engineering, medical technology, and public school music added to list of majors. (October 21) Stadium-Dormitory dedicated. (November 19) Brock Hall dedicated.
1950	(April 7) R.O.T.C. established on campus. (September) Academic reorganization into three colleges: Arts and Sciences under Dean Maxwell A. Smith, Applied Arts under Dean Paul Palmer, and Fine Arts under Dean Harold Cadek (Fine Arts discontinued as a college in 1956). (October 4) Evening college was named

	"Chattanooga College."
1951	(June) Addition to administration building (Founders Hall) completed.
1952	(January 17) Danforth Chapel dedicated.
1953	(fall) Major in social work established.
	(December) Mortar Board chapter installed.
1954	3-2 engineering program with UT approved; similar agreements made later with Vanderbilt, Georgia Tech, MIT, and New York University.
1955	(June 6) Lupton Patten succeeded Morrow Chamberlain as board chairman.
	(October 20-21) Seventieth anniversary convocation.
	Start of fundraising drive for $5 million.
1956	(August) Development Office established.
1957	(June 29) Dedication of the Manker Patten Tennis Center.
	(September) August W. Eberle appointed to the new post of provost and also became acting dean of the College of Applied Arts. James W. Livingood succeeded Maxwell Smith as dean of Arts and Sciences.
1958	(June) William E. Brock, Jr. succeeded Lupton Patten as board chairman.
	(October 17) President David Lockmiller resigned to accept appointment as president of Ohio Wesleyan University.
	(October 19) Dedication of George Thomas Hunter Hall, named for George T. Hunter, the

Coca-Cola bottler who established Benwood Foundation.

(October 25) Dedication of the Student Center (later re-named Guerry Center for Alexander and Charlotte Guerry.)

1959 (January 31) LeRoy A. Martin elected president. (June) M.Ed. degree in education authorized.

1961 (March 26) Dedication of Joseph O. Cadek Hall. (May 30) Master's degree in business administration authorized. Establishment of the Alexander and Charlotte Guerry Professorships. The first designees: Maxwell A. Smith, Irvine W. Grote, Edwin S. Lindsey, and Paul Palmer.

1962 (October) In excess of $100,000 raised for first time during annual sustaining fund drive.

1963 (March) $181,000 grant from Ford Foundation for a three-year Asian studies program on campus.

1964 (May 26) Board of trustees voted to admit qualified students "without regard to race" beginning with graduate students in the summer term of 1964 and with undergraduates in September 1965.

1965 August W. Eberle resigned as provost and dean of the College of Applied Arts.
(September 23) Dedication of Maclellan Gymnasium.
(September 28) Board announced that LeRoy

Martin would be named chancellor when his successor as president was selected.

1966 (February 18) William H. Masterson elected president.

1967 (September 15) University began its 82nd academic year with an enrollment of 1,756 full-time students.
(November 18) A.C. "Scrappy" Moore retired as head football coach; Harold Wilkes named to the head coaching position.
(December 16) Bold Venture campaign for $9 million launched under the chairmanship of the Reverend James L. Fowle.

1968 (January 12) Dedication of Stagmaier Hall.
(February-March) Tennessee Higher Education Commission recommended the establishment of The University of Tennessee at Chattanooga; Governor Buford Ellington signed into law two acts of General Assembly authorizing establishment of the school and an initial capital outlay of $5 million.
(April 2) Chattanooga City Commission voted to close the portion of Oak Street running through campus.
(April 25) Board resolved to proceed with negotiations to transfer the university's operating assets to the University of Tennessee. The board of trustees consisted of Everett Allen, George Awad, Creed F. Bates, Sebert Brewer,

William E. Brock, Jr. (chairman), Robert H. Caldwell, Harry C. Carbaugh, Gordon L. Davenport, Joseph H. Davenport, Jr., Thomas O. Duff, Jr., W. Max Finley, the Reverend James F. Fowle, J. Burton Frierson Jr., Ruth Golden Holmberg, Alex Guerry, Jr., DeSales Harrison, Dr. Carl A. Hartung, B. Eugene Hatfield, Otto J. Hubbuch, John L. Hutcheson, Jr., James B. Irvine, Jr., H. Clay Evans Johnson, Summerfield K. Johnston, Will S. Keese, Jr., David A. Lockmiller, John T. Lupton II, Edwin O. Martin, Olan Mills II, Richard L. Moore, Jr., Don Overmeyer, Z. Cartter Patten, Albert F. Porzelius, Scott L. Probasco, Jr., Robert P. Purse, Jr., William G. Raoul, Thomas T. Rowland, John Ross Scott, M.B. Seretean, J. Polk Smartt, Gordon P. Street, Richard C. Thatcher, Jr., Charles W. Wheland, Jack E. Whitaker, Harry R. White, Earl W. Winger, Raymond B. Witt, Jr., and Edwin C. Woodworth.

(April 25) Board approved guidelines for transferring operating assets to the University of Tennessee System.

1969 (March 4) Representatives of UC and UT executed the "Agreement of Merger and Plan of Transition."

(July 1) The University of Tennessee at Chattanooga established; University of Chattanooga Foundation began operation

	with an initial endowment of $6.3 million. Enrollment of 3,741 students; tuition of $315 for in-state students. (August 27) Chattanooga City College merged as a component of UTC.
1970	(April) Grote Hall dedicated. (August 31) Edward Boling succeeded Andrew Holt as president of UT. (August) B.S. Nursing enrolled first students.
1973	(July 1) James E. Drinnon, Jr. succeeded William Masterson as chancellor of UTC.
1974	(January 17) Library moved into a new $5.4 million building; named the T. Cartter and Margaret Rawlings Lupton Library in 1985. (September) University Center opened on Vine St.
1975	(May) Student Village, with 106 apartments, opened (later renamed the Boling Apartments to honor Edward J. and Carolyn Boling).
1976	(April 23) Holt Hall dedicated. Start of the Tennessee Tomorrow Campaign. Scott L. Probasco, Jr. Chair of Free Enterprise established by estate of Burkett Miller. First endowed chair on the UTC campus. Dr. J. R. Clark named to chair in 1993.
1977	Men's basketball team won NCAA Division II national championship.
1978	(August) UTC Athletics moved to NCAA Division I and joined the Southern Conference.

1979	(December) Brock Scholars program established with $1.5 million endowment. Children's Center opened.
1980	(fall) Dedication of the Fine Arts Center. (December) Chancellor James Drinnon resigned, effective January 1, 1981.
1981	(April) First biennial Southern Writers Conference held on UTC campus. (July 1) Frederick W. Obear elected chancellor. (August) Adult Services Center opened.
1982	Lockmiller Apartments opened. (August 1) Original license granted by the Federal Communications Commission to WUTC, FM 88.1. (December) Dedication of the UTC Arena ("Roundhouse"), a 12,000-seat, 211,000 square-foot sports and entertainment facility.
1985	(August 31) Burkett Miller Chair of Excellence in Management and Technology funded by the Tonya Memorial Foundation with matching state funds. Dr. Ron Cox named chair holder in 1996. (October) Frist Hall acquired. Building opened for use in November 1986 and dedicated in June 1987.
1986	(January 10) American National Bank Chair of Excellence in Humanities (later changed to SunTrust Bank Chair of Excellence in Humanities) funded by the American National Bank and the University of Chattanooga

Foundation with matching state funds. Dr. Bill McClay named chair holder in 1999. Provident Life and Accident Insurance Company Chair of Excellence in Applied Mathematics funded by the Provident Life and Accident Insurance Company and the University of Chattanooga Foundation with matching state funds. Dr. Jerald Dauer named chair holder in 1988. George R. West Jr. Chair of Excellence in Communication and Public Affairs funded by the Westend Foundation with matching state funds. Dr. David Sachsman named chair holder in 1991.

(August) Lockmiller Apartments Phase II opened.

(August-May) University celebrated its centennial.

1987 (April) Fellowship of Southern Writers established and UTC's Lupton Library chosen as home to the Fellowship archives. The Archives dedicated in 1989 and named in honor of Connor Professor of American Literature Arlie Herron in 1999.

(February 16) Walter M. Cline Chair of Excellence in Rehabilitation Technology funded by JoAnn and Haley Cline and the University of Chattanooga Foundation with matching state funds. Dr. Michael Whittle named chair holder in 1989. J. Burton Frierson, Jr. Chair of

Excellence in Business Leadership funded by Dixie Yarns and the University of Chattanooga Foundation. Dr. Mark Mendenhall named chair holder in 1989. Chair of Excellence in Judaic Studies funded by the University of Chattanooga Foundation and private gifts with matching state funds. Dr. Irven Resnick named chair holder in 1990.

1988 Lamar Alexander elected president of the University of Tennessee.

(December 31) Three-year Centennial Campaign closed. More than $23 million raised toward original goal of $15 million.

(May) Southeast Center for Education in the Arts to support discipline-based arts education in music, theatre, and the visual arts throughout the region funded by grants from the Getty Trust and Lyndhurst Foundation.

(October 21) Clarence E. Harris Chair of Excellence in Business Administration and Entrepreneurship funded by Clarence Harris, a 1964 graduate of the University of Chattanooga, making him the first alumnus to match state funding for a chair. Dr. Richard Becherer named chair holder in 1995. Lyndhurst Chair of Excellence in Arts Education funded by the Lyndhurst Foundation with matching state funds. Dr. Kim Wheetley named chair holder in 1996.

1990 (September) Siskin Memorial Hospital and

	Foundation property acquired.
1991	Joseph E. Johnson succeeded Lamar Alexander as president of UT.
1992	Challenger Center opened.
	Anonymous gift of land across McCallie Avenue to the University of Chattanooga Foundation opened prospect of campus expansion south of McCallie Avenue. Community and campus plans call for the construction of housing and recreational facilities with groundbreaking in 2000.
	(February) New physical plant and administration building opened.
	(July) Vine Street closed to vehicular traffic. City of Chattanooga approved permanent closing in 1994.
	(October 29) New WUTC transmission tower on Signal Mountain completed
1993	(August) Village Apartments Phase I opened. Phase II opened in 1997.
1995	Academic divisions consisted of the college of arts and sciences, college of education and applied professional studies, college of engineering and computer science, college of health and human services, and school of business administration. 260 full-time faculty; 46 bachelor's and 16 master's programs; 103-acre campus. Enrollment of 8,331; in-state tuition of $996; total of 25,414 graduates since merger with UT in 1969.

1997
(October 1) WUTC became the primary National Public Radio station for the region, combining NPR's informational programming with a jazz music format.
(December) Metropolitan Hospital property acquired. University began using facility in 1998.
U.S. News & World Report ranked UTC third in the "best buy" category among regional universities in the South.
Market value of UC Foundation endowment placed at $77.4 million.
(August 1) Bill W. Stacy succeeded Frederick Obear as chancellor.
(February) Scrappy, new mascot, adopted with new athletics logos and wordmarks.
(October) UTC Football Mocs moved to Finley Stadium/Davenport Field, a community facility in the city's Southside district. Opening crowd of more than 22,000. Mocs left historic Chamberlain Field, the second oldest stadium in continuous use in the country.

1998
(February) Fletcher Hall dedicated following two-year renovation.
(April) UTC Lady Mocs Softball team began playing in the new Frost Stadium, the Stadium of 1,000 Dreams, constructed by the City of Chattanooga, UTC and private sources at nearby Warner Park.

1998 (August) Ed.S. in Advanced Educational Practice initiated. First post-master's degree program.

1999 (January) O.D. McKee Chair of Excellence in Dyslexia and Exceptional Learning funded by the McKee family.

APPENDIX B

Presidents – Chancellors

Edward S. Lewis	President 1886-1889
John F. Spence	Chancellor 1889-1891
	President 1891-1893
Isaac W. Joyce	Chancellor 1891-1896
John H. Race	President 1897-1914
Fred W. Hixson	President 1914-1920
Arlo A. Brown	President 1921-1929
Alexander Guerry	President 1929-1938
Archie M. Palmer	President 1938-1942
David A. Lockmiller	President 1942-1959
LeRoy A. Martin	President 1959-1966
	Chancellor 1966-1969
William H. Masterson	President 1966-1969
	Chancellor 1969-1973
James E. Drinnon, Jr.	Chancellor 1973-1981
Frederick W. Obear	Chancellor 1981-1997
Bill W. Stacy	Chancellor 1997-

APPENDIX C

Members of the Board of Trustees
University of Chattanooga

Presidents – Chairmen

Bishop J.M. Walden	1886-1889
Capt. H.S. Chamberlain	1889-1897, 1898-1916
Bishop D.A. Goodsell	1897-1898
Bishop T.S. Henderson	1916-1921
Z.W. Wheland	1921-1932
Morrow Chamberlain	1932-1955
Lupton Patten	1955-1958
W.E. Brock, Jr.	1958-1969

Trustees

Adams, J.W.	1886-1917
Allen, Everett	1949-1969
Allison, M.M.	1917-1931
Anderson, Bishop William F.	1907-1916
Annis, J.E.	1896-1916
Avery, Clarence	1941-1953
Awad, George J.	1964-1969
Banfield, William	1901-1921
Bates, Creed F.	1886-1887
Bates, Creed F., Jr.	1939-1969
Bayless, J.W.	1900-1922
Beck H.C.	1886-1888; 1892-1915

Bishop, J.W.	1920-1951
Black, Henry C.	1928-1933
Brewer, Sebert	1954-1969
Bristol, Bishop F.M.	1916-1924
Brock, W.E.	1913-1950
Brock, W.E., Jr.	1950-1969
Brown, Arlo A.	1921-1929
Brown, Sam C.	1923-1926
Brown, Bishop Wallace E.	1932-1939
Burnette, William A.	1928-1932
Caldwell, the Reverend L.B.	1889-1898
Caldwell, Robert H.	1961-1969
Carbaugh, Harry	1943-1969
Carder, J.O.	1920-1922
Cardwell, Noel	1929-1938
Carter, Earl P.	1942-1961
Carter, the Reverend T.C.	1886-1894
Case, H.B.	1889-1897
Chamberlain, H.S.	1886-1916
Chamberlain, Morrow	1916-1959
Cone, M.D.	1889-1896
Cooke, the Reverend R.J.	1886-1889
Cranston, the Reverend Earl	1889-1896
Davenport, Gordon L.	1964-1969
Davenport, Joseph H., Jr.	1967-1969
Davenport, R.B.	1910-1918
Davis, James A.	1964-1967
Duff, T.O.	1930-1961
Duff, Thomas O., Jr.	1964-1967

Ellington, the Reverend L.D.	1886-1889
Evans, F.C.	1916-1918
Faxon, R.S.	1914-1918
Ferger, Herman	1907-1925
Finlay, Edward	1938-1947
Finley, W. Max	1954-1969
Fisher, J.W.	1900-1928
Fisher, R.J.	1892-1900
Fletcher, John S.	1917-1961
Flint, Bishop Charles W.	1936-1939
Foster, J.W.F.	1898-1908
Fowle, the Reverend James L.	1956-1969
Fowler, J.A.	1900-1938
Francisco, the Reverend G.T.	1906-1915
Freeman, the Reverend J.L.	1886-1889
Frierson, J. Burton, Jr.	1938-1969
Fuller, the Reverend F.E.	1896-1900
Gahagan, A.J.	1886-1889
Galbraith, W.A.	1888-1889
Gaston, W.S.	1894-1901
Gilman, W.D., Jr.	1938-1947
Goodsell, Bishop D.A.	1895-1904
Grigsby, J.A.	1914-1944
Griswold, D.H.	1934-1956
Guerry, Alexander	1929-1948
Guerry, Alexander, Jr.	1959-1969
Guerry, Charlotte Patten	1951-1959
Hamilton, Bishop J.W.	1895-1904
Hardwich, George L.	1917-1924

Hardy, Richard	1924-1927
Harris, the Reverend W.K.	1916-1939
Harrison, DeSales	1961-1969
Harrison, J. Frank	1960-1969
Hartung, Carl A.	1967-1969
Harvey, W. Stephens	1964-1968
Hartzell, Bishop J.C.	1888-1896
Hatfield, B. Eugene	1967-1969
Hawkins, Alvin	1886-1887
Henderson, Bishop T.S.	1912-1921
Hicks, Judge Ken	1924-1933
Hixson, F.W.	1914-1921
Holmberg, Ruth Sulzberger (Golden)	1957-1969
Hooper, the Reverend W.W.	1889-1904
Hoxsie, J.B.	1886-1887
Hubbuch, Otto	1944-1969
Hutcheson, John L., Jr.	1959-1969
Hutson, C.H.	1916-1929
Hypes, the Reverend W.L.	1889-1896
Irvine, James B. Jr.	1964-1969
Johnson, H. Clay Evans	1959-1969
Johnston, Summerfield K.	1947-1969
Joyce, Bishop I.W.	1888-1895
Julian, M.L.	1887-1888
Keeney, Bishop Frederick	1928-1936
Keese, William S., Jr.	1954-1969
Kern, Bishop Paul B.	1939-1952
Key, Judge D.M.	1886-1889
Kruesi, P.J.	1928-1955

Leete, Bishop Frederick D.	1919-1921
Lewis, the Reverend E.S.	1886-1889]
Little, C.D.	1939-1957
Lockmiller, G.F.	1914-1939
Long, the Reverend C.S.	1886-1887
Loomis, J.F.	1886-1895
Lupton, J.T.	1909-1912; 1917-1934
Lupton, J.T. II	1956-1969
Lupton, Thomas, A., Jr.	1964-1969
Maclellan, Robert J.	1935-1956
Maclellan, Robert L.	1956-1969
Mallalieu, Bishop W.F.	1889-1893
Manker, the Reverend J.J.	1886-1889; 1909-1916
Mann, the Reverend J.W.	1886-1889
Marshall, the Reverend J.K.P.	1889-1892
Martin, the Reverend B.M.	1916-1924
Martin, Edwin O.	1957-1969
Matthews, E.H.	1889-1897
McDonald, Roy	1943-1955
McNeill, the Reverend J.W.	1886-1889
Melear, the Reverend J.M.	1921-1954
Meyer, Douglas A.	1964-1968
Millard, the Reverend R.M.	1926-1930
Miller, Felix	1939-1960
Miller, S.E.	1916-1918
Mills, Olan II	1967-1969
Mitchell, the Reverend James	1886-1889
Moore, the Reverend D.H.	1889-1901
Moore, Richard L., Jr.	1964-1969

Morgan, Q.A.	1934-1939
Nelson, Stacy E.	1925-1961
Nicholson, Bishop Thomas	1916-1929
Overmyer, Donald H.	1949-1968
Parham, C.L.	1906-1915
Patten, D. Manker	1926-1940
Patten, George H.	1922-1942
Patten, John A.	1894-1916
Patten, Mrs. John A.	1916-1941
Patten, Lupton	1941-1959
Patten, Z.C. Jr.	1917-1948
Patten, Z. Cartter	1955-1969
Payne, C.V.	1887-1888
Pearson, the Reverend John	1895-1914
Petty, the Reverend J.S.	1892-1901
Pierce, the Reverend Ralph	1886-1889
Porzelius, A.F.	1935-1961
Preston, T.R.	1943-1953
Probasco, H.S.	1909-1919
Probasco, Scott L.	1921-1955
Probasco, Scott L., Jr.	1956-1969
Purse, R.P.	1920-1935
Purse, R.P., Jr.	1935-1969
Race, the Reverend John H.	1898-1954
Ramsey, Judge J.W.	1886-1887
Raoul, William G.	1964-1969
Rathmell, Dr. J.R.	1886-1889
Rawlings, J.W.	1920-1921
Read, S.R.	1922-1942

Rees, D.E.	1886-1889
Rhodes, L.W.	1929-1956
Richardson, Bishop E.G.	1921-1929
Riker, the Reverend E.B.	1887-1890
Roberson, the Reverend J.D.	1886-1889
Roberts, M.S.	1919-1941
Robinette, the Reverend J.J.	1886-1889
Rogers, the Reverend W.H.	1886-1889
Rowland, Thomas T.	1967-1969
Ruble, the Reverend J.A.	1888-1889; 1893-1906
Rule, William	1886-1903
Rust, the Reverend R.H.	1895-1914
Rust, the Reverend R.S.	1886-1906
Scott, John Ross	1927-1969
Seretean, M.B.	1967-1969
Short, Bishop Roy H.	1952-1961
Smartt, J. Polk	1954-1969
Smith, Bishop H. Lester	1928-1932
Spellmeyer, Bishop Henry	1904-1909
Spence, the Reverend J.F.	1889-1893
Stagmaier, John	1932-1943
Street, Gordon P.	1956-1969
Sulzberger, Mrs. Arthur Hays	1945-1957
Thatcher, Richard C., Jr.	1967-1969
Thirkield, Bishop W.P.	1899-1907; 1924-1928
Thompson, S.H.	1914-1917
Thompson, T.C.	1909-1937
Thrall, Victor W.	1924-1926
Thurman, the Reverend J.A.	1886-1889

Townsend, W.B.	1922-1934
Underwood, F.L.	1920-1942
Van Deman, Dr. J.H.	1886-1889
Vaughan, the Reverend E.H.	1886-1888
Walden, Bishop J.M.	1886-1914
Walsh, the Reverend J.D.	1889-1927
Wareing, the Reverend E.C.	1920-1924
Warner, the Reverend T.C.	1886-1887
Wasson, E. Hornsby	1961-1967
Wester, S.D.	1886-1890
Wheland, Charles W.	1957-1969
Wheland, Z.W.	1909-1956
Whitaker, J.E.	1961-1969
White, Harry R.	1964-1969
Wilder, General J.T.	1886-1888
Wilson, Bishop L.B.	1904-1912
Winger, Earl	1947-1969
Witt, Raymond B., Jr.	1955-1969
Wood, D. Hewitt	1939-1945
Wood, P.H.	1945-1963
Woodworth, C.N.	1917-1928
Woodworth, D., Jr.	1886-1889
Woodworth, Edwin C.	1934-1957
Wright, the Reverend J.C.	1886-1887

APPENDIX D

Members of the Board of Trustees
University of Chattanooga Foundation, Inc.

Chairmen

William E. Brock, Jr.	1969-1970
John T. Lupton II	1970-1972
Joseph H. Davenport, Jr.	1972-1974
James B. Irvine, Jr.	1974-1977
Thomas O. Duff, Jr.	1977-1980
Harry R. White	1980-1983
James D. Kennedy, Jr.	1983-1987
H. Clay Evans Johnson	1987-1988
Raymond B. Witt, Jr.	1988-1990
H. Carey Hanlin	1990-1991
Daniel K. Frierson	1991-1993
Ray L. Nation	1993-1995
John P. Guerry	1995-1999

Trustees

Herbert G. Adcox

Lamar Alexander
Ex-Officio Trustee

Everett Allen, Sr.

John R. Anderson*
Alumni Associate Trustee
1995-1996 Elected Trustee

Lee Anderson*

Harry B. Au, Jr.
Alumni Associate Trustee

George J. Awad

Col. Creed F. Bates

Rev. Herman Battle

James C. Berry

A. Vincent Blunt, III

Edward Boling
Ex-Officio Trustee

Llewellyn Boyd

Tom Braly

Sebert Brewer

Frank Brock

W.E. Brock Jr.

William G. Brown

Richard W. Buhrman

L. Hardwick Caldwell, III*

Robert H. Caldwell, Sr.*

Harry C. Carbaugh
Life Trustee

Forrest Cate, Jr.

E.Y. Chapin, III

Gary Chazen

George M. Clark, Jr.

Nancy Collum
Alumni Associate Trustee

Peter T. Cooper*

Thomas A. Cubine

Bruce Dahrling
Ex-Officio Trustee

Gordon L. Davenport

Joseph H. Davenport, Jr.

Joseph H. Davenport, III*

Trustees

Leland Davenport*

Susan F. Davenport

James A. Davis
Alumni Associate Trustee

Joseph F. Decosimo*

Roger W. Dickson*
UT Trustee

James E. Drinnon, Jr.*
Ex-Officio Trustee

Thomas O. Duff, Jr.

A.L. Dyer

W. Max Finley

James Fowle

C. Duffy Franck, Jr.

A. Russell Friberg, Jr.
Ex-Officio Trustee

Amy H. Frierson
Ex-Officio Trustee

Daniel K. Frierson*

J. Burton Frierson

Jim Frierson*
Ex-Officio Trustee

Louise Griffith*
Trustee Emerita

Alexander Guerry

Charlotte Guerry
Life Trustee

John P. Guerry*

Zan Guerry*

H. Carey Hanlin

Ken G. Harpe
Alumni Associate Trustee

Clarence E. Harris

DeSales Harrison

J. Frank Harrison

Carl Hartung

Steven Harvey
Alumni Associate Trustee

B. Eugene Hatfield

William Hatfield

Clifford L. Hendrix, Jr.*

James L. Hill*

Trustees

Jayne Holder*
Alumni Associate Trustee

Brice L. Holland*

Ruth S. Holmberg*

David L. Hopkins, Jr.
Alumni Associate Trustee

Robert Hopper
Alumni Associate Trustee

Otto J. Hubbuch
Life Trustee

Mai Bell Hurley
Ex-Officio Trustee

John L. Hutcheson, Jr.

W. Frank Hutcheson

James B. Irvine, Jr.

James L. Jackson
Alumni Associate Trustee

H. Clay Evans Johnson*

Joseph E. Johnson*
Ex-Officio Trustee

Summerfield K. Johnston, Jr.*

Will S. Keese, Jr.

James D. Kennedy, Jr.*

William Kilbride
Ex-Officio Trustee

Frank J. Kinser*
UT Trustee

Paul J. Kinser
UT Trustee

Paul J. Kruesi
Honorary Trustee

Charlotte Landis
Ex-Officio Trustee

David A. Lockmiller*
Life Trustee

William R. Love
Ex-Officio Trustee

John T. Lupton

Thomas A. Lupton, Jr.*

James W. Lynch

Hugh O. Maclellan, Sr.

Robert H. Maclellan*

Robert L. Maclellan

Earl A. Marler, Jr.

Trustees

Edwin O. Martin
Life Trustee

William H. Masterson
Ex-Officio Trustee

Frank W. McDonald*

Ellsworth McKee

Joni McNeil
Alumni Associate Trustee

Herbert McQueen

Norma P. Mills*

Olan Mills, II

Alice Lupton Montague

Chris Moore*
Ex-Officio Trustee

Mary Navarré Moore

Richard L. Moore, Jr.

Elbert N. Mullis
Ex-Officio Trustee

Angelo Napolitano*
Alumni Associate Trustee

Ray L. Nation*

David Noblitt*
Alumni Associate Trustee

Herbert L. Oakes

Frederick W. Obear
Ex-Officio Trustee

Donald Overmyer

W.A. Bryan Patten*

Z. Cartter Patten

William D. Pettway, Jr.

Joseph Petty
Alumni Associate Trustee

P. Robert Philp

Charles L. Pierce
Alumni Associate Trustee

Albert W. Pitner
Alumni Associate Trustee

Albert Porzelius
Life Trustee

Mervin Pregulman*

Scott L. Probasco, Jr.*

Robert P. Purse, Jr.
Life Trustee

Trustees

William G. Raoul

Edward Richey
Ex-Officio Trustee

Howard Roddy*

Susan Rogers
Alumni Associate Trustee

Thomas T. Rowland

Diane Ryder
Alumni Associate Trustee

Carolyn Schaerer
Alumni Associate Trustee

Frank V. Schriner, Jr.*

John Ross Scott
Life Trustee
M.B. Seretean

Bishop Roy H. Short
Honorary Trustee

J. Polk Smartt

Frances S. Smith*
Ex-Officio Trustee
Elected Trustee

Howard P. Sompayrac
Alumni Associate Trustee

Bill W. Stacy*
Ex-Officio Trustee

Paul M. Starnes*
United Methodist Trustee

Judith F. Stone*

John C. Stophel*

Gordon P. Street
Life Trustee

Ruth L. Street

Robert J. Sudderth, Jr.*

Gloria Sutton
Ex-Officio Trustee

William L. Taylor, Jr.*

Marie Thatcher
Alumni Associate Trustee

R.C. Thatcher, Jr.

John C. Thornton*
Ex-Officio Trustee
Elected Trustee

Jean Troy
United Methodist Trustee

Frank Trundle, Sr.
Alumni Associate Trustee

Trustees

John Vorder Bruegge

Ronald K. Wade
Alumni Associate Trustee

James Walden

Robert Kirk Walker*

Hornsby Wasson

Herman E. Welch

Charles W. Wheland

Jack E. Whitaker

Phil B. Whitaker*

Harry R. White

Thomas A. Williams

Earl W. Winger
Life Trustee

Raymond B. Witt, Jr.*

Edwin C. Woodworth
Life Trustee

Lynn Woodworth

Spencer H. Wright*

JoAnn Cline Yates*

Colon W. York

*Current members 1998-99

APPENDIX E

Guerry Professorships

1961	Irvine Walter Grote (Chemistry)
	Edwin Samuel Lindsey (English)
	Paul Lester Palmer (Education and Psychology)
	Maxwell Austin Smith (Modern Languages)
1962	Wilbur Kingsley Butts (Biology)
	Culver Haygood Smith (History)
	James Weston Livingood (History)
	Terrell Louise Tatum (Modern Languages)
1965	Winston Louis Massey (Mathematics)
	Myron Stanley McCay (Physics)
1966	Dorothy Hackett Ward (Theatre and Speech)
	William O. Swan (Chemistry)
1968	Karel Hujer (Physics and Astronomy)
1973	George Coleman Connor (English)
1974	Ziad Keilany (Economics)
	George Ayers Cress (Art)
1975	Arthur George Vieth (Economics and Business Administration)
	Benjamin Harrison Gross (Chemistry)
1976	Edward J. Green (Psychology)
1977	William H. Masterson (History)
1981	Charles Hyder (Education)
	Paul Ramsey (English)
1986	Fred C. Armstrong (Economics)

1989	Jane W. Harbaugh (History)
1990	Lloyd D. Davis (Education)
	Thomas G. Waddell (Chemistry)
1992	James A. Ward, III (History)

APPENDIX F

Merger Agreement Between the University of Chattanooga and the University of Tennessee

AGREEMENT AND PLAN OF TRANSITION

THIS AGREEMENT AND PLAN OF TRANSITION, made and entered into this 4th day of March, 1969, by and between THE UNIVERSITY OF TENNESSEE, a public educational corporation organized and existing under the laws of the State of Tennessee, and the UNIVERSITY OF CHATTANOOGA, an educational corporation, organized and existing under the laws of the State of Tennessee.

WITNESSETH

WHEREAS, the Board of Trustees of the University of Tennessee has been vitally concerned for some time with the lack of public aided higher education in the Chattanooga-Hamilton County area, and with what its response should be in meeting this need for higher education in that metropolitan area; and

WHEREAS, the Eighty-Sixth General Assembly of the State of Tennessee authorized the Board of Trustees of the University of Tennessee to establish a campus of the University of Tennessee at Chattanooga to be known as "THE UNIVERSITY OF TENNESSEE AT CHATTANOOGA"; and

WHEREAS, the Board of Trustees of the University of Chattanooga has felt and has expressed a similar sincere concern for providing quality higher education and educational leadership suitable to the physical growth and to the economic and cultural development of southeastern Tennessee and of the State; and

WHEREAS, the Tennessee Higher Education Commission recommended and a plan has been agreed upon whereby both institutions may serve, more effectively and efficiently, the increasing needs of the State relative to educational services with additional opportunities for the young people of the State at both undergraduate and graduate levels and directly benefiting civic, business, industrial and agricultural interests and the general welfare of our State; and

WHEREAS, the solution and response reflected here will enhance the work contributions and aspirations of all who, with justifiable pride, are responsible for the fine institution created and nurtured by The Methodist Church and now known as the University of Chattanooga, and will achieve real economy for the State and more effectively utilize its resources as Tennessee meets increasing enrollments and educational demands by assuming the costs of continuing support and improvement without the initial capital outlay required to start a new institution through incorporation and establish a comprehensive institution within its system of higher education; and

WHEREAS, it has been determined by the respective boards and by the Tennessee Higher Education Commission that it is in the best possible interests of the parties hereto acting in their fiduciary capacities, and of the State of Tennessee to transfer to The University of Tennessee such assets as are hereinafter described so that the institution of higher education now known as the University of Chattanooga will become part of The University of Tennessee, to be governed by the Board of Trustees of The University of Tennessee and for which the State of Tennessee shall be financially responsible, and

WHEREAS, The University of Tennessee is willing to accept the transfer of said assets and responsibilities and the University of Chattanooga is willing to transfer such assets upon the terms and conditions of this plan for quality education;

NOW THEREFORE, the institutions hereby agree as follows:

I.

(a) "UC" means the University of Chattanooga, a Tennessee corporation, and/or the Board of Trustees of the University of Chattanooga.

(b) "UT" means The University of Tennessee, a State institution existing under the laws of Tennessee, and/or the Board of Trustees of The University of Tennessee.

(c) "UTC" means The University of Tennessee at Chattanooga, located at Chattanooga, Tennessee, from and after the effective date and refers to a major campus of The University of Tennessee.

(d) "Date of Agreement" means the date of this instrument as stated above.

(e) "Effective Date" means the date on which UT will assume possession and operation of UTC and shall be July 1, 1969.

II.

In consideration of UT's agreeing, as it hereby does, to assume the responsibility for maintaining and operating an institution of higher learning in Chattanooga-Hamilton County, Tennessee, hereinafter referred to as UTC, as a major campus and part of UT exercising its care and management therefor to preserve its present high standards, to provide for its sound growth and secure enhancement of it as a first class institution, according to a plan of transition calling for specific action by UT particularly stipulated by paragraphs III to X, inclusive, of this instrument, and in consideration of The University of Tennessee's paying One Million ($1,000,000.00) Dollars out of the bond proceeds for capital outlay aforesaid to UC for the land, buildings, equipment, library holdings, and other physical assets of the University of Chattanooga, which will be delivered free of debt except such as is represented by self-liquidating, revenue-producing projects; and in consideration of specified undertakings to be performed by UC particularly stipulated by paragraphs XI to XIV, inclusive, of this instrument, together with the mutual covenants and provisions of these parties hereinafter contained, this Agreement and Plan of Transition is by the parties entered into so that, subject to the terms and conditions set forth, the University of Chattanooga's educational operating function will, on the Effective Date, be fully transferred to The University of Tennessee, which shall continue to be governed by the laws of the State of Tennessee with UT receiving and assuming, after the date of transfer, such assets of the University of Chattanooga as provided for herein.

III.

It will be the policy and commitment of The University of Tennessee to seek financial resources and distribute state appropriations and other future unrestricted funds, after the Effective Date hereof to the Chattanooga campus on the same basis as that of other units of the University system, so that for equivalent programs equivalent resources will be made available on the Chattanooga campus as on the Knoxville campus and other campuses of The University of Tennessee. The University of Tennessee, in cooperation with local governments in the Chattanooga area, will begin to acquire additional land adjacent to the University of Chattanooga campus prior to July 1, 1969, for the necessary expansion of the program.

IV.

The name of the resulting institution will be "THE UNIVERSITY OF TENNESSEE AT CHATTANOOGA," that name being deemed descriptive of its broad function, its location and the fact that it is a major campus of The University of Tennessee, UTC will be administered by a Chancellor who will be the chief executive of "The University of Tennessee at Chattanooga." He shall be employed by the Board of Trustees of The University of Tennessee and shall serve under and report and be responsible to the President of The University of Tennessee and through that officer to the Board of Trustees of The University of Tennessee. His powers and responsibilities as prescribed by the President and the UT Board will be those usually associated with that educational office, and consistent with the fact that he will be the chief executive officer of UTC. The Chancellor will be responsible for the administration of the institution, and the other administrative officers on the Chattanooga campus will be responsible to him. The position of Chancellor has been offered to Dr. W.H. Masterson, President of the University of Chattanooga.

V.

The faculty of UTC will have the same academic freedom as faculty members on other campuses including but not limited to determination of course content, methods of instruction and evaluation, determination of curriculum, and other academic matters, consistent with system-wide policies about these matters. The determination of the exact program to be established and maintained, including curricula, division into colleges and schools, education for the professions, scope of educational services, library growth plan, research program and continuing (adult) education, are matters of informed educational judgment consistent with system-wide policies. Academic programs of presently enrolled students at the University of Chattanooga will be honored and continued through graduation.

VI.

All regular employees of the University of Chattanooga as of the Effective Date will be offered employment with The University of Tennessee at Chattanooga. The term "regular employee" shall be determined by UC in accordance with established practice. (Exhibit A lists such employees as of 9-1-68.) Those regular UC employees who enter UTC employment on the Effective Date and who meet eligibility requirements shall be entitled to participate in UT's programs of fringe benefits, including the joint contributory retirement system, group insurance plans, etc., to the same extent and with the same employee contributions thereto applicable to other UT employees. UT will honor tenure commitments of UC on the Effective Date. Employment with UC prior to Effective Date will be counted as service for any initial eligibility requirements for participation in the retirement system of UT and not otherwise. As to such personnel, salary adjustments will be made by UTC on the Effective Date so as to make the combined total of an employee's compensation and the employer's contribution to the UT retirement system for the employee's account no less favorable to the employee than the combined total of salary and employer retirement contributions in effect at UC immediately preceding the Effective Date. This adjustment to UTC employment may result in the employee's receiving a larger percentage in salary and a smaller percentage in retirement contributions paid by the employer than would be the case if UC employment should continue, but it is contemplated that the employee may elect to have a portion of his salary adjustment used to purchase additional retirement annuities for himself to supplement those purchased under UT's joint contributory system. (Exhibit B lists UC personnel participating in UC retirement plans as of 9-1-68.)

In addition to the salary adjustments mentioned above, further adjustments in salary will be made for UTC employees in order to make these salaries consistent with those offered similar UT personnel of the Knoxville campus for comparable levels of work in similar fields, it being intended that UTC become a doctoral-granting institution as soon as practicable. The parties agree that the UTC salary schedule must be such as to attract the calibre of faculty necessary to support a doctoral program.

The parties hereto are aware that differences now exist with reference to certain fringe benefit programs, which differences vary in degree among the individuals involved, being affected by age, length of service, salary level, etc.

In most instances the net effect will be minor but in some instances the difference may be significant. It will be the objective of UC Foundation to provide funds to assist the individual faculty and staff members through a reasonable period of transition in those instances where they are substantially affected because of the differences in the two programs.

Under like circumstances and conditions, equal treatment will be given all individuals.

The two areas of benefits which are of principal concern are group life and disability insurance programs – specifics cannot be spelled out in details and generalization could be misunderstood because each individual situation is different.

In each area of benefit the programs of UT and UC will differ but on balance the net effect on the individual, in most cases, will be minor. However, where age, accompanied by many years of service at UC, is a major reason for an important difference in benefits for which the individual can qualify under the UT program, the UC Foundation will devise an assistance program in such situation and continue it for a reasonable period of time.

VII.

The admissions and retention standards at UTC will not be lower than those of any other UT campus. Student activities will be financed and operated as on other campuses of UT. The identity and individuality of the athletic programs of UTC will be preserved. School colors, songs and the like will be determined on UTC campus. Athletics grants-in-aid will be made within the framework of the UT system policy and the standards of NCAA. Academic scholarship programs will be financed as on the other UT campuses except that the scholarship program may be supplemented by funds from the University of Chattanooga Foundation, Inc. as described hereinafter.

The UTC Development and Alumni activities will be financed as on Knoxville and other UT campuses and will be operated during a transition period in a way that my achieve maximum understanding, support and cooperation from UC and UTC alumni toward the furtherance of the UT system and its commitment to academic excellence. The UTC

Development Office, through flexibility in its local operation, will seek to maintain and expand its fund raising efforts in a manner best suited to the furtherance of UT, UTC and any endowment funds.

VIII.

The Administration of the UT system, including the Chancellor of UTC, shall move to implement the transition of the University of Chattanooga into The University of Tennessee and the operation of UTC through development of internal policies and procedures for UTC as a major campus of The University of Tennessee. Since it will be impossible at this time or at the Effective Date to foresee all aspects of the proper merger of UC into UT, the Board of UT hereby declares that the development of the required policies and procedures shall be assessed against the Board's controlling consideration, i.e., that the most effective ways be chosen by which the two institutions may be drawn together so that UTC shall serve adequately the needs of southeastern Tennessee with higher education of quality and excellence.

IX.

After the date of Agreement, UT shall request of the General Assembly of Tennessee through the Tennessee Higher Education Commission that it provide for the University of Tennessee campuses and programs by State appropriations made in like manner as appropriations are now made for the maintenance and operation of The University of Tennessee. UT will serve a liaison function with the Tennessee Higher

Education Commission, the Governor and other State officials, and the General Assembly in planning a legislative budget for fiscal year 1970 for UTC as an essential element of UT.

X.

UT agrees that the real and personal property and Current Restricted Fund balances transferred to it by UC under the terms of this Agreement, or the proceeds thereof, and as specifically set forth in the Audit of UC, will be used after the Effective Date only for the benefit of UTC.

XI.

UC will furnish to UT within sixty (60) days after date of this Agreement the following:

(a) A list of all realty owned or under the control of UC (other than held as a part of the Endowment Fund) and such originals or true copies of all deeds or instruments under which UC acquired an interest;

(b) Satisfactory evidence showing unpaid accounts to contractors, laborers and materialmen for which mechanics', laborers' materialmens' liens may be established against UC and/or its property, and evidence showing bond or other protection thereon, if any;

(c) Complete information relating to policies of insurance in effect, all existing contracts and commitments which either involve payment of more than $5,000.00 each or which, regardless of amount, might extend beyond July 1, 1969. A current list of all regular employees (Exhibit A) and the rate of compensation of each;

(d) Other data and information requested by UT in order to plan an orderly transition and merger on the Effective Date, including but not limited to financial data, enrollment data, and budgets.

XII.

UC will cause an audit to be prepared of the institution by the independent Certified Public Accountants normally employed by UC, including financial statements of all funds of UC, general funds, restricted funds, endowment funds, loan funds, and all other funds of UC, in which there will be reflected all assets, liabilities, revenues, expenditures, and fund balances of said funds as of June 30, 1969, the fiscal year then ended.

The audit shall be made in accordance with generally accepted auditing standards, shall include examination or verification of all securities, and shall include the professional opinion of the Certified Public Accountant on the representations contained in the financial statements, and UC shall furnish UT copies of the audit report as soon as it is received.

XIII.

From and after the date of this Agreement and prior to the Effective Date UC will conduct its affairs in a normal manner and will advise UT of any transaction deemed to be unusual or abnormal and substantial, providing UT adequate opportunity to participate in any such decision. In order that UT may become conversant with the academic, business, fiscal, and financial operations of UC from and after the date of this Agreement, UC shall make available to appropriate personnel of UT for purposes of review and analysis any and all records of transactions having to do with operations of UC as may affect the functions described herein. UC shall operate during the fiscal year 1969 in accordance with the detailed budget approved by the Board of Trustees of UC. UT shall be provided a copy of such budget and personnel representing UT shall have complete access to transactions relative to such budget as they take place. UT personnel will have complete scrutiny and functional reconnaissance of activities of UC during the current year in exactly the same manner as UT system personnel carry on similar activities with each campus of UT; except in the case of UC, the functional personnel of UT will have no supervisory or veto powers during such period.

UC agrees to operate under the provisions of the 1969 budget approved by the UC Board of Trustees and to make no changes in said budget except as may be approved by the UC Board of Trustees and with the knowledge of UT.

In order that UT and UC personnel be in a position to plan for appropriations request and submission of budget data to the Sate Commission on Higher Education prior to January, 1969, and which is prior to the Effective Date of this contract, it is recognized that UT personnel immediately become acquainted with current UC operations if adequate preparations are to be made as required by higher state authorities.

During this period, namely fiscal 1969, UC and UT personnel will plan in detail for the operation of UTC starting July 1, 1969, in accordance with present UT procedures and as amended by instructions of the Commission on Higher Education, and the executive or the legislative branch of State Government.

Incremental expenditures applicable to fiscal year 1970, when the institution will be UTC, may be required to be made during fiscal year 1969. Such will be determined in joint consultation with personnel of UT and UC, and UT will provide the necessary funding for carrying out such immediate expenditures as are determined necessary. Activities relating to the normal operations of UC for the fiscal year 1969 will be carried on as usual by UC personnel under the authority of UC Board of Trustees, but with full knowledge, but not necessarily the concurrence of UT personnel.

Personnel of UC will operate under its budget as approved by the UC Board of Trustees and UT personnel will review this operation in exactly the same manner as said UT personnel supervises the budgetary operations of the various campuses of The University of Tennessee under the budget approved by the Board of Trustees of The University of Tennessee.

XIV.

UC will transfer to UT title to the assets, real, personal, tangible and intangible, including the real property described in Exhibit E attached hereto and hereby made a part hereof, held in its name whether of record or not on the Effective Date. Such shall include all such assets whether a part of the

Plant Fund and Current Restricted Funds or otherwise described in the audit of UC as of June 30, 1969 by Ernst and Ernst; and shall exclude all Endowment Funds reflected in such audit. UT shall use such property and their proceeds for the use and benefit of UTC. Assets to be transferred shall include books, papers, records and files under custody or control for the use of UC, together will all annual giving pledges, contracts and other entitlements of UC, except to the extent provided in paragraph XV and as such may pertain to endowment or corporate records, said transfer to be by appropriate instruments of transfer irrevocably made by UC and accepted by UT; provided, however, that UT shall have the option to refuse to accept delivery of instruments of transfer as to any item or items of assets involving duties and responsibilities inconsistent with UT policies or involving duties and responsibilities adjudged by UT to be too onerous to justify acceptance. UC shall deliver title to all real property free of all debts except those covering financing or self-liquidating revenue-producing projects.

XV.

Prior to the Effective Date UC proposes to amend its Charter by changing its name to the University of Chattanooga Foundation, Inc. and by amending its objectives and purposes so as to remove any requirement that it maintain and operate an educational institution with a faculty, student body and other normal indicia of an operating educational institution. The purpose of the University of Chattanooga Foundation, Inc. will be the support of higher education through special programs and projects of The University of Tennessee at Chattanooga in order to enrich its educational program over and above the level possible with normal operating and capital funds available to University of Tennessee. To the extent not otherwise committed pursuant to the terms of this Agreement, income and corpus from said Foundation will be disbursed solely for the benefit of The University of Tennessee at Chattanooga as the Trustees of such Foundation may determine. It is intended that UTC will be the beneficiary of such income and corpus in unique and innovative means and methods designed to effect a continuing movement toward academic excellence. Initiation of projects and ideas will come primarily from the Chancellor of UTC and his staff but the Foundation Trustees may consider requests from other sources. The University of Chattanooga Foundation, Inc. Trustees will possess the final decision although no funds may be disbursed to UTC, or be spent on its behalf without prior approval of the President of UT and The Board of Trustees of UT.

The University of Chattanooga has received funds during its history and has accepted such funds upon certain specified terms and conditions. These funds are designated restricted endowment funds and are to be retained in the endowment of the educational foundation. Such Funds are more specifically described in Exhibit F to this Agreement. To the extent the perpetuation of the purpose of such funds require administrative action and decisions by the UTC Chancellor and his administrative staff, but no disbursement of funds derived from state sources, UT agrees to authorize whatever

UTC administrative actions as are necessary to perpetuate such trusts so long as the money to support such originate with the University of Chattanooga Foundation, Inc.

XVI.

From and after the effective date, the Board of Trustees of UC shall relinquish all control, responsibility and supervision vested by law, or exercised in fact, over and to the institution and assets now known as UC which shall thereafter be both owned and operated by UT, a state institution, as provided in this Agreement, except as to such assets as retained in the University of Chattanooga Foundation, Inc.

All gifts, bequests and devises made to the University of Chattanooga which have presently vested and unpaid pledges to the Bold Venture Campaign shall remain endowment property of the University of Chattanooga and such gifts, bequests and devises, as between The University of Tennessee at Chattanooga and the University of Chattanooga Foundation, Inc., shall not be affected by the fact that the testator or settlor died prior to this Agreement without knowledge of it; or that the testator or settlor died prior to this Agreement with knowledge that this change was planned; nor shall such gifts, bequests and devises be affected by the fact that the will or trust in which they are contained was executed prior to the time that the creator had knowledge of the change or was made subsequent to that time.

All gifts, bequests and devises presently existing or hereafter made to the University of Chattanooga which will vest immediately upon the death of the testator or settlor shall remain endowment property of the University of Chattanooga Foundation, Inc. and such gifts, bequests and devises, as between The University of Tennessee at Chattanooga and the University of Chattanooga Foundation, Inc., shall not be affected by the fact that the testator or settlor died subsequent to this Agreement but without knowledge of it; or that the testator or settlor died subsequent to this Agreement and had knowledge of it, whether the gift, bequest or devise is contained in a will or trust made prior to this Agreement or subsequent to it; nor shall such gifts, bequests and devises be affected by the fact that the will or trust in which they are contained was made prior to the time the testator or settler had knowledge of the change or was made subsequent to that time.

All gifts, bequests and devises presently existing or hereafter made to the University of Chattanooga which depend upon some contingent future event to vest shall remain the property of the University of Chattanooga and such gifts, bequests and devises, as between The University of Tennessee at Chattanooga and the University of Chattanooga Foundation, Inc. shall not be affected by the fact that the testator or settlor died prior to this Agreement without knowledge of it; or that the testator or settlor died prior to this Agreement with knowledge that this change was planned; or that the testator or settlor died subsequent to this Agreement but without knowledge of it; or that the testator or settlor died subsequent to this Agreement and had knowledge of it, whether the gift, bequest or devise is contained in a will or trust make prior to this Agreement or subsequent to it; nor shall such gifts, bequests and devises be affected by the fact that the will or trust in which they are contained was made prior to the time the testator or settlor had knowledge of the change or was made subsequent to that time.

The University of Tennessee agrees to seek state appropriations as well as other financial support and resources for UTC on the same basis as for other campuses of UT, and will (to the extent permitted by law) distribute such upon the same basis, so that for equivalent programs per student equal resources will be available at UTC or at Knoxville and other campuses of UT. The income from the University of Chattanooga Foundation, Inc. will be distributed by its Trustees to UTC for designated uses and purposes, with the consent of UT, for enrichment of the education program, faculty and staff benefits, scholarships and chairs, and for other similar purposes.

XVII.

When UC amends its Charter as provided in paragraph XV, it shall continue its present corporate existence and powers for such time as may be reasonably necessary, and shall, as promptly thereafter as possible, adopt a resolution amending its Charter providing for the necessary powers to conduct such business as provided in paragraph XV and repealing and deleting all other powers of UC corporation, file and record same, and furnish a copy to UT.

XVIII.

The obligation of UT and of UC to effect the Agreed Plan of Transition shall be subject to the following conditions: (1) The representations herein contained shall be substantially accurate in all material respects, and each institution shall have performed all obligations and complied with all covenants required by the Agreement to be performed or complied with by it prior to the Effective Date hereof. (2) No material adverse change in financial condition shall have occurred, nor any material loss or damage to property or assets, whether or not covered by insurance, which change, loss or damage would materially affect or impair the ability of the other institution on the Effective Date. In the event a loss or damage is covered by insurance, any insurance on account of such damage shall be paid to UT, or if no such proceeds have been collected by the Effective Date, UC shall assign its right to collect such proceeds to UT. (3) The Legislature of the State of Tennessee, in the opinion of the UT Board of Trustees, has appropriated sufficient funds for the operation of UTC. (4) The execution of the terms of this Agreement will not conflict or result in a breach of, or constitute a default under, any agreement or instrument to which the other institution is a party except to the extent that the same shall have been cured by waiver, consent of the other institution or otherwise.

XIX.

The University of Chattanooga was granted a Corporate Charter by the State of Tennessee in 1889 upon application from members of the Methodist Episcopal Church. The

University utilized real property leased from The Freedman's Aid Society of the Methodist Episcopal Church, an Ohio corporation from 1889 until 1909 when the real property was deeded to the University of Chattanooga by the Methodist Church with notes given for the purchase price being guaranteed by J.F. Annis and J.A. Patten. There has been a close relationship between the Methodist Church and the University of Chattanooga during its existence as is evident from an original charter provision requiring that "at least two thirds of the Trustees shall be members in good standing in The Methodist Episcopal Church." This provision was removed from the Charter in 1935. Because of the long history of such close association with The Methodist Church, the fact that UC has accepted gifts under varied circumstances and conditions over a long period of time, both coupled with the unusual nature of the joint educational venture contemplated by this agreement which is without legal precedent in Tennessee, legal counsel for UC have advised that the execution of this Agreement and the changes set forth herein be specifically conditioned upon approval of such acts by the Chancery Court of Hamilton County, Tennessee. The execution of this Agreement shall be subject to and conditioned upon an appropriate final decree of such Chancery Court or appropriate appellate court. UC will transfer to UT whatever right, title and interest it may have in the assets to be transferred as set forth in pertinent exhibits hereto and cannot warrant as to the clear title to any such property. UC shall make a full disclosure within the scope of its available records and knowledge and will further cooperate to remedy any defects found to exist and within its power to correct without substantial financial expenditures.

XX.

In assuming supervision and control of, and responsibility for the educational activity now carried on by UC, UT agrees to maintain and perpetuate the institutions and traditions of the University of Chattanooga. In pursuance thereof UT agrees to maintain the current names of buildings, rooms, stadium, dormitories, endowed chairs, endowed scholarship programs, lectureships and similar items reflecting those whose contribution to the University of Chattanooga has been outstanding meriting such continued acknowledgment thereof.

The institutional identity of the Chattanooga campus will be maintained in the Southern Association of Colleges and Schools, Southern University Conference, The Tennessee College Association, American Alumni Council, American College Public Relations Association, Association of American Colleges and all other similar organizations.

XXI.

UC and UT each obligates itself at any time and from time to time to execute all necessary papers, documents, legal conveyances and other instruments required to effectuate the purposes and intents of this Agreement.

(a) UC has made substantial financial payments as of the date of this Agreement with respect to a new science building to be erected on Vine Street and Baldwin. Included are the purchase price for the real property, architect's fees and other similar expenses. In the interim prior to June 30, 1969, substantial additional payments will be required. UT agrees to reimburse the University of Chattanooga Foundation, Inc. for such expenditures at the time of the transfer of operating control by UC to UT. The University of Tennessee further agrees to assume all obligations of the University of Chattanooga under the terms and conditions of the HEFA grant agreement, dated February 28, 1967 between the University of Chattanooga and U.S. Office of Education for the construction of the new science and engineering building, Profect (sic) No. Tenn. 4-4-00359-0 (Formerly Project No. Tenn. 4-2605).

(b) The Manker Patten Tennis Center and related realty may be transferred by UC in such manner as UC may determine and independently of the transfer to UT of the realty to comprise the original UTC campus.

XXII.

This agreement embodies the entire Agreement between UT and UC with respect to the merger of these institutions, and there have been and are no agreements, representations or warranties relating thereto between the parties other than those set forth herein or herein provided. Either may waive any inaccuracies in the representations by the other with any of the covenants or conditions herein; any such waiver by either shall be sufficiently authorized for the purposes of this Agreement if authorized or ratified in writing by the party granting the waiver.

XXIII.

All notices, requests, demands shall be in writing and shall be deemed to be duly given if delivered or mailed, first class, registered or certified mail, (1) if to UT to President, The University of Tennessee, Knoxville, Tennessee 37916, and (2) if to UC to President, University of Chattanooga, Chattanooga, Tennessee, 37403.

XXIV.

UT and UC both understand and agree that further refinement of this Agreement may be desirable, and both pledge themselves to accept amendments hereto reflecting such matters.

XXV.

The parties hereto are deeply sensitive that the success of the transfer herein contemplated depends upon the good faith and integrity of the respective Boards and their executive officers, and to the end that opportunities for quality higher education in Tennessee be advanced and greater facilities therefor be made available to the youth of the State, the parties hereto will work closely together for the accomplishment of the aims of this Agreement.

XXVI.

This contract may be executed in four counterparts, each of which is an original.

IN WITNESS WHEREOF, the Parties hereto, pursuant to authority given to their respective Boards have caused this Agreement and Plan of Transition to be entered into and signed by their respective officers in their corporation names, and their corporate seals to be affixed hereunto, and to be attested by their respective Secretaries or Assistant Secretaries, all in accordance with their respective Resolutions, copies attached, which authorized this action and designated the officers so executing to act in that capacity, all as of the day and date above set forth.

UNIVERSITY OF CHATTANOOGA

By   W.E. Brock

Attest:
Raymond B. Witt
Secretary

THE UNIVERSITY OF TENNESSEE

By
       A.D. Holt, President

Attest:

Secretary   John C. Baugh

Index

Abernathy, Thomas P., 227
Academic Freedom, 87, 108, 118
Ackerman, George, 44, 45
Adams, Frank, 21
Adams, John Wesley, 17, 18, 42
Alexander, Lamar, 177
Allegheny College, 84
Allen, Everett, 122, 152, 154, 235
Alpha Society, 225
American Medical Association, 80
American Temperance University, 46
America Trust and Banking Company, 101, 105
Anderson, William F., 73, 74, 185
Annenberg Foundation, 178
Annis, J.E., 59, 225
Area, Ron, 174
Arena (UTC), 167, 238
Armstrong, Walter P., 205
Association of American Universities, 88
Association of Urban Universities, 231
Athens Female College, 7

Bach, Bert C., 164, 213
Baisden, Frank, 86
Bales, Paul, 227
Bara, Theda, 82
Barnum, Phineas T., 24
Bates, Creed F., 36
Bates, Creed F., Jr., 154
Baugh, John C., 207

Bayless, John W, 60
Baylor School, 91-92, 93, 94, 134, 136, 146
Becherer, Richard, 240
Beck, Henry Clay, 17, 41, 181
Bell, Georgia, 113
Bender, A.L., 158
Benwood Foundation, 144, 234
Berry College, 119
Birmingham Barons, 122
Blount College, 141
Board of Education (Methodist Episcopal Church, North), 71
Bold Venture Campaign, 137-138, 146, 150, 154
Boling Apartments, 165, 237
Boling, Edward J., 141, 142, 143, 156
 and UC merger, 147, 148
 as UT president, 159, 161-162, 164-165, 169, 170, 175-177
Bolton, David, 61, 184, 185
Bond, Claude, 213
Boston University, 22
Boult, Reber, 208
Bradford, George, 188
Breland, Walker, 213
Bretske Hall, 100, 118, 232
Bretske, Stanley F., 99, 107, 112, 117, 120, 122
Brewer, Sebert, 235
Briggs, Garrett, 213
Brock Candy Company, 99, 115
Brock Hall, 119, 232
Brock, Ray L., Jr., 155, 200
Brock Scholars Program, 165, 238

Brock, William E., 76, 89, 227
Brock, William E., Jr., 124, 131, 147, 148, 149, 153, 154, 156, 253
Brown, Arlo Ayres, 84, 85, 86, 87-88, 91
Brown, Karla, 213
Brown vs. Board of Education, 126
Brownley, Floyd, 164
Brownlow, William G., 6-7, 8, 12
Brumbaugh, A.J., 203
Bryan, William Jennings, 86
Bryant, Paul "Bear", 122
Buttrick, Wallace, 73, 75
Butts, Wallace, 122, 193
Butts, Wilbur K., 260
Byrd, Admiral Richard, 96

Cadek Conservatory, 106
Cadek Hall, 125, 234
Cadek, Harold, 232
Cadek, Ottokar, 106
Caldwell, Robert H., 236
Callaway, Joe, 106
Carbaugh, Harry C., 236
Carnegie, Andrew, 54-55, 69
Carnegie Foundation, 72, 73, 78
Carnegie Library (Chattanooga), 55
Carson and Newman College, 57
Carter, Thomas C,. 29, 30-31
Case, Halbert B., 29
Caulkins, Wilford, 21, 26, 30-31, 32-33, 34, 35, 36, 182
Center of Excellence in Computer Applications, 178
Central High School (Chattanooga), 70
Challenger Center, 178, 241
Chamberlain Field, 88, 186, 224, 242
Chamberlain, Hiram S., 3, 14, 17, 20, 41, 44
Chamberlain, Morrow, 117, 227, 229, 233
Chancellor's Roundtable, 177
Chattanooga Art Association, 97
Chattanooga Chamber of Commerce, 75, 130, 140, 158
Chattanooga City College, 157-158
Chattanooga College of Law, 93
Chattanooga Golf and Country Club, 75
Chattanooga Kiwanis Club, 88
Chattanooga Medicine Company, 59, 80, 93, 101, 115
Chattanooga National Bank (See also First National Bank), 100-101
Chattanooga Savings Bank, 59, 90
Chattanooga State Technical Institute, 130
Chattanooga Symphony Orchestra, 105
Chattanooga University
 academic divisions of, 23, 38
 and Freedmen's Aid Society, 19-21
 and race relations, 3, 28-38, 48
 buildings of, 18-19
 campus of, 1-2
 coeducation at, 24-26
 curricula of, 22, 181-182
 extracurriculum at, 24-25

groundbreaking for, 1-5, 18
in merger with Grant
   Memorial, 39-40, 41
formation of, 14-18, 181
Clement, Frank G., 130, 141
Cleveland State Community
   College, 130, 205
Cline, Haley, 239
Cline, Jo Ann, 239
Cline, Walter M., 239
Cobleigh, E. A., 55-56, 183-184
Colby, Margaret Smith, 227
College Training Detachments, 112
Commercial National Bank
   (Chattanooga), 105
Conference on Southern
   Literature, 178
Connor, George C., 108, 121, 192-193, 260
Consacro, Peter, 165
Coolidge, Ellen, 227
Cornelius, David W., 227
Cornelius, Orrelle F., 86
Cox, Ron, 238
Cress, George A., 120, 121, 260
Cumberland University, 111

Dabney, Charles W., Jr., 57
Danforth, Addie, 69
Danforth Chapel, 233
Daniels, Jonathan, 59
Darrow, Clarence, 86
Darwinism, 86-87
Dauer, Jerald, 239
Davenport, Gordon L., 207
Davenport, Joseph H., Jr., 207, 253
Davis, Lloyd D., 261
Depauw University, 78

Dickey, James, 120
Dixie Yarns, Inc., 240
Douglas, Ben, 143
Downing, W. T., 79
Drew Theological Seminary, 88
Drinnon, James E., Jr., 162, 163-165, 166-167, 168-169, 177
Duff, Thomas O., Jr., 207, 253
Dyer, Lee, 213

East Tennessee State University, 130, 140
East Tennessee Wesleyan
   College, 7-8, 9, 12, 13, 30
Eberle, August W., 110, 115-117, 131, 132-133, 196-197
Edwards, John W., 227
Ellington, Buford, 140, 141, 142, 144, 148, 158, 200, 201
Emory University, 127, 132
Erlanger Hospital, 113
Erskine, John, 96
Evans, H. Clay, 225

Faxon, Ross, 225
Fellowship of Southern Writers, 178, 239
Fenix, Robert W., 193
Ferger, Herman, 225
Fine Arts Center, 165, 238
Finlay, Ed, 93
Finley, Max, 153
Finley Stadium-Davenport
   Field, 242
First Methodist Church
   (Chattanooga), 3, 13-14, 17, 36, 68, 80
First National Bank (See also
   Chattanooga National Bank), 90, 100-101

Fisher, Anna A. 185
Fisher, E. Bruce, 205
Fisher, Edward M., 200
Fisher, John W., 76, 225
Fisher, Robert J., 60
Fleming, Arthur, 123
Fletcher Hall, 242
Fletcher, John S., 89, 117, 185, 227
Fletcher Library, 107-108, 119, 230
Folger, John F., 204
Founders Hall, 79, 225
Fowle, James L., 235, 236
Fowler, J. A., 225
Francisco, G. T., 225
Freedmen's Aid and Southern Education Society (See Freedmen's Aid Society)
Freedmen's Aid Society, 10-11, 14, 39, 40, 71
   and Chattanooga University, 15-18, 19-21
   and U.S. Grant University, 42, 44, 45, 52, 54, 55, 58, 60, 67
   racial policies of, 30, 35, 37-38, 48
Freedmen's Bureau, 11
Freemen, J. L., 181
Frierson, Daniel K., 253
Frierson, J. Burton, Jr., 148, 149, 152, 194, 239
Frist Hall, 238
Fritz, Robert, 213
Fulton, Robert C., 213
Furman University, 119

Gahagan, Andrew Jackson, 14, 17, 40
General Education Board, 72, 73, 74
Georgia Arts Commission, 120
Getty Trust, 240
Gibbs, Louis, 28-29
G. I. Bill, 113
Gill, Edith, 227
Gilman Paint and Varnish Company, 115
Girls' Preparatory School, 136
Grant Memorial University (See also U.S. Grant University), 30, 36, 37, 39, 41
Grant, Ulysses S., 2, 183
Green, Edward J., 260
Green, Wyman, R., 227
Grigsby, J. A. 225
Griscom, Isobel, 227
Gross, Benjamin H., 260
Grote Hall, 159, 237
Grote, Irvine W., 125, 159, 260
Guerry, Alexander, 59, 91, 101, 105, 106-107, 111
   at Baylor School, 93-94, 188
   background of, 92
   views of, 95, 97, 102-103
Guerry, Alexander, Jr., 207
Guerry Center, 234
Guerry, Charlotte Patten, 93-94, 101, 188
Guerry, John P., 253
Guerry Professorships, 125, 139, 234, 260
Guerry, William Alexander, 92

Hales, William, Jr., 213
Hamilton, John W., 48, 49-50, 52, 54, 182
Hamilton National Bank, 105
Hanlin, H. Carey, 253

290

Harbaugh, Jane W., 164, 211, 261
Harris, Clarence E., 240
Harris, Thomas A., 199
Harris, W. K., 227
Harrison, DeSales, 236
Hartung, Carl A., 236
Hartzell, Joseph Crane, 39, 41-42, 43, 44, 48
Hatfield, B. Eugene, 236
Hawkins, Alvin, 181
Hawkins, Mrs. Richard M. 205
Hayes, Rutherford B., 163
Herron, Arlie, 239
Hicks, Ken, 227
High Museum, 120
Hixson, Fred W., 78, 81, 83-84, 186
Hixson, Jerome, 81, 85
Holmberg, Ruth S. (Golden), 207
Holston Annual Conference, 3, 10, 12, 13, 29, 83, 84
  and Chattanooga University, 14, 15, 39
  and U.S. Grant University, 57
  formation of, 7
Holston Methodist, 182
Holt, Andrew D., 141, 142, 143, 144, 158, 159-160, 161
  and UC Foundation, 152
  in UC-UT merger, 146, 147, 148, 149, 154, 155, 156
  retirement of, 156-157
Holt Hall, 165, 237
Hood, Robin, 120
Hooper, Frank F., 226
Hooper Hall, 80, 121, 225
Hooper, Wesley W., 21, 62-63, 70, 185

Hoxsie, J. B., 181
Hubbuch, Otto, Jr., 236
Hujer, Karel, 260
Hullihen, Elizabeth, 185
Hullihen, Walter, 65, 185
Hunter, George T., 233
Hunter Hall, 233
Hutcheson, John L., Jr., 207
Hutson, C. H., 227
Hyder, Charles M., 164, 213, 260

Indiana University, 115, 116
Industrial Research Institute, 115
Interstate Life and Accident Insurance Company, 105
Irvine, James B., Jr., 152, 153, 253

Johnson, B.H., 31
Johnson, Claudius O., 227
Johnson, H. Clay Evans, 148, 152, 253
Johnson, Joseph E., 142, 177
Johnston, Summerfield K., 236
Jones, John M., 144
Journal of Southern History, 134
Journal of the American Medical Association, 80
Joyce, Isaac, 43, 47

Keeney, Frederick, 228
Keese, Will S., Jr., 236
Keilany, Ziad, 139, 260
Keith, Leroy, Jr., 213
Kelley, Margaret, 176-177
Kelley, Ralph, 139
Kennedy, James D., Jr., 253
Key, David M., 42, 181

Kinser, Paul J., 162, 200, 213
Kirkendoll, C. A., 205
Kirkland, James, 71
Kline, Earl K., 227
Knoxville University, 8-9
Knoxville *Whig*, 6
Kruesi, Paul, 89, 117, 228

LaFollette, Phillip, 103
Larson, David, 174
Leatherman, George A., 227
Levine, Lawrence D., 200
Lewis, Edward S., 22, 27, 28, 36, 37, 38, 44, 182
Lilienthal, David, 96, 103
Lindsey, Edwin S., 87, 107, 125, 227, 260
Little Rock University, 22
Livingood, James W., 115, 233, 260
Lockmiller Apartments, 238, 239
Lockmiller, David A., 110, 116-117, 124
  background of, 111
  views of, 114, 118, 123, 191, 193-194
Lockmiller, G. F., 61, 111, 184
Long, John R., 205
Loomis, J. F., 41, 181
Luce, Henry R., 96
Lupton, Cartter, 124, 128, 138, 159, 194
Lupton, John T., 91, 94, 124, 228
Lupton, John T. II, 128, 134, 138, 145, 147, 148, 206, 253
Lupton Library, 159, 165, 237, 239
Lupton, Margaret R. 159

Lupton, Thomas A., 205
Lyndhurst Foundation, 165, 240

MacGaw, Grace, 191
MacKinlay, Mary H., 227
Maclellan Gymnasium, 125, 234
Maclellan, Robert L., 147, 148, 149, 154
Mahoney, J. J., 76
Maier, Robert H., 213
Mallalieu, W. F., 27, 32
Manker, John J., 3, 13-15, 20, 21, 23, 28-30, 38, 41, 59
Manker Patten Tennis Center, 233
Mann, John W., 181
Martin, Edwin O., 110, 111, 124
Martin, Francis, 185
Martin, LeRoy A., 124, 126, 127, 132, 134
Maryville College, 119, 127
Massey, Winston L., 260
Masterson, William H., 134-136, 158, 260
  as UTC chancellor, 157, 161-162
  in UT-UC merger, 140, 143, 147, 149
  views of, 137, 139
McAdoo, William Gibbs, 180
McAllister, Hill, 103
McCallie, J. Park, 92
McCallie School, 92, 93, 136, 146
McCay, Myron S., 260
McClay, Bill, 239
McDonald, Roy, 118
McKee, O.D., 243
McLemore, James S., 227
Melear, J. M., 228

Memphis State University (See also University of Memphis), 146
Mendenhall, Mark, 240
Methodist Advocate, 29, 30, 83
Methodist Episcopal Church (North), 1-4
   and Chattanooga University, 17, 18, 20, 23-24
   and University of Chattanooga 78, 83, 84, 85, 88, 91, 104, 111, 155
   and U.S. Grant University, 46, 47
   formation of, 5
   General Conference of, 7, 10, 32, 33, 35, 39, 44, 45
   in East Tennessee, 6, 11, 51-52, 54, 57, 87
Methodist Episcopal Church (South), 1, 5-7, 12, 51
Metropolitan Hospital, 242
Middle Tennessee State University, 129, 200
Mifflin, Al Clark, Jr., 205
Millard, R. M., 228
Miller, Burkett, 238
Miller, William E., 149
Mills, Olan II, 236
Milton, George Fort, 76
Mitchell, James, 181
Moccasin, 224
Moon, James E., 213
Moore, Andrew C. "Scrappy," 122-123, 193, 235
Moore, Richard L., Jr., 236
Morgan, Arthur, 103
Morgan, H. A., 103
Mortar Board, 233
Moser, Barry, 120

Myers, Charles Haven, 80
Myers, Roland H., 205

Nation, Ray L., 253
National College Football Hall of Fame, 122
Neel, Warren C., 213
Nelson, Stacy E., 228
New York *Herald Tribune*, 17
New York *Independent*, 48, 182
New York Stock Exchange, 97-98
New York *Times*, 96
Newcomb, John T., 222
Neyland Stadium, 123
Nichols, Roy F., 197
Nicholson, Thomas, 228
North Carolina State College, 110
Norwood, Barbara, 213

Oak Street closure, 139
Oak Street Stadium, 88, 96, 112, 227
Oakland University, 170
Obear, Frederick W., 171, 176-177, 178
   and UT System, 175-176
   background of, 170
   views of, 172, 173-174
Ochs, Adolph S., 96
Ochs, Martin, 204
Ohio State University, 163
Ohio Wesleyan University, 13, 123, 193-194
"Old Main," 18-19, 42, 47, 58, 79
Overmyer, Don, 154
Owen, Blynn, 227

Packard, Sandra, 174
Palmer, Archie M., 107, 108-109
Palmer, Paul L., 115, 125, 226, 232, 260
Patten Chapel, 80, 208
Patten, Edith Manker, 80, 228
Patten, George H., 228
Patten House, 232
Patten, John A., 14, 58-59, 68, 72, 73, 78, 80, 93
Patten, Lupton, 117, 124, 233
Patten, Manker, D., 228
Patten, Z. C., 89, 228
Pearne, Thomas H., 7
Pearson, John, 185
Pearsons, Daniel K., 67-68
Peerless Woolen Mills, 115
Perkins, Frances, 103
Perry, Ruth C., 227
Pfeiffer Hall, 118, 232
Phelps, Clyde W., 227
Phi Beta Gamma, 65
Phi Beta Kappa, 78, 111, 129
Pilgrim Congregational Church, 80
Porzelius, Albert F., 236
Pouder, W. R., 187
Pound, Roscoe, 96, 103
Powell, Claude Jack, 200
Powell, Sam H., 200
Prados, John W., 169, 175-176, 212
Prescott, Frank, 107, 187
President's House, 72, 153
Presnell, Mary A., 21, 25, 26, 34, 38
Preston, Thomas R., 75
Prince, John W., 227
Princeton University, 50

Pritchett, Henry Smith, 78
Probasco, Harry, 75, 79, 225
Probasco, Scott L., 89, 228
Probasco, Scott L., Jr., 144-145, 147, 148, 152, 156, 213
Provident Life and Accident Insurance Company, 147, 239
Purse, R. P., 228

Race, Alice, 49, 50, 51, 58
Race Hall, 80, 225
Race, John H., 48, 49, 50-52, 58, 59, 60-62, 70, 76-78, 85-86, 111
    and Andrew Carnegie, 54-55, 69
    as fundraiser, 66-69, 72-74, 75
    views of, 53, 56-57
Race Relations in U.S., 28-35, 37-39, 48, 126-128, 234
Ramsey, John W., 181
Ramsey, Paul, 139, 260
Raoul, William G., 148, 149
Rathmell, John R., 181
Read, Daniel, 25
Read, Harold, 206
Reconstruction Finance Corporation, 101
Redd, William C., 227
Renneisen, Charles, 174
Reserve Officers Training Corps, 115, 128
Resnick, Irven, 240
Reynolds, Paul, 203
Rhodes College, 119, 136
Rice University, 161
Richardson, E. G., 228
Roane Iron Company, 17
Roberson, J. D., 181
Roberts, Gene, 172

Roberts, M. S., 228
Roberts, S. B., 142
Robertson, E. A., 21
Rockefeller Foundation, 75
Rockefeller, John D., 72
Rockne, Knute, 95
Rogers, C. H., 187
Rogers, W. H., 16, 181
Roosevelt, Franklin D., 101
Rowley, Erastus, 7
Rule, William, 181
Russell, J. B., 69
Rust, Richard S., 3, 11-12, 29
   and Chattanooga University, 15-17, 20-21, 22, 23, 30, 31, 34
   and John Spence, 36
   and race relations, 37, 39
Rust University, 21

Sachsman, David, 239
Sadd, Walter, 75
Scarritt College, 127
Schietinger, E. F., 203
Schonblom, Eric, 175, 213
Scopes Trial, 86
Scott, John Ross, 236
Shuptrine, Herbert, 120
Shuton, Mary, 185
Simpson, (Bishop) Matthew, 6
Siskin Memorial Hospital, 240-241
Smartt, J. Polk, 236
Smith, Culver H., 260
Smith, H. Lester, 228
Smith, Judy, 113
Smith, Maxwell A. 115, 125, 227, 232, 260
Snodgrass, William, 142
Snow, Louis F., 227

Southeastern Center for Education in the Arts, 178, 240
Southern Association of Colleges and Secondary Schools, 71
Southern Regional Education Board, 144, 202, 203
Southern Writers Conference, 238
Spence, John Fletcher, 7, 12-13, 14
   and Chattanooga University, 15, 36
   at Grant Memorial University, 37, 39, 40
   at U.S. Grant University, 41-42, 43, 44, 46
Stacy, Bill W., 179
Stadium-Dormitory, 118, 122
Stagmaier Hall, 138, 235
Steudel, Robert, 21
Stone Fort Land Company, 59
Stophel, John C. 213
Street, Gordon P., 207
Student Army Training Corps, 82
SunTrust Bank, 238
Swan, William O., 260
Swift, Mrs. G. W., 69

Tatum, Terrell L., 227, 260
Taylor, Jerome, 149
T. C. Thompson Children's Hospital, 113
Temple, Charles M., 164, 169
Tennessee Higher Education Commission, 142, 144, 147, 166, 171, 174-176, 204, 205

Tennessee State Board of Education, 140
Tennessee Technological University, 130, 200
Tennessee Valley Authority, 96, 103
Tennessee Wesleyan College, 21, 61-62, 124
Thatcher, Richard C., Jr., 236
Third Presbyterian Church, 112
Thirkield, W. P., 228
Thomas, Frank, 95, 122, 227
Thomas, Norman, 96
Thompson, T. C., 75, 225
Tietze, Godfrey, 227
Tinnon, Ann S., 213
Title Guaranty & Trust Company, 17
Tonya Memorial Foundation, 238
Townsend, W. B., 228
Traylor, Horace, 128, 158
Tulane University, 67, 127
Tusculum College, 57

Underwood, F. L., 228
United Methodist Church, 155
University Center, 159, 165, 237
University Lookout, 41
University of Alabama, 95
University of Chattanooga
 and academic freedom, 87, 108, 118
 and town-gown relations, 85, 88-89, 96, 106, 177
 athletic programs of, 65-66, 95, 121, 122-123
 campus of (*See also individual buildings*), 69-70, 75, 79-80, 105, 139, 150
 curricula of, 70, 87-88, 113, 115, 125, 129, 191, 231
 desegregation of, 126-128, 234
 endowment of, 75-76, 89-90, 101, 104, 118-119
 enrollments of, 88, 114, 125, 145, 226, 227, 235
 evening college of, 97
 extracurriculum at, 82, 83-84, 87, 96, 113
 in merger with UT, 139-140, 143, 145, 146-156, 174-176, 262-286
 Institutes of Justice at, 96, 103-104
 motto of, 225
 professional schools of, 73, 74, 75
 summer school of, 86
University of Chattanooga Athletic Association, 121-122
University of Chattanooga Foundation, 150-152, 162, 165-166, 177, 178
University of Chicago, 88
University of Georgia, 122
University of Memphis (See also Memphis State University), 140
University of Mississippi, 126, 127
University of New Hampshire, 170
University of North Carolina, 124
University of Pennsylvania, 134
University of Tennessee, 14, 25, 57, 65, 115, 121, 123, 141-142
 Alumni Association of, 200

Development Council of, 144
in merger with UC, 140, 144-145, 146-156, 262-286
Martin branch of, 141
Space Institute of, 141
System of, 157, 160, 162, 174-175
University of Tennessee at Chattanooga
and Chattanooga City College, 158
and UT System, 160-162, 170, 174-175
campus of (*See also individual buildings*), 159, 165, 178
curricula of, 167, 174-176, 178
endowed chairs at, 237, 238, 239, 240, 243
enrollments of, 159, 167, 177-178, 237, 241
Faculty Council of, 169-170, 175
formation of, 142-143, 144-145, 148-157, 165
tuition of, 237, 241
University of the South, 1, 25, 66, 92, 106, 107, 127
University of Virginia, 96
U. S. Grant University
athletic programs of, 65-66
campus of, 42, 52-53
curricula of, 43, 47, 53, 63-64
endowment of, 66-69
enrollments of, 56, 63
extracurriculum at, 64-65
formation of, 41
preparatory department of, 54, 61, 62, 71
professional schools of, 46, 47, 53, 55-56, 62, 64, 183-184

Van Deman, J. H., 181
Vanderbilt University, 1, 23, 24, 25, 67, 71, 84, 88, 127, 129
Vaughn, E. H., 181
Vieth, Arthur, 137, 260
Village Apartments, 241
Vine Street Closure, 241
Volunteer State Life Insurance Company, 59

Waddell, Thomas G. 213, 261
Walden, John M., 17, 20, 31, 36, 37, 180
Walker, Patricia, 213
Walker, Robert Kirk, 140, 142, 158, 199-200, 202
Walsh, J. D., 225
Walters, Herbert, 149
Ward, Dorothy Hackett, 121, 192-193, 260
Ward, James A., III, 261
Wareing, Ernest C., 186
Warf, Howard, 201
Warner, T. C., 36, 181
Warren, Henry W., 15, 16
Washington College, 57
Wasson, E. Hornsby, 207
WDOD, 97
West, George R., Jr., 239
Westend Foundation, 239
Wester, Samuel D., 181
Western Christian Advocate, 78, 186
Whaley, Betty, 213
Wheetley, Kim, 240
Wheland, Charles W., 236
Wheland, Z. W., 14, 89, 185, 225
Whitaker, Jack E., 236
Whitaker, Phil, 93
White, Harry R., 236, 253

Whiteside, Hugh, 5
Whittle, Michael, 239
Wilder, John T., 14, 17
Wiley, Isaac, 1-5, 17, 18
Wilkes, Harold, 122, 123, 235
Williams, Godwin, Jr., 200
Wilson, William 28-29, 182
Wilson, Woodrow, 81, 83
Winchester, Maude L., 185
Winder, Charles H., 185
Wine of Cardui, 80
Winger, Earl W., 207
Witt, Raymond B., Jr., 154-155, 189, 253
Woodard, Prince, 203
Woodworth, C.N., 228
Woodworth, David, 14, 17
Woodworth, David, Jr., 181
Woodworth, Edwin C., 236
Worthington, Joseph, 69
Wright, William A., 61, 184, 185
Wriston, Henry W., 137
WUTC, 238, 242
Wyoming Seminary, 50

Zion College (See Chattanooga City College)